GOD AND ME

Reasons for Faith

NICK HAWKES

Hawkesflight Media

Contents

God and Me: Reasons for Faith	vii
Introduction	ix
1. The Cosmos, Meaning, and Me	1
2. Creation, Evolution, and Me	32
3. Jesus, Evidence, and Me	51
4. History, Morality, and Me	82
5. Philosophy, Truth, and Me	101
6. Quantum Physics, Atheism, and Me	128
7. Suffering, Grief, and Me	152
8. Other Faiths, Christianity, and Me	173
9. Church, Its Moral Failure, and Me	196
10. Sex, the Bible, and Me	224
11. Life After Death, and Me	248
12. A Personal Note	264
Notes	269
Acknowledgments	281
About the Author	283
Also by Nick Hawkes	285

God and Me: Reasons for Faith

Copyright © 2020 Nick Hawkes
All rights reserved.

Hawkesflight Media

No part of this book may be reproduced in any form or by any electronic or mechanical means, including information storage and retrieval systems, without written permission from the author, except for the use of brief quotations in a book review.

ISBN: 978-0-6451202-5-7
www.author-nick.com

Scripture quotations taken from The Holy Bible, New International Version® NIV®
Copyright © 1973 1978, 1984 2011 by Biblica, Inc ™
Used by permission. All rights reserved worldwide.

To my wife Mary, who has loved me beyond reason.

God and Me: Reasons for Faith

by

Nick Hawkes

Introduction

Let's begin with you. Who are you...and why do you exist? It is the most profound question you will ever ask, so it's worth taking some care over the answer.

The current sociological climate is not kind to people seeking to answer this question. Most philosophers and opinion leaders of our time simply tell you that you are a rather oddly shaped bag of subatomic particles that came from nothing, as a result of nothing.

My fervent hope is that we will be able to say something more truthful and helpful in the pages that follow.

I have had the privilege of interacting with young adults for most of my life. The question they ask, in those beautiful still moments when the time is right to ask the really important things is: Do I have meaning? It was the question put to me by a medical student in India who struggled to believe he was significant in a nation of 1.3 billion people. It was the question put to me by a sexually confused young man in Sparta, Illinois.

Getting anyone to be still enough to ask this question is not easy. Today's society abhors deep thinking and gives you all sorts of toys to trivialize and fill up your day. This brings to mind an aphorism of

Introduction

the seventeenth century French scientist and theologian, Blaise Pascal who said, "All of humanity's problems stem from man's inability to sit quietly in a room alone."[1] I do hope you find time to look at the stars at night and think. Otherwise, you will be swept along by the mainstream secular/atheistic culture of our time, which will leave you lying on the scrap heap of meaninglessness – where you will slowly desiccate and lose your humanity.

The journey ahead will therefore take a modicum of courage. The easy way is to do nothing and to lazily and uncritically adsorb the culture of the day. This is so terribly dangerous. One of the reasons for this is that a lot of the atheistic culture promulgated by media's opinion leaders is parasitic on true science. I use the word parasitic quite deliberately. Today's culture bombards us continually with the message that rationalism means not embracing the idea of God. It holds up in glittering lights the idea that being an atheist means that you are your own person, and that you are grown up and no longer need the childish notion of a divine being. Those who still believe in the quaint idea of God are to be scorned, ridiculed and pitied.

In reality, nothing is further from the truth. However, to discover this truth will take courage, because it is the nature of society to force you to conform to its thinking.

The truth of who you are is not only vitally important for you, but also for the generation that follows you. To illustrate this, let me tell you a story.

It only takes one generation

Following the 16th century Reformation in Europe, ninety percent of Hungary and Poland was Protestant. However, within one generation, both countries were solidly Roman Catholic. The reason for this extraordinary turnaround was that the aristocracy of both nations hired Catholic Jesuits to educate their children.

It only took one generation.

Without passing judgment about whether it was a good thing for Poland and Hungary to be Catholic, this story should remind us of

Introduction

the importance of being eternally vigilant about whom we allow to educate our children. If your son or daughter is being educated in the humanities department of a Western university, you can almost guarantee they will finish college indoctrinated with an anti-West, anti-Christian culture.

Sadly, too many churches have given up their responsibility for teaching young adults a robust, reasoned faith. As a result, the mournful atheistic world-view of our society is taking over their minds, leaving them anxious, angry, self-obsessed and struggling under the burden of meaninglessness.

It is a woeful indictment of Western Christianity that most churches have never taught the rational and scientific case for God in a cogent way. Even worse, some have insisted that their people believe scientifically absurd (and theologically unnecessary) things about creation. All I can say is that church leaders who do this will be accountable to God for putting pitfalls in front of people seeking God. And we are not just talking about a lack of good teaching on science: most churches have not taught the basics of the philosophical reasons why faith in God is morally, historically, and existentially reasonable.

There are generally two reasons for this. The first is because too many pastors, ministers and priests are uninformed. Whilst they may be able to give you the latest theories on theological topics like the atonement, many remain ignorant of the issues young people are really seeking answers to: issues such as the scientific credibility of faith, suffering, and other faiths. As such, the church has not given its young adults the philosophical foundations they need to engage with the atheistic tsunami waiting to deluge them at university and in the workplace.

The other reason young people leave the church is that its ministers, particularly in Protestant churches, have not had a passion for the gospel. Some of the reasons for this can be traced back to the 1960s, a time when America was in turmoil. Once revered pillars of society, including religious institutions, were being protested against, and the Nihilistic winds of postmodernism were being felt every-

Introduction

where. It was a time when young adults could avoid being sent to Vietnam if they went to college. (You may be interested to know that Bill Clinton, Joe Biden, and Dick Cheney all had 'student deferments,' but it cannot be said it was because they wanted to avoid Vietnam.) One of the certain ways to avoid the draft was if you trained as a cleric. This resulted in an influx of ordinands who brought with them, from their seminaries and universities, a radicalized liberal culture. It was a culture that put a priority on being critical of the gospel rather than proclaiming it. People in their congregations, including many adults today, were not taught why conventional Christianity is valid. These people picked up on the hopelessness of liberal theology and left the church.

It only takes the loss of one generation.

So, what can we do to avoid being the generation that drops the baton? How will you and I influence the next generation? Let's pick up our responsibility and leave a worthy legacy. For me, it means writing this book.

The first six chapters are designed to give people a rational foundation for Christianity. Chapters 7 through 10 have a different function. They are designed to address the common faith-blocking issues of our time. The final chapter (Chapter 11) unpacks the substance of the hope Christians look forward to.

Before we launch into the book, may I teach you the basics of how to do theology? It will only take a few seconds, honest. It is a helpful thing to know if you have ever wanted to know what the Bible says about any tricky subject you are exploring.

I also want to share this with you because you will occasionally see octagons in this book. Let me explain:

Octagons

Whenever you are faced with a tough theological question, a good practice is to go to the Bible and identify those key truths that are relevant to the question, truths which you can be certain about. These truths act like fences that keep you from straying into danger.

You can then circle your tough question with these truths

Introduction

(fences). This allows you to say that the answer to the question has to be contained somewhere within that ring of truths.

When I do this, I usually end up with an octagon, i.e. eight truths within which the answer is contained. In fact, I have ended up with an octagon so many times, that I now try to end up with one. This helps ensure that I have covered the subject thoroughly and that I'm not charging off in any direction based only on one or two verses of Scripture.

Here's an example of one I put together to answer the question: "What makes prayer effective?"

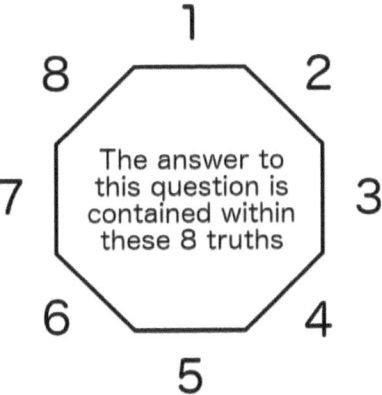

1. Be confident that prayer changes things (James 4:2; 5:14-16).
2. Seek God's agenda (Matthew 6:10).
3. Fix issues that arise through being careless of God and others e.g. Disobeying God (Zechariah 7:13); Not being honest to God about your sins (Psalm 66:18; James 5:16); Not forgiving others (Mark 11:25); Having divided or selfish motives (James 4:2-3); Being inconsiderate to your spouse (1 Peter 3:7); Not caring about those who need help (Proverbs 21:13).
4. Pray as often as you can (1 Thessalonians 5:15).
5. Be bold and wholehearted in prayer (Luke 11:5-8; Deuteronomy 4:29; Jeremiah 29:13; Hebrews 11:6).

6. Persist in prayer. Don't give up (Luke 18:1-8). Believe that God will answer (Mark 11:24).
7. Have faith, even if that faith is as small as a mustard seed (Matthew 17:20-21). Don't doubt (James 1:5-8).
8. Follow the pattern taught by Jesus regarding prayer (Matthew 6:5-15).

Now we have laid the foundation, let's uncover the truth about you.

1

The Cosmos, Meaning, and Me

Does the remarkable being that is 'you' have significance? Do you have meaning?

One of the biggest clues to the answer is found in the cosmos. If it can be shown that the universe displays evidence of design and purpose, it will be a fair indication that you also have purpose.

I suspect that deep down in your soul, you instinctively know that your existence *has* meaning, despite the atheistic clamoring of our age that tells you otherwise. It would be very wise to listen to that inner voice of yours, and here's why.

The universe you live in displays no evidence of being the product of random chaos. In fact, its grandeur, size, and level of order should blow your mind. Here's a little teaser to get you thinking:

There are four forces that build the universe. These will be mentioned later, but for now, I'll just mention just two of them: 'the electromagnetic force' and 'the gravitational force'. The significant thing to note is that the ratio of the strengths of the electromagnetic and gravitational forces needs to be very close to the observed value of 10^{40}, (that's 1 followed by 40 0s!) if planets capable of developing life are to form.[1]

This fact alone should give you a fair indication that the universe has been remarkably fine-tuned to allow for intelligent life to flourish on the third planet out from a middle-aged star. Once we know that the universe is carefully designed, then we are half way to discovering that we also are designed – and therefore have meaning.

If we are to look for clues for the hand of God in the universe, we will need to open our eyes. In other words, we will need to wake up from the deadly slumber of the atheistic reductionist and his horrible, blinkered, half-human world. Not for him the wonder of the cosmos, Beethoven, Mother Teresa, comedy, and laughter. For him, nothing is true; his sense of wonder has no significance. Any sense of needing something greater than self to believe in cannot be countenanced. The only truth allowed is the truth that there is no truth. Everything is meaningless, for he is convinced that he is nothing but a chance collection of atoms.

Please let that not be you. I invite you to take off the blinkers and see the bigness of reality. Give yourself permission to wonder and be amazed, to recover the childlike delight of saying "Wow!" I say this, because I think you are meant to. There is good evidence that God has hung his business card in the cosmos and invites us to see it. A three-thousand-year-old songwriter certainly seemed to think so. The psalmist writes in the Old Testament:

> The heavens declare the glory of God;
> the skies proclaim the work of his hands.
> Day after day they pour forth speech;
> night after night they reveal knowledge.
> They have no speech, they use no words;
> no sound is heard from them.
> Yet their voice goes out into all the earth,
> their words to the ends of the world *(Psalm 19:1-4)*

I believe it is reasonable to suggest that the outrageous splendor and order of the cosmos is an invitation for us to consider the possibility of a Creator, and perhaps learn a few things about him.

The universe is certainly pretty big when viewed from a human perspective. It's about 97 billion light years in size. As light scurries along at the goodly pace of 300,000 kilometers a second, (186,000 miles a second) it can go a very long way in 97 billion years! The very size of the universe may tempt you to believe that you have no significance in it. But this is not so. The British particle physicist, John Polkinghorne, says that the universe has to be as big as it is for life to develop on any one planet. The size of the universe was necessary so that planets and galaxies were far enough apart to avoid gravity clumping them back together before intelligent life could evolve.[2] I hope that makes you feel better.

If it doesn't, then perhaps this quip from the Scottish comedian Arnold Brown will: "I sometimes look at the stars and think: how significant I am."

So, in summary: Why is the universe so big and splendid? Two reasons: 1) to allow life to develop on at least one planet. 2) God is showing off (Psalm 19:1-4).

Dare to Wonder

Let's have a bit of fun and wonder at some amazing things in the cosmos.

There is a star, (a white dwarf) which scientists have nicknamed, Lucy. It sits in the constellation of Centaurus about 50 light years from Earth. It is only 4,000 kilometers in diameter and is the crystallized carbon remains of a once large star. However, the form of this crystallized carbon is none other than diamond. Yes: diamond! That's why scientists have nicknamed it Lucy (after the song: "Lucy in the sky with diamonds" by the Beatles). That's one very big diamond – some ten billion, trillion, trillion carats!

Amazed?

Try this:

The interstellar gas cloud, Sagittarius B, contains a billion, billion, billion liters of alcohol. Tragically, it's not drinkable.

And what about this:

One of Jupiter's moons (Europa) gets squeezed back and forth by Jupiter's gravity like a rubber ball – so much so that it gets hot through friction. The reason this is significant is that it gets hot enough to melt the ice under its surface into water, which could potentially allow life to develop.

I'm telling you these things to encourage you to be amazed at existence. Please don't take it for granted.

How do atheists explain the universe? They either shrug and don't let themselves think about it – which is culpable, intellectual laziness...or they say that everything came from nothing, as a result of nothing, via a mechanism that has never been discovered and for which there is no precedent – which is pretty ridiculous. It is certainly unscientific. The very notion that everything comes from nothing fractures the law of 'cause and effect' that underpins all science.[3]

The most obvious answer to the intrinsic order and creativity of the universe is that there is a mind behind it all. And to deny the significance of this order by postulating the existence of an infinite number of universes is simply avoiding the issue...because the question remains: why did the first universe exist?

Coincidences

You are a leftover. Even more astounding: our universe is made of leftovers.

For every one billion particles of anti-matter in the early universe, there were a billion and one particles of matter. When matter and anti-matter met, they annihilated each other – leaving relatively few leftover particles of matter. The universe, and everything in it, is built from these leftovers – tiny remaining bits of matter that were not canceled out by anti-matter.

Now, here's the thing: Was this a cosmic accident, or was this an intentional outcome?

Rather a lot of things got annihilated in a massive bang in order for you to exist. It's as if God chose to introduce his creation with a giant fireworks display.

Certainly, the opening chapters of the Bible teach us God

delights in his creation. He called it "good." The opening chapters also teach that God delights in having a loving relationship with us.

Now, the big thing is: What are you going do with this information? Will you allow the extraordinary 'show and tell' of the cosmos to prompt you to explore the mind behind it all? Quite frankly, it's difficult to think what else God could have done to invite your faith – short of forcing you.

You are made of star stuff

Let's talk about stars.

Stars are a crucial part of our universe – and the mechanism by which they are made is fascinating. They are made on tendrils of cosmic dust. These are known as 'elephant trunks' and they poke out of giant dust clouds. Elephant trunks can be one light year long, so they're pretty big. Blobs of dust float off them into space. Gravity then causes the dust in these blobs to clump together, and to do so with such force that hydrogen is fused into helium, producing a massive release of heat. When that happens, hey presto! You have a star. Gravity keeps pressing in, causing this reaction to continue over billions of years. This amazing scenario has given enough time to allow life to evolve on planet Earth.

Stars like our Sun are, in fact, giant ovens that cook up hydrogen and helium to form all the atoms in the periodic table up to the weight of iron. Heavier elements can only be made with the exceedingly high temperatures and pressures that occur when big stars (at least eight times bigger than our sun) die in super nova explosions, or when two neutron stars collide. The debris from these explosions scatters atoms into the cosmos. Some of these atoms then clump together to form planets such as our Earth.

It's worth pondering what this means for a moment. Look at yourself in a mirror. Every atom that exists within you was once cooked up inside a star. You are made of star stuff! You truly are a walking cosmic drama.

. . .

Chance or design?

The English physicist and astronomer, Fred Hoyle (1915–2001) had his atheistic convictions shaken a number of times during his life. It happened once when he was trying to work out how a carbon atom could be made. As all living things are carbon-based, it was a relevant question. The trouble was, making carbon inside a star from the component atoms of beryllium and helium seemed impossible. The necessary intermediate reaction states were just too unstable to allow time for a carbon atom to be made. Fred therefore reasoned that there had to be a special 'resonance state' within the nucleus of carbon which would allow reaction rates to increase dramatically, and this energy state would need to correlate exactly to the temperature found inside a star. He managed to persuade a research team at California Institute of Technology to look for this proposed resonance state.

They found it at the temperature Hoyle predicted. When they did, Hoyle wrote:

> *A common sense interpretation of the facts suggests that a superintellect has monkeyed with physics, as well as with chemistry and biology, and that there are no blind forces worth speaking about in nature.*[4]

Coincidences like this have even caused the physicist, Stephen Hawking, who was ambivalent and sometimes antagonistic about faith, to wonder about religious implications. He once said, "The odds against a universe like ours emerging out of something like the Big Bang are enormous. I think there are clearly religious implications."[5]

I think he's right.

Fine-tuning

The fact that our universe seems remarkably conducive to the evolution of intelligent life has led to the development of the 'anthropic principle'. This is the idea that the universe exists in a very precise way that has allowed the existence of humankind. (Anthropic literally means 'of humankind'.)

The scientific finding that underpins the anthropic principle is the level of fine-tuning necessary for our universe to produce life. (Skip this section if you don't like numbers...but let me say, the details are amazing. This is geek heaven!)

There are four forces that build the universe: 1) gravity, 2) the electromagnetic force, 3) the strong nuclear force, and 4) the weak nuclear force. Geraint Lewis, professor of astrophysics at the Sydney Institute for Astronomy, says that these building blocks of the universe come with tight specifications and they never vary. If you fiddle with these fundamental forces just slightly, things go badly wrong.[6]

It appears that the forces that build the universe have to be just right.

A neutron needed to be about 1 percent heavier than a proton for atoms to form and support the chemistry of life.

The ratio of the electromagnetic force to the gravitational force between a pair of protons is approximately 10^{36}. If this number was smaller, only a small and short-lived universe could exist.

The strong nuclear force is the force that holds atoms together. This force had to be precisely right to allow 0.7% of its mass to be converted into energy. If the amount of matter converted were slightly smaller, the universe would consist only of hydrogen. If the amount of matter converted were slightly bigger, nuclear fusion would occur so quickly that no hydrogen would remain, and no galaxies, stars, or planets could have formed.[7]

The fine-tuning surrounding the 'big bang' is also impressive. The radiation left over from the big bang is referred to as the 'cosmic microwave background.' It is responsible for warming the universe $2.725°C$ above absolute zero. (Absolute zero is minus $273.15°C$, or minus $459.67°F$). The radiation is detectable in space at one part in 100,000. If this number were any smaller, the universe would exist only as a collection of gas. No galaxies, stars, or planets would exist. Conversely, if the number were any bigger, the universe would only consist of large black holes.

Now, let's get to some really big numbers.

Quantum mechanics predicts that empty space is teeming with 'virtual particles'. Quantum mechanics requires its particles to temporarily split into two particles momentarily, forming 'virtual particles'. These particles possess energy and, importantly, possess the requisite negative pressure to generate the cosmic repulsion that causes the universe to expand.[8]

Scientists tried to work out how much dark energy would be provided by all these virtual particles that inhabit the quantum vacuum. They came to a conclusion that it was 10^{93} grams per cubic centimeter, (a huge number, that suggests that a thimble full of empty space has a mass density of a million trillion, trillion, trillion, trillion, trillion, trillion, trillion tonnes—which is absurd). Scientists then worked out that the actual value of dark energy is 10^{120th} of their calculated value of 10^{93}! Scientists wondered how they could get it so wrong! But when they applied this correction factor of 10^{120}, the equation for the dark energy force worked brilliantly. But here's the thing: if the correction factor was 10^{119} (just one less) the consequence would be lethal in terms of allowing life to develop in the universe. That's how finely tuned the universe is![9] The English cosmologist, Paul Davies writes: "The odds of this happening by chance is same as tossing a coin and getting heads no fewer than 400 times in a row." He goes on to call this "the biggest fix in the universe".[10]

And there's more:

The rate at which the universe expands had to be finely tuned to one part in 10^{55}. If the universe had expanded any faster, matter would expand too quickly for stars, planets and galaxies to form. If the universe had expanded more slowly, the universe would have collapsed under the force of gravity before any stars could form.

Finally, the mass density of the universe had to be finely tuned to permit life – to a degree of one part in 10^{59}! If the universe were slightly more massive, an overabundance of deuterium from the big bang would cause stars to burn too rapidly for the formation of complex life. If the universe were slightly less massive, a lack of helium would result in a shortage of the heavy elements necessary for life to develop.

Some say when viewing this apparent fine-tuning that these figures are not special, because there might be other combinations of factors that could give rise to life. Indeed, that is so. But it should not blind us to the incontrovertible fact that our universe has very specific parameters that have allowed sentient life to develop. The same people who say there may be other combinations of factors that result in life also need to take seriously the trillions and trillions of other combinations that could have occurred which they know would *not* result in sentient life.

The extraordinary numbers presented here suggest that the universe is very precisely constructed to allow life to exist. This points to the existence of a Mind. Nothing in human experience can explain the existence of anything so extraordinarily fine-tuned other than consciousness.

So, whilst atheists may claim they are rationalists, this is not so. They have to believe the impossible – that all these numbers were arrived at by chance, which is absurd. It is much more reasonable to believe in the existence of a mind behind it all. This means that those who seek that mind are the true rationalists.

I invite you to be one of them.

Anthony Flew (1923 - 2010)

Anthony Flew was professor of Philosophy at Reading University in the UK. He was the intellectual spokesperson for atheism in the late twentieth century. Whilst he was not the only mouthpiece for atheism at this time, he was the one who gave atheism its academic backbone. As such, atheists lionized him.

It therefore came as a shock when he announced in 2004 that he now believed in the existence of God – and he'd done so as a result of learning about the 'fine tuning' of the universe.[11]

As you might imagine, this threw the atheistic community into disarray. If you search the Internet, you will discover even now that some atheists still don't believe it, and claim that a Christian writer put words into his mouth. Others were less kind and suggested Flew had become old and senile.

Flew responded by saying that his whole life "has been guided by the principle of Socrates: "Follow the evidence, wherever it leads.""[12]

Monkeys with computers

Many atheists have claimed that a universe such as ours containing intelligent life could have arisen by chance – in the same way that a group of monkeys typing on computers could eventually type out a Shakespearean sonnet.

The Jewish Physicist, Gerry Schroeder, has exposed this idea as a myth.[13] He reports on the fact that the British National Council of Arts actually placed a computer in a cage with six monkeys for one month. In that time, they'd managed to produce an impressive fifty pages of typing – but not one word.

This should be of no surprise.

Schroeder tells us that a Shakespearean sonnet is 14 lines long – and contains about 488 characters. This means that it would take 26 (the number of letters in the alphabet) multiplied by itself 488 times to have a chance of typing the sonnet by chance. This equates to 1 chance in 10...with 690 zeros after it! To put this into perspective, this is significantly more than the number of protons, electrons, and neutrons in the observable universe (which has been calculated to be 10...with a paltry 80 zeros after it).

In case you want to know what 10...with 690 zeros after it looks like, here it is. It is 10, with:

000,000,000,000,000,000,000,000,000,000,000,000,000,000,000,
000,000,000,000,000,000,000,000,000,000,000,000,000,000,000,
000,000,000,000,000,000,000,000,000,000,000,000,000,000,000,
000,000,000,000,000,000,000,000,000,000,000,000,000,000,000,
000,000,000,000,000,000,000,000,000,000,000,000,000,000,000,
000,000,000,000,000,000,000,000,000,000,000,000,000,000,000,
000,000,000,000,000,000,000,000,000,000,000,000,000,000,000,

000,000,000,000,000,000,000,000,000,000,000,000,000,000,000,
000,000,000,000,000,000,000,000,000,000,000,000,000,000,000,
000,000,000,000,000,000,000,000,000,000,000,000,000,000,000,
000,000,000,000,000,000,000,000,000,000,000,000,000,000,000,
000,000,000,000,000,000,000,000,000,000,000,000,000,000,000,
000,000,000,000,000,000,000,000,000,000,000,000,000,000,000,
000,000,000,000,000,000,000,000,000,000,000,000,000,000,000,
000,000,000,000,000,000,000,000,000,000,000,000,000,000,000,
000,000,000,000,000 after it!

And that is just the chance of typing one 14 line Shakespearean sonnet! Imagine the number of chances you would need to get the zillions of things in place to produce a universe capable of producing intelligent life!

We should not ask the impossible from the concept of infinity. It is an abuse of mathematics to use the term 'infinity' like a magician's hat from which you can pull anything you want. It becomes even more of an abuse if your motive for doing so is to avoid taking the existence of God seriously.

So, what can we conclude? Two things:

1. The miracle of our universe's existence should not be dismissed or taken for granted.
2. It is quite rational to suggest that there is a mind behind the existence of our universe.

To believe that the facts and figures detailed here are no more than happy coincidences, requires significantly more faith than that of the Christian who believes there is a mind behind it all.

Black holes

Come with me "to the dark side" for a while.

Cosmologists tell us that black holes will eventually consume all matter in the universe. This means that the only things that will be left in the universe will be black holes. The question is: do black holes then become the eternal prison for all the information of the universe?

As it turns out, the information in black holes may not be lost. Stephen Hawking has shown that black holes are not completely black. They glow slightly with radiation (which has been labeled, 'Hawking radiation'). This means that black holes slowly lose mass, erode, and die over a period of trillions of years. Hawking suggests that the information that has been swallowed by the black hole is radiated back out into the universe, or even to another universe. Therefor, as the English cosmologist, Brian Cox, says: "it would seem that black holes are not tombs, but gateways."[14]

It is significant that the language of scientists is now sounding remarkably theological. Here are two further statements from Brian Cox:

> *Black holes tell us that our intuitive understanding of space and time are wrong, and that a deeper reality exists ... Space and time are not fundamentally a property of nature. They emerge from a deeper reality in which neither exists.*[15]

These words cast a shadow over the thinking of 'materialist reductionists' who reduce humanity to 'materials' and say there is nothing more that makes humans significant. It seems that scientists are now whispering theological truth to us!

Another intriguing phenomenon to emerge from the study of black holes is that evidence it gives for the interconnectedness of reality. (This was something also hinted at by 'quantum entanglement' – of which more will be said later.') Scientists are suggesting that information contained within a half-eroded black hole becomes the 'same place' as distant information emitted eons earlier through Hawking radiation.[16] If this confuses you, you are in good company! The exact mechanism of this is currently baffling scientists and is still being worked out.

So, where does this leave us?

If we have dispensed with space-time as the fundamental reality and have replaced it with 'information,' that is highly significant. Information, by definition, is not something that is randomly and chaotically configured. It is something that is ordered. This suggests that at the heart of reality is order... and that seems to suggest 'Mind'.

So, here's the question: Does this deeper reality have a divine origin? Is this deeper reality God?

Brian Cox would insist, quite rightly, that this deeper reality might be natural, not supernatural. Certainly, no one can rightly posit God simply because they have reduced reality to information. To do that is to fall into the discredited thinking of inventing a 'God of the gaps.' But what we can say is that the discovery of a deeper reality beyond space-time is totally consistent with theistic belief.

Beginnings

The only thing known to humankind that has ever produced significant 'order' from nothing is intelligence. Chance alone can't do it. Time can't do it. Energy alone can't do it. It has been the experience of humanity that only a mind directing energy can do it. To believe, as atheists do, that everything came from nothing as a result of nothing, is not a rational position.

This reality raises the interesting question of 'beginnings'.

Was there a beginning to the universe?

Alexander Vilenkin is professor of evolutionary science at Tufts University. In 2003, he, along with cosmologists Alvin Borde and Alan Guth, proved that any expanding universe cannot have an infinite past. It must have had a beginning. He says: "All the evidence we have says that the universe had a beginning."[17]

It would seem that we can't avoid the reality of this.' Vilenkin says unequivocally:

> *It is said that an argument is what convinces reasonable men, and a proof is what it takes to convince even an unreasonable man. With the proof now in place, cosmologists can no longer hide behind the possibility of a past-eternal*

universe. There is no escape; they have to face the problem of a cosmic beginning.[18]

The English humorist and author, Terry Pratchett, encapsulated the logical difficulty of atheism when it comes to explaining the origins of the universe, when he wrote: "In the beginning there was nothing...which exploded."[19]

Sir Anthony Kenny is, or has been, a professor of philosophy in both Cambridge and Oxford. He also highlights the atheist's dilemma, saying: "A proponent of the Big Bang theory, at least if he is an atheist, must believe that the universe came from nothing and by nothing."[20]

The cosmologist, Paul Davies, also puts the issue starkly: "...the coming into being of the universe, as discussed in modern science ...is not just a matter of imposing some sort of organization ...upon a previous incoherent state, but literally the coming-into-being of all physical things from nothing."[21]

Multiverses

The British cosmologist and astrophysicist, Martin Rees, was Master of Trinity College, Cambridge from 2004 to 2012 and President of the Royal Society between 2005 and 2010. He has been one of those who have championed the idea of multiverses, that is to say: a universe that successively seeds new universes. This effectively creates a scenario in which universes exist forever...and circumvents the thorny issue of a universe having a beginning.

A significant aspect of this theory is the idea that each re-born universe develops its own physical laws – most of which, it is presumed, don't allow for complex life to develop. However, because there are an infinite number of successive universes, a universe (such as ours) must eventually chance upon a set of scientific rules that enable intelligent life to develop.

The physicist and theologian, John Polkinghorne highlights the bleakness of this view, describing such universes as: "occasional islands of meaningfulness in an engulfing sea of absurdity."[22]

Paul Davies, strongly disagrees with the idea that multiverses solve the issue of beginnings. He says it simply moves the issue up a level. Why do any universes exist at all? Where does the information come from that allows even one universe to have the physical laws necessary to allow sentient life to develop? [23]

Anthony Flew makes the point that, "If the existence of one universe requires an explanation, multiple universes require a much bigger explanation."[24]

It must also be said that the issue is not just *that* we exist, but the *manner* of our existence. The self-observing life form we call "humanity" is not simply a blob of brain able to know itself to be alive for a brief moment of time. It is significantly more. It is Einstein, Beethoven or Florence Nightingale. It is humor, compassion, creativity, love, heroism and science. It is also a shy but persistent ache that compels most of humanity to reach toward a higher being, someone who will give us meaning. The life form that is 'us' really is very remarkable – too remarkable, I suggest, to lazily dismiss as a chance product of an infinite number of universes.

I've heard someone explain the significance of this with this analogy.

Suppose some drug smugglers had tampered with your traveling case while you were touring in a foreign country and customs officials find five kilograms of heroin inside it. The judge refuses to believe you are innocent and condemns you to be shot by a firing squad. You are led out of prison, placed against a wall, and blindfolded. Ten of the army's top marksmen stand eight paces away. At a command from the officer, they cock their weapons. Then you hear, "Ready, aim...FIRE!"

To your amazement, you discover that you are still alive. You feel all over your body, but don't find any bullet holes. Might I suggest that at this point you would do more than shrug with indifference and say, "Well, since I'm here to report on the situation, I must have fluked a set of circumstances that has enabled me to do so." No. You would justifiably seek some sort of explanation.

Caution needs to be exercised when using the term 'infinite' to dilute the significance of the existence of humankind. As I said earlier, the word 'infinite' is not a magician's hat from which anything can be produced. We still need to ask: 'Who' or 'what' began the first universe? Why has 'chance' been given the opportunity to build a universe able to develop humankind?

You do not explain a book simply by pointing to a library of books. Neither do you explain our ordered universe by pointing to the possibility of an infinite number of universes. It is simply not helpful to say that all possible universes exist. To do so comes dangerously close to suppressing inquiry. The twentieth century German mathematician, David Hilbert warns that: "The infinite is nowhere to be found in reality. It neither exists in nature, nor provides a legitimate basis for rational thought ...the role that remains for "infinite" to play is solely that of an idea."[25]

The Oxford philosopher, Richard Swinburne also makes the point that it is crazy to postulate trillions of universes to explain the features of one universe, when postulating one entity (God) will do the job.[26]

The scientific laws of 'cause and effect' mean it is reasonable for us to seek the ultimate cause of the universe, and the ultimate source of the scientific laws by which it operates. Both things point to the existence of mind.

This leads us to consider the question: Isn't science irreconcilable with Christian faith?

Is faith in science irreconcilable with Christian faith?
No.

Perhaps I should expand on this. The logic is pretty simple. If God (as he has revealed himself in the Bible) exists, then *all* truth has its origin in God. This means that both scientific truth and theological truth come from the essence of who God is. Therefore, the two disciplines cannot fight each other. The two disciplines answer different questions, but they must at least make room for each other. It might even be expected that each discipline frames the other so they can dance together.

Essentially, science asks the question, 'how' whilst theology asks the question, 'why'. As such, theology goes deeper. It explores why things are. It seeks to do more than to say lazily, "things exist because they do." Theology puts science in a bigger context. This brings to mind Einstein's aphorism: "Science without religion is lame, and religion without science is blind."

So: If we are really wondering about God, let's read his invitation to get to know him in the cosmos.

Science at war with Christianity
"Science is rational and Christianity is not"...such is the claim of many strident atheists. Many go further and say Christianity is actively at war with science, suppressing its truth.

In reality, this claim is but one of the myths some people wrap around themselves in order to hide from truth and stay huddled within the rhetoric of their own kind. Colin Russell (1928 – 2013) was professor of history at Cambridge and the UK's 'Open University'. He wrote:

The common belief that...the actual relations between religion and science over the last few centuries have been marked by deep and enduring hostility...is not only historically inaccurate, but actually a caricature so grotesque that what needs to be explained is how it could possibly have achieved any degree of respectability.[27]

The truth about Christianity's relationship with science is far more complex.

It may surprise you, but it is not just Christians who display faith, scientists need it too. They need to have faith that the universe is put together in a way that is ordered, consistent, and open to rational inquiry. If they didn't have faith in these realities, they couldn't do science. This has led to some of the world's top scientists saying that belief in God is scientifically reasonable. Paul Davies, a mathematical physicist and cosmologist says:

I belong to the group of scientists who do not subscribe to a conventional religion but nevertheless deny that the universe is a purposeless accident. Through my scientific work I have come to believe more and more strongly that the universe is put together with an ingenuity so astonishing that I cannot accept it merely as a brute fact.[28]

Here's another interesting fact:

Robert Grosseteste and Roger Bacon were clerics in the church in the 13th century. Both men were responsible for revolutionizing how science was done. Until they turned up in history, science was largely restricted to passive observation. However, when Grosseteste and Bacon arrived, they introduced the notion of experimentation. It can therefore be said that experimental science (at least in the West) was born in the Christian church.

In fact, it is very hard to imagine how science could have flourished in the West without Christianity. This was because science was sometimes seen as a spiritual discipline. Why? Science helped to uncover the creative hand of God. Many of the world's top scientists today say the same thing, as we shall see later.

One of the key events in history used by atheists to ridicule Christianity and support their claim that Christianity is inherently anti-science, is the story of the Roman Catholic Church putting Galileo on trial for heresy. They did so because Galileo taught that the earth was not the center of the universe but a heavenly body that circled the sun – an idea that had been revived a century earlier by Copernicus.

The real story is, again, more complex...and it's a ripping yarn, so it's worth telling.

Galileo's tiff with the Catholic Church

Galileo lived at a time when the Roman Catholic Church was desperately trying to regain control in the face of the Reformation, which saw different groups of Protestants going off in a thousand different theological directions. In response to this, the Catholic Church called the Council of Trent (1545–63) at which they decided that only doctors of the church were allowed to give definitive interpretations of Scripture.

Galileo, however, fractured this ruling and was giving interpretations of scripture in the light of his scientific findings. He taught his heliocentric model of the universe as fact, despite the Catholic Church only permitting him to teach it as a hypothesis. (This is worth noting as it shows that the church was not trying to suppress his scientific inquiry.) The Catholic authorities instructed Galileo to get proof for this theory, and then let the church's doctors of divinity interpret the significance of his findings for the church.

The problem was, Galileo didn't actually have the knockout proof for his heliocentric theory of the earth circling the sun. Proof could only come from measuring the parallax of a distant star (measuring its different angle from the Earth six months apart). It was actually Aristotle who defined this requirement (which he'd become convinced of as a result of his study of Pythagoras). Unfortunately, the instrument needed to measure parallax to the required level of precision didn't exist. Ptolemy, Copernicus, and Tycho Brahe had tried, but failed. Galileo also tried, but failed. In desperation, he asked the German astronomer Johannes Kepler for help, but Kepler couldn't deliver either. It wasn't until 1832 that the German scientist Friedrich Bessel built an instrument capable of measuring the parallax of a distant star.

Galileo could actually be obstinate and even wrong when it came to science. For instance, he ascribed the movement of the ocean's tides to the heliocentric motion of the earth, even though Kepler had shown that tides were linked to the timing of the moon's orbit.

In reality, Galileo's fight was not so much with the Catholic Church but with the Aristotelian philosophers whose understanding of the universe was particularly challenged by Galileo's hypothesis. Put simply, Aristotle taught that the sun, moon and stars orbited the Earth in perfect circles – the initial motion being caused by God. Right at the edge of space (or 'aether' as he called it) stars existed that didn't move at all.[29]

Galileo's hypothesis challenged this thinking, and the Aristotelians refused to look through Galileo's new invention (the telescope) at Jupiter's moons to see evidence of his theory for themselves. One of these was Guilio Libri, professor of Aristotelian Philosophy at Pisa. Another was Cesare Cremonini, Professor of Aristotelian Philosophy at the university of Padua. He was friendlier toward Galileo than Libri and did look through the telescope, but he complained it gave him a headache and said he wouldn't do it again! (In reality, it would have cost him his job if he gave credence to Galileo's theory.)

Galileo fueled antipathy with the church by putting the theological objections of Pope Urban VIII (who was once kindly disposed toward Galileo) into the mouth of the fool, Simplicitus, in a satirical book he wrote. It was therefore not surprising that the church brought Galileo to trial on 22 June 1633. Galileo was required, under threat of torture, to "abjure, curse and detest" his Copernican theories.

So there you have it in a nutshell.

I hope the story reminds you to be careful with atheistic claims that Christianity is inherently anti-science.

If there is a mind behind the universe, (as is suggested by the remarkable order and fine-tuning of events that caused it to exist), then scientific truth and theological truth have the same origin – God. Therefore, the two disciplines cannot, or should not, fight. They should, however, be allowed to answer different questions. As we said earlier: science answers the question 'how' whilst theology answers the question 'why'.

...and 'why' is a very, very, interesting question.

Both science and Christianity require faith

It is not the case that science is driven by skepticism, observation, and experiment, while Christianity requires you to believe "six impossible things before breakfast." Science and Christianity are *both* built on evidence...and both require faith.

The cosmologist, Paul Davies, makes the point that scientists can only do their work on the assumption that nature is ordered, rational, and intelligible. If the universe was chaotic, they couldn't do their work. When scientists begin their investigations, they expect to encounter a universe that is set out in elegant mathematical order.[30] Davies goes on to say that the intelligibility of the cosmos is reflected in the laws of physics – the fundamental rules that determine how nature runs. These laws of physics are regarded as sacrosanct; phenomena that have always existed in our universe.

The obvious question prompted by this is: Where did these laws come from? After all, the idea that they exist without reason is anti-rational.

The relevance of this is that scientists need faith to do their work. They need to have faith that something, or someone, has ordered the universe so that it is accessible to rational inquiry. Paul Davies says bluntly, "Until science comes up with a testable theory of the laws of the universe, its claim to be free of faith is manifestly bogus."[31]

The Nobel Prize winning physicist, Max Planck (considered to be the founder of quantum theory) put this truth in an even more extreme way. He simply said: "Both religion and science require a belief in God."[32]

Wow!

Why can we understand the universe?

It's worth dwelling for a moment on this remarkable feature of the universe – that it is not only ordered, but it is ordered in such a way that our minds can unlock the secrets of how it works. It's almost as if we were meant to understand it. In other words; it is not only the universe that has been fine-tuned, but the human mind seems to have been fine-tuned to be able to lay bare its workings.

The big question, of course, is: Why?

John Polkinghorne suggests that the answer is found in God. He says: "If the universe is the creation of a rational God, and we are creatures made in the divine image, then it is entirely logical that there is order in the universe, and that it is accessible to our minds."[33]

Einstein's recognition of the rational nature of reality and its accessibility to the human mind led him to say: "I have never found a better expression than (religion) for this trust in the rational nature of reality, and of its peculiar accessibility to the human mind."[34]

Willful atheism

As I write this chapter, I am seeking to present facts that suggest faith in God is rational and reasonable. However, I am under no illusion that 'facts' will always be the key that unlocks faith in the heart of an atheist. Most atheists hold their position for emotional reasons rather than rational ones (as will be seen in a later chapter). Thomas Nagel, professor of philosophy at New York University, displays something of this reality when he says:

> *I want atheism to be true, and I am made uneasy by the fact that some of the most intelligent and well-informed people I know are religious believers. It isn't just that I don't believe in God and naturally, hope there is no God! I don't want there to be a God.*[35]

It is therefore worth pausing for a moment so we can consider the reality of 'willful atheism'.

I used to think that the apostle Paul was being a bit unreasonable when he said that there was no excuse for not believing in God, because the evidence for God can be seen clearly in creation. He wrote: "For since the creation of the world God's invisible qualities – his eternal power and divine nature – have been clearly seen, being understood from what has been made, so that people are without excuse" (Romans 1:20).

Now, however, I am not so sure Paul was being extreme.

In his book, *Jesus Among Other Gods*, the Christian apologist, the late (and sadly, morally disgraced) Ravi Zacharias, makes the point that the problem posed by many atheists is not the absence of evidence, but the suppression of evidence.[36] In other words, whilst many atheists trot off intellectual excuses for not believing in God, what they are actually doing is refusing to have an honest look at the evidence that does exist. They are doing exactly what the apostle Paul accuses them of in Romans 1:18 – they are 'suppressing' evidence.

What makes this particularly odious is that they are doing this whilst claiming to stand on the intellectually high ground of reason. I respectfully want to suggest that such people need to come at Christians with something more substantial than the claim that the universe came from nothing, as a result of nothing, via a mechanism of which science has no proof.

Despite lack of scientific evidence, some have tried to make this very claim. The American scientist, Lawrence Krauss, (a strident atheist) wrote a book called *A Universe from Nothing*. It is a philosophically muddled book in which he speculates that it is possible for a universe to come from nothing—provided some parameters (such as quantum fields and the physical laws that govern them) are already in existence to allow it. He wants to call the empty space of the cosmos 'nothing' whilst also insisting that this 'nothing' is actually a cauldron of virtual particles which can pop into physical existence when interacting with powerful fields. But as Neil Ormerod, Professor of Theology at Australian Catholic University, has pointed out: "Scientifically this may well be correct, but it clearly does not address the question of whether something *can* (italics mine) come from nothing." [37] Krauss' great mistake, of course, is to fail to understand what 'nothing' really means.

The inherent hubris of humankind means that many simply *don't want* God to exist. This is presumably because any God presents a challenge to their autonomy. They don't want to make God the Lord of their life, as it would be inconvenient to their life-style.

I must hasten to say that many morally good atheists do exist, and some of them have legitimate intellectual problems with theism – 'suffering' being one of them. However, if you bring to an intellectual debate a mindset of not actually *wanting* there to be a God, then you will not come with an open mind. You will come to the debate with a self-blinding bias.

What surprises me is the passion people can display who want to believe there is no God. It's good to be aware of it because you can be attacked by raw emotion and ridicule rather than reason if you challenge their thinking. So, have the wisdom to know when to speak and when to keep silent.

The leading atheistic philosopher in the early twentieth century, Bertrand Russell, was once asked what he would say to God by way of explanation when asked why he didn't believe in him. His reply was: "Not enough evidence; not enough evidence"... which raises the really good question: What would enough evidence look like?

What if God answered this question by creating a universe of unimaginable wonder – a universe constructed according to the rules of very advanced mathematics? Would that cause atheists to accept the probable existence of God? And what if the universe had many factors finely tuned to a degree of many, many trillionths of exactitude so as to allow life to develop on at least one planet? Could atheists reasonably dismiss that as coincidental? How many trillionths would an atheist need before he or she reviewed their position?

In Bertrand Russell's case, he simply refused to look at the evidence. During a 1948 debate with the Jesuit philosopher, Father Frederick Copleston, he said: "I do think the notion of the world having an explanation is a mistake. I don't see why one would expect it to have."[38] This comment from a leading academic is an extraordinary one. Russell's answer to the existence of mind-boggling complexity, codes, and fine-tuning of the universe, was simply not to ask any questions about it. This, I submit, is not being intellectually honest.

Not everyone is interested in seeking truth. I once heard an atheist say: "If life has no purpose, why work it out?" It seems to be a sentiment that reflects the philosophy of many in society, which is odd, because it is an illogical, circular argument. If you don't at least *try* to work out what the meaning of life is, you will, rather unsurprisingly, come to the conclusion that life has no purpose.

Many don't bother trying to 'work life out' because it results in a highly desirable outcome – the freedom to do what they like. Unfortunately, it also carries with it an attendant outcome that is highly toxic to human well-being: they consign themselves to meaninglessness.

Being able to 'do what you like,' and having 'no meaning,' is a dreadful cocktail of convictions that have resulted in the worst human abuses seen in history. It is also a mournful expression of hopelessness that can find little expression outside of deep depression. I would want to spare you that, so please don't stick your head in the sand and surround yourself with ignorance when it comes to God.

Quotes from the great scientific minds of history

Let's pause at this point and luxuriate in the wisdom of the great scientific minds of history.

We'll begin with **Albert Einstein**.

If you Google 'Einstein and Christianity' you will discover an unseemly squabble between Christians wanting to claim Einstein was a Christian, and atheists who want to insist he was an atheist. Each wants Einstein, and his brilliance, to be on their side to lend them credibility.

The truth concerning Einstein is actually much more interesting – and, I submit, significant.

Einstein was a brilliant scientist. He was not, however, a brilliant theologian...and it is perhaps unfair for people to expect him to be one. Theology was not his area of study. What is significant is that science took Einstein as far as it could toward God. Einstein's scientific study convinced him of God's existence. It gave him good reasons to believe in a higher being. However, that was as far as he was able to go. Although he was firmly convinced of the historical reality of Jesus Christ, theology was not his forte. He was not able to give a conventional Christian definition to the God he'd become convinced of through science.

Einstein's parents were atheistic Jews, so he didn't have a Christian heritage. He had also observed some overbearing behavior from church institutions, and this did nothing to endear him to conventional Christianity. As such, Einstein contented himself in being a theist. Why? Because that's where the science took him. He did not believe in a God who was interested in us personally. His brand of theism could best be described as deism.[39] Sometimes, in his uncertainty, he described himself as an agnostic (someone who isn't sure about God's existence.)[40] But he made it quite clear that he was not, and never had been, an atheist (someone who is convinced that there is no God.)[41]

The significance of Einstein's story is that science took one the greatest minds of modern history to God. Therefore, to suggest that science must inevitably do the opposite is quite wrong.

Here are some of his quotes:

I'm not an atheist, and I don't think I can call myself a pantheist. We are in the position of a little child entering a huge library filled with books in many languages. The child knows someone must have written those books. It does not know how. It does not understand the languages in which they are written. The child dimly suspects a mysterious order in the books but doesn't know what it is. That, it seems to me, is the attitude of even the most intelligent human being toward God.[42]

In view of such harmony in the cosmos, which I, with my limited human mind, am able to recognize, there are yet people who say there is no God. But what really makes me angry is that they quote me for the support of such views.[43]

I want to know how God created this world ...I want to know His thoughts. The rest are details.[44]

The French biochemist, **Louis Pasteur** (1822 - 1882) was one of the fathers of modern medicine.

Posterity will one day laugh at the foolishness of modern materialistic philosophers. The more I study nature, the more I stand amazed at the work of the Creator. I pray while I am engaged at my work in the laboratory.[45]

The Scottish scientist, **James Clerk Maxwell** (1831 - 1879) was responsible for formulating the classical electromagnetic theory.

> *Science is incompetent to reason upon the creation of matter itself out of nothing. We have reached the utmost limit of our thinking faculties when we have admitted that because matter cannot be eternal and self-existent it must have been created.*[46]

Charles Darwin (1809 - 1882) was an English naturalist who gave scientific evidence for biological evolution.

> *I have never been an atheist in the sense of denying the existence of God.*[47]

> *Another source of conviction in the existence of God, connected with the reason and not with the feelings, impresses me as having much more weight. This follows from the extreme difficulty or rather impossibility of conceiving this immense and wonderful universe, including man with his capacity of looking far backward and far into futurity, as the result of blind chance or necessity. When thus reflecting I feel compelled to look to a First Cause having an intelligent mind in some degree analogous to that of man; and I deserve to be called a Theist.*[48]

Arno Penzias and his colleague Robert Wilson discovered the cosmic microwave background radiation left over from the 'Big Bang.' They were awarded a Nobel Prize for their work in 1978. Arno Penzias wrote:

> *The best data we have* (concerning the Big Bang) *are exactly what I would have predicted, had I nothing to go on but the five books of Moses, the Psalms, the Bible as a whole.*[49]

> *If there are a bunch of fruit trees, one can say that whoever created these fruit trees wanted some apples. In other words, by looking at the order in the world, we can infer purpose and from purpose we begin to get some knowledge of the Creator, the Planner of all this. This is, then, how I look at God. I look at God through the works of God's hands and from those works imply intentions. From these intentions, I receive an impression of the Almighty.*[50]

Astronomy leads us to a unique event, a universe which was created out of nothing, one with the very delicate balance needed to provide exactly the conditions required to permit life, and one which has an underlying (one might say 'supernatural') plan.[51]

Christopher Isham (theoretical physicist at Imperial College London, and one of Britain's leading quantum cosmologists)

Perhaps the best argument ...that the Big Bang supports theism is the obvious unease with which it is greeted by some atheist physicists. At times this has led to scientific ideas ...being advanced with a tenacity which so exceeds their intrinsic worth, that one can only suspect the operation of psychological forces lying very much deeper than the usual academic desire of a theorist to support his or her theory.[52]

Werner Heisenberg (1901 - 1976) was an eminent German quantum physicist.

In the course of my life I have repeatedly been compelled to ponder on the relationship of these two regions of thought [science and religion], *for I have never been able to doubt the reality of that to which they point.*[53]

Freeman Dyson (1923 - 2020, theoretical physicist)

The more I examine the universe and study the details of its architecture, the more evidence I find that the universe in some sense knew we were coming.[54]

I hope you enjoy reading the wisdom of some of the finest minds in history, and have allowed it to enrich you.

Worshiping nature

Atheists who appeal to rationally understandable scientific processes as the cause of everything, come dangerously close to nature worship. They are appealing to something they see in the universe – scientific process – and saying it made everything.

Christians would say they are worshiping a process rather than the creator of the process. There is little difference between doing this and worshiping a tree rather than the creator of the tree. Please don't do it.

Perhaps a small discourse is warranted here on the 'laws of nature'.

Laws of nature are simply mental conclusions we come to as a result of seeing observable regularities in nature. They are not gods. They do, however, point to 'order' and 'regularity' – an order and regularity that can reasonably be ascribed to a 'mind'.

Isaac Newton made the point that the fact that we have a 'law of gravity' tells us only how things behave under the influence of whatever gravity is. It tells us nothing about the what/how/whence of gravity and how it can reach across the squillions of kilometers of empty space and pull things in.

So please don't ask anything of the 'laws of nature' they can't deliver – or turn them into gods.

Where you stand with 'The Enlightenment' will determine what you see

It is difficult to overstate the seismic shift in philosophic thinking brought about by The Enlightenment of the 17th century. Prior to The Enlightenment, the cultural philosophy of the time was based on Aristotelian thinking which factored in an 'ultimate cause' when studying natural science, (see: Aristotle's 'Four Causes'). However, The Enlightenment instituted new principles for doing science that removed all consideration of an ultimate cause. This way of thinking was articulated particularly by the English philosopher, Francis Bacon (1561-1626), who is considered to be the father of modern 'scientific method'.

The reason I mention this seismic change in thinking is this: It seems curiously circular to follow Francis Bacon's directions for rational inquiry and exclude all thought of God – then look at science and be surprised that you see no God!

. . .

Making sense of our ending

The marvels of the cosmos, and the marvels of creation, are designed to encourage us to reach out to God. The Bible says in Acts 17:27: "God did this (create the world) so that people would seek him and perhaps reach out for him and find him, though he is not far from each one of us."

So...I invite you to reach out. I do so because all evidence suggests that there will be an ending. You will physically end. And interestingly, so will our solar system. Scientists tell us that our sun will die in 4.5 billion years' time. If you manage to escape to another solar system, you are not out of the woods, because the universe itself is due to die and fade away in what is known as 'heat death'.

The British astrophysicist and theologian, David Wilkinson, writes about how non-Christian scientists are feeling about a world without hope. In his book, *Christian Eschatology and the Physical Universe*, he says: "This end of Universe in the heat death of futility raises a great deal of pessimism within the scientific community."[55] Certainly, the 20th century atheistic philosopher, Bertrand Russell, didn't express much hope. He said:

> ...*The world which science presents for our belief is even more purposeless, and more void of meaning ...all the labors of the ages, all the devotion, all the inspiration, all the noonday brightness of human genius, are destined to extinction ...and the whole temple of man's achievements must inevitably be buried beneath the debris of a universe in ruins.*[56]

Paul Davies echoes this sentiment and says: An "almost empty universe growing steadily more cold and dark for all eternity is profoundly depressing."[57]

The huge question each of us needs to answer is: Why? Why does anything exist, if it's all just going to end? What on earth am I here for?

The Bible makes it clear that this is a question God expects us to ask. The Apostle Paul says that it is reasonable for people to look at existence, ponder its meaning, and let it introduce the possibility of God (Romans 1:19-20).

Conclusion

I mentioned in the introduction to this book that atheism is parasitic on science. What I mean by this is that it tries to suck academic credibility from science, whilst giving nothing of intellectual substance back in return. I hope that this chapter makes it clear that any claim by atheists that their position stands on the high ground of rationality is bogus.

I can think of no better way to end than with a quote attributed to the great quantum physicist, Werner Heisenberg. "The first gulp from the glass of natural sciences will make you an atheist, but at the bottom of the glass God is waiting for you."[58]

2

Creation, Evolution, and Me

It may be a little unsettling but the fact is: a chimpanzee and a human being have 98.8 per cent of their DNA in common. We are very close cousins, biologically speaking. However, we are also very different. Only humans have the ability to reach for the stars and comprehend the cosmos. Through the agency of mathematics and the beautiful equations that define the laws of nature, we have unlocked many of the secrets of the universe. Perhaps our ability to do so is actually an *invitation* for us to explore it.

Some scientists are asking why humankind has this extraordinary power to understand things. The particle physicist and theologian, John Polkinghorne, marvels that the universe is so astonishingly open to us and so rationally transparent to our inquiry. In his view, the fact that we understand the subatomic world of quantum theory, and the cosmic implications of general relativity, goes far beyond anything that could conceivably be required by evolution.[1]

Our universe is extraordinarily intelligible to us, and it allows mathematics to unlock its secrets. For Christians, this is not surprising. As we said in the last chapter: If a rational God created the universe, then it is entirely to be expected that its workings will be open to our inquiry.

The first book in the Bible says that humankind is the result of a deliberate act of self-expression on the part of God. It records God saying: "Let us make humankind in our image, in our likeness" (Genesis 1:26). It is therefore to be expected that we, like God, are rational beings.

However, being made in God's image means a lot more than being rational. It also means:

- The big-heartedness of God lives in us.
- The passion for good to win lives in us.
- The creativity of God lives in us.
- The desire for significance lives in us.
- The ache for the love of God lives in us.
- The hunger for the eternity of God lives in us.

It also explains why:

- Death is obscene to us.
- Lack of meaning is obscene to us.
- Lack of relationships is obscene to us.
- Lack of a purpose is obscene to us.
- Lack of being able to give and receive love is obscene to us.

No other religion in the history of the world has made the claim that we are made in God's image.

Christians believe that because we have been made in God's image, we have the ability to make spiritual, intellectual, and moral judgments in a way that no other created being can – even those to which we are closely related biologically. Dr. Ian Tattersall, in his book, *Becoming Human*, reminds us that humanity represents a totally unprecedented entity on Earth.[2]

Therefore, don't write yourself off! Don't think of yourself as simply being a species of animal that has climbed to the top of the evolutionary pole, and since become toxic to the rest of the planet.

There is another very important significance to being human. If you are made in the image of God, it means you were created to relate to God. It logically follows that if you are not relating to God, you have fallen short of your calling, and you are operating merely on the level of the rest of the animals.

Is God necessary to make life?

The idea of God creating everything took a bit of battering in 1953 when Harold Urey and Stanley Miller, researchers at the University of Chicago, introduced some electrical sparks to a mixture of gasses and water that simulated the Earth's early atmosphere. After a few days, the water discolored with a mixture of a few simple amino acids. As amino acids are the building blocks of proteins, the basis of all life, some people claimed that the idea of God was redundant. Brute circumstances can fluke the existence of amino acids. The mystery of how proteins and life came about was solved.

Alas, this is not so. Leaving aside the rather obvious fact that God began with nothing – no laboratory, no flasks, no chemicals, no physical laws – the fact is, whilst making amino acids is relatively easy, making proteins capable of sustaining life is mind-bogglingly difficult.

To build a protein, you have to put amino acids in precisely the right sequence. As a typical protein consists of two hundred amino acids, the likelihood of making one protein by chance would be equivalent to spinning a slot machine with two hundred wheels, each with twenty symbols (to represent twenty of the most common amino acids)...and then getting the winning combination.

You don't reckon that's a big deal? Let me explain. It would require you to spin the wheels more times than there are atoms in the universe.[3]

And if that is not enough, there needs to be a sophisticated organization that will protect the acidic environment of DNA from the alkaline environment of proteins. (A living cell is lot more than a blob of soup!)

It would appear that God is not redundant after all.

Notwithstanding his atheistic convictions, the English physicist and astronomer, Fred Hoyle wrote that the likelihood of chance alone being responsible for making even the simplest of living cells, was about the same as that of a tornado sweeping through a junkyard and assembling a Boeing 747 airplane.[4]

The British philosopher, Anthony Flew, says that we need to ask: "How can a universe of mindless matter produce beings with intrinsic ends, self-replication capabilities, and 'coded chemistry?'"[5] He goes on to wonder why living matter has "an inherent goal, or end-centered organization, that is nowhere present in the matter that preceded it."[6]

It's a good question, but we need to be careful. When talking about living matter having "intrinsic ends" and "an inherent goal", we are not talking about evolution. Evolution is blind. It doesn't try to get anywhere. It just selects mutations that help an organism adapt to a particular ecological niche. Flew is talking something more elemental. He is talking about how mindless matter can result in complex life forms that have a drive to reproduce, adapt and thrive.

Paul Davies makes the point that life is more than complex chemical reactions. The living cell operates according to coded information. As such, the cell is "an information storing, processing and replicating system." He goes on to say, "The problem of how meaningful or semantic information can emerge spontaneously from a collection of mindless molecules subject to blind and purposeless forces presents a deep conceptual challenge."[7]

Flew reminds us that there is "no law of nature that instructs matter to produce end-directed, self-replicating entities."[8] The fact that it does so is therefore a mystery. He goes on to quote the Nobel Prize-winning physiologist, George Wald, who said, "We choose to believe the impossible: that life arose spontaneously by chance."[9]

Flew concludes that "the only satisfactory explanation for the origin of such 'end-directed, self-replicating' life as we see on earth is an infinitely intelligent Mind."[10]

Is Christianity scientifically credible?

According to a South Australian survey conducted in 2001, eighty percent of tertiary trained people (who don't attend church) believe that Christianity is not scientifically credible.[11] In other words, they believe you have to commit intellectual suicide to be a Christian. I can't imagine this statistic has improved much in the intervening years.

Whichever way you view it, this statistic is deeply concerning.

Christians have no right to put obstacles to others coming to faith by requiring them to believe things that are scientifically absurd. Exaggerated claims have been publicized by some Christian organizations aimed at discrediting the evolutionary theory. Sadly, their writings are often distortions of scientific truth. As a result, they have achieved little other than to fuel a sub-culture amongst Christians that holds views not seen to be credible by most scientists – and many Christians.

Equally, secular scientists need to be careful that they don't trumpet the claim that evolution discredits the existence of God. Whilst evolution is a plausible mechanism that explains the development of biological diversity, it cannot explain why such a mechanism exists, how the universe began, why it is so amazingly ordered, and why we can understand it.

Some have questioned the ability of evolutionary theory to explain all of the biological complexity we see in life, and have done so for legitimate scientific reasons. These views should be respected, but it needs to be said that such scientists are a minority group. Despite this, no scientific theory should be dismissed on ideological grounds – whether these ideologies are religious or atheistic. Any theory needs to be held up to rigorous scientific scrutiny and be accepted or rejected solely on that basis.

Other people seek to discredit evolutionary theory because they believe that by doing so they are protecting the status of the Bible as the infallible word of God. This is regrettable as they fail to understand that Scripture contains the consistent principles of God mediated through the writings of people living in a particular historical context. Those seeking to protect the Bible in this way do not appreciate, for example, that the opening chapters of Genesis are not primarily concerned with science's 'how' and 'when', but theology's 'who' and 'why'. As such, they try to impose on scripture dogma the original authors (and God) never intended. This stresses the importance of interpreting a biblical text rightly, according to its literary genre.

When interpreting the Bible, our job is to look past those features in scripture that reflect the cultural context of the time (such as the necessity for women to wear veils), and see beyond them to the timeless principles that are consistent with *all* of scripture. This will reveal those principles God wants all people, at every period of history, to understand and live by.

Is the Earth really 4.5 billion years old?

It's very easy to be chronologically arrogant and sneer at the work of Archbishop, James Ussher (1581 - 1656), when viewing him from the perspective of today. To do so, would be a pity. By the standards of his time, he was considered to be a very bright chap who published widely throughout his life. He was renowned for his mastery of Semitic and classical languages, and for his knowledge of history. Ussher used the chronologies and dates mentioned in the Bible to work out that God must have created the world in 4004BC.

Scientists have since told us that the universe is 13.8 billion years old, and the Earth 4.5 billion years old.

So much for the Bible and Bishop Ussher!

But let's not be too rude. It is easy to forget that science was in its infancy in the early seventeenth century, and the discipline of reading the Bible in the way its original authors intended was not always appreciated. We might permit ourselves to say that Bishop Ussher would have done well to note what one of the great fathers of the Christian church, St. Augustine (354 - 430AD), wrote, [12] and perhaps a little of what the reformer John Calvin (1509 - 1564) also wrote. Both men were critical of those who turned to the Scriptures for answers to cosmological questions the writers of the Bible never intended to teach. Calvin said bluntly, "He who would learn astronomy and other recondite arts, let him go elsewhere."[13]

The big question is: Has evolution fully explained the origin and design of the marvelous range of species that live on our planet?

The short answer is that evolution has nothing to say about the origin of life on the planet, but is a remarkably useful and well-attested theory that explains the design of species that live, or have lived, on Earth.

There are two mistakes that can be made when considering evolution. The first is not to accept the full significance of it. The second is to over-blow the significance of it.

It is worth remembering that evolution only occurs in living organisms. As such, it cannot explain the extraordinary chemical and structural organization necessary to build the first living cell. Neither can it explain the existence of a universe able to develop sentient life.

One of those seeking to keep evolutionary biologists honest in their claims is the Jewish agnostic, David Berlinski. Berlinski (a mathematician and historian) is a senior fellow of the Discovery Institute's Center for Science and Culture. He is author of the book *The Devil's Delusion: Atheism and Its Scientific Pretension*, which he wrote in response to Richard Dawkins' book *The God Delusion*.[14] Berlinski believes that evolution may not give a fully adequate explanation of the existence of all living things. In saying this, Berlinski is, in fact, simply voicing a misgiving that Darwin himself had. When writing about there being no (or not enough) evidence of pre-Cambrian life forms, Darwin wrote: "To the question, why we do not find records of these vast primordial periods, I can give no satisfactory answer ...The case at present must remain inexplicable; and may be truly urged as a valid argument against the views here entertained."[15]

Darwin's misgiving was picked up by the American scientist and college professor, Stephen Meyer, in his book *Darwin's Doubt*.[16] It was a book that caused an unholy furor amongst biologists. Meyer's main argument is the mathematically impossible time scale required to support the emergence of new genes required to drive the explosion of new species during the Cambrian period. This difficulty had been picked up earlier at the 1966 Wistar Conference at the University of Pennsylvania. On this occasion, mathematicians, engineers, and biologists tried to define the mechanism that drove evolution. They agreed that evolution happened, but they weren't sure how. Where did the innovations come from? Were they accidental or did they arise as a result of a system embedded within life forms? The mathematicians said to the group of rather frustrated biologists, that they couldn't make the math explain what the biologists were observing.

Stephen Gould and Niles Eldredge, the American evolutionary biologists, sought to solve the dilemma by positing the theory of 'punctuated equilibrium'. This suggested that there were bursts of biological development (evolution) in history that were followed by long stable periods in which there was little change. This, of course, prompts the question of 'how,' and 'why'.

It would seem that there are questions still to be answered. Berlinski, for example, wonders why there is a lack of major transitional fossils, and how the ingenious design of the eye could have evolved incrementally. He also wonders why sharks have shown little evidence of evolution in the last sixty million years.[17]

Unsurprisingly, his questionings have drawn a sharp response from Richard Dawkins, whose sensibilities have been sensitized both by his anti-theistic convictions, and by the overblown claims of biblical literalists. Dawkins' response cannot, however, be entirely dismissed as blinkered atheistic thinking. Evolutionary biologists have identified plausible explanations to the biological phenomena Berlinski refers to. Berlinski does, however, serve to remind all scientists to hold their position with a degree of humility, and with a readiness to re-examine their theories in the light of new evidence.

Richard Dawkins

It's worth dwelling for a moment on Richard Dawkins, the

Oxford biologist who has been one of the most strident and vociferous atheists attacking Christianity in recent years.

The anti-Christian diatribes of Dawkins have resonated well with people in the West living in a post-Christian age. Many have applauded him...and in so doing, have participated in promoting the worldwide phenomenon of Christianity being the most persecuted religion in the world.

Dawkins' anti-Christian diatribes have arrived at a perfect time in history. They have arrived at a time that is not only post-Christian, but also post-truth. As such he can claim in his book *The God Delusion* that:

- Jesus may not have existed. He uses the term: "Jesus (if he existed)" frequently.
- Jesus' command to "love your neighbor" really meant loving only fellow Jews.
- Hitler was a Christian. [18]
- There are almost no serious academics in Oxford University who are Christian.
- Christianity encouraged slavery.
- Christianity is hateful toward women. [19]

These are outrageous distortions of truth. Nonetheless, his acolytes seem to love it and accept what he says uncritically. All I can say to them is: "Shame on you. Do not for a moment, think that by applauding Dawkins' diatribes that you are standing on the intellectual high ground of truth."

Amazingly, Dawkins is so wedded to his evolutionary convictions, that he asks his readers to trust him in believing that evolutionary processes similar to those found in biology will be found to explain how the universe developed.

Wow! Is a scientist really asking us to believe in something before a single piece of evidence has been found to indicate its truth?

I think I've said enough! Let's return to real empirical science.

. . .

Geological evidence

Geochronology is the science of determining the age of rocks, fossils, and sediments, usually by using radioactive dating methods. One of the most useful radioactive dating methods, centers on the use of zircon crystals.

Zircon crystals are small crystals that form within rocks such as granite. Here's the interesting bit: In its molten state, zircon rejects lead. When zircon is first formed, it contains no lead. It does, however, contain uranium. Uranium exists as a number of isotopes that decay over huge periods of time into lead. This means that if you know the radioactive half-life of the uranium isotopes, and can measure how much of it has turned into lead, then you can date the age of the zircon in the rocks.

The uranium isotope ^{238}U decays into lead (^{206}Pb) with a half-life of 4.47 billion years. ^{235}U, another common uranium isotope, decays into ^{207}Pb with a half-life of 0.704 billion years. As both isotopes usually occur in zircon, you have two dating mechanisms for rocks containing zircon.

But how accurate are they?

The two uranium/lead dating mechanisms are accurate to within 1%, and both show that the earth is billions of years old.

Those wishing to hold on to Bishop Ussher's idea of the earth being 'young' have claimed that radioactive dating is wrong because it assumes:

1. The decay rate has been constant throughout time.
2. The isotope levels in the specimen have not been altered during its history by the addition or removal of either parent or daughter elements.
3. When the rock was formed, it may have already contained an amount of daughter material.

So, what can we say?

Firstly: Geologists have assumed that the decay rate has remained constant throughout time, and have done so because there is no evidence to the contrary. Secondly: Geologists have methods for detecting loss or removal of the parent or daughter elements, and so can account for it. Thirdly: it is known from laboratory tests that molten zircon really does reject lead. We can therefore be very sure that zircon contained no lead in its early molten state.

So, the earth really is very old.

I hope that helps.

Charlie (Charles Darwin)

Charles Darwin (1809-1882) was an English naturalist. He traveled the world in a ship called *The Beagle*, collecting and recording information on wildlife and fossils.

From what he observed, he concluded that some individuals of a species were able to adapt slightly in a way that made them better able to thrive in a particular environmental niche. Because they were able to thrive, the characteristics that gave them an advantage over other individuals of the same species were passed on to more offspring, causing their numbers to increase. Nature therefore selected the 'survival of the fittest'. Its continual selection of what worked best ensured that all living species were able to continually adapt and develop so that they became ever more specialized at thriving in a particular ecological niche. This meant that nature did the selection and drove organisms to become more complicated. God was no longer necessary.

As Charles anticipated, this rocked the faith of many people, a fact that caused him to be reticent in publishing his findings.

It's worth pausing a moment to consider why Charles Darwin lost his Christian faith.

Charles did not grow up with a Christian heritage. He studied theology at Cambridge largely at the insistence of his father after Charles had failed as a medical student. He had initially studied medicine at Edinburgh. However, the fact that he couldn't stand the sight of blood, and that he spent too much time collecting beetles and barnacles, meant that he flunked his course. His father, a doctor, reasoned that if Charles became a Church of England cleric, Charles would have all the time he needed to indulge his naturalist pursuits. Certainly, British clerics were at the forefront of biological research at the time.

Despite his parents coming from a largely Unitarian background, (and him having the celebrity atheist, Erasmus Darwin, as a grandparent,) Charles aligned himself with Christianity in his early years. Later in life, however, he lost his Christian convictions – although he never lost his belief in the existence of God.

Charles lost his faith for three reasons.

The first was his research, which indicated that God did not necessarily intend the existence of specific life forms, as Christianity appeared to suggest. The second was the death of his daughter Annie, and the suffering he saw in nature. This caused Darwin to struggle with the idea that a loving God existed. (He had a poorly developed theology of suffering.) The third reason was Darwin's struggle with the idea that God could eternally condemn good people to hell because they weren't Christians.

However, despite walking away from Christianity, Darwin remained a theist. He said, "I have never been an atheist in the sense of denying the existence of God."[20]

Darwin's convictions caused a good deal of consternation in the church, but not universally so. The novelist and cleric, Charles Kingsley, wrote that he found it, "just as noble a conception of Deity to believe that he created primal forms capable of self-development."[21] Frederick Temple, the future Archbishop of Canterbury, also preached that, "the finger of God could be seen at work in the laws of nature," and that there was, "no need to oppose the extension of natural law into new territory."[22]

Cosmic chance, suffering, and hope

Darwin's theory of evolution prompts the question: Is humankind special, or are we just the product of chance? Similarly, Darwin's problem with a God who allows suffering is also worth exploring. So, what can we say?

Firstly, the suggestion that God has set up a giant game of cosmic chance and has no idea what the final outcome will be, is a profoundly un-Christian idea. Christians understand that God stands outside of time and therefore knows full well what the outcomes of 'life' will be. He fully saw the development of humankind *before* he began his act of creation. As such, God intended humankind, even though the evolutionary pathway that resulted in us coming into being was long and convoluted. As such, we are not simply the chance winners of an evolutionary game of dice...and that's probably worth a smile.

Secondly, Christians understand that the existence of suffering suggests something is amiss. Suffering is a consequence of humankind going down a path God never intended, and this has not only impacted humanity, but all of creation. (We shall devote a chapter to the subject of suffering later.) Meanwhile, as we wait for God to institute his perfect 'end game', we can be assured that God shares our pain, and promises to be with us as we navigate our way through it.

Ways of thinking about the creation accounts in Genesis

Dr. David Wilkinson is, at the time of writing, Principal of St. John's College, Durham University. He is not only a theologian, but also one of Britain's top astrophysicists. I once heard him go through the different theories regarding how the creation accounts in the first three chapters of the Bible have been understood. [23] I've researched them a bit more (so all mistakes are mine!) and can now present them here for you.

1) Genesis is a scientific textbook

This idea was promoted in the 20th century by the American young-earth creationist, Henry M. Morris (1918-2006).[24] Young earth creationists take seriously the work of Bishop James Ussher, who, as we've said earlier, concluded from his study of biblical genealogies, that the Earth was created in 4004BC.

In order for Henry Morris to conclude the earth was only 6,000 years old, he believed that God made the earth with a partial appearance of age. Despite this, Morris firmly dismisses the significance of geological fossil records, and the theory of biological diversification through evolution.

Morris backed his claims by suggesting that the speed of light had changed through history. Sadly for Morris, it was found that his 'error bars' were so huge that there was, in reality, no evidence for the change in the speed of light.

To support the evidence for a young earth, some have claimed that human footsteps have been found, together with dinosaur footprints, in the petrified mud of the Paluxy River in Texas.[25]

However, on closer inspection, the allegedly human footprints showed no regularity of direction or stride length, and were found to be either depressions of weathered rock, or the footprints of a small dinosaur. This new evidence was so convincing that John D. Morris, (son of Henry Morris), head of the Institute for Creation Research, reported in the January 1986 issue of his publication *Impact* that "it would now be improper for creationists to continue to use the Paluxy data as evidence against evolution."

2) The universe was made old with perfect 'antiquing'

This idea was promoted by Phillip Gosse, the English naturalist (1810-1888). Gosse argued in his book *Omphalos* (the Greek word for 'navel') that if God created everything from nothing (*ex nihilo*), there would be traces of an existence that had never occurred. So whilst Adam did not require a navel (as he was never born), he must nonetheless have had one. Similarly, some trees had growth rings that they never grew, and fossil records existed of life that had never actually existed.

The rather obvious problem with this theory is: Why would God create things in this way? If he did, it would suggest that God was a deceiver.

It is fair to say that this idea is one that few have taken seriously.

3) Gap Creationism

Thomas Chalmers (1780-1847), a Scottish theologian and political economist, promoted this idea. Chalmers believed that the six days of creation involved literal 24-hour days, but that there was a gap of time between the first and the second verses of Genesis, between God creating the heavens and the earth, and God creating the things that existed on the earth. This, he felt, gave an explanation for the great age of the earth. He further speculated that this gap in time was the result of Satan's 'fall', which caused the earth to become "formless and empty" (Genesis 1:1). God then reconstructed the universe (in a process called 'ruin reconstruction').

The Gap theory therefore allows for fossil animals.

4) Day-age creationism

Hugh Miller (1802-1856), a Scottish geologist and theologian, promoted this theory. He believed that the 'six days' were really 'six ages'. These ages correspond to six different geological rock strata: Azoic, Silurian, Carboniferous, Permian, Oolitic and Tertiary.

This idea, in a less specific form, is still believed by some Christians today who cite Psalm 90:4 and 2 Peter 3:8 as indications that 'a day' could equate to 'a thousand years'. 2 Peter 3:8 says: "But do not forget this one thing, dear friends: With the Lord a day is like a thousand years, and a thousand years are like a day." It has to be said, however, that these Bible verses were written to teach the timelessness of God. They were not designed to teach that God's year equals one thousand human years.

Having said that, the sequence of events listed in Genesis reflects moderately well the sequence scientists now understand must have happened in the formation of planet Earth – particularly if you allow that "birds" (Genesis 1:20) could actually refer to flying insects. (The Hebrew word, *owph*, literally means 'a creature with wings'.) But whilst this is so, such a translation is unlikely. The repeated phrase "and there was evening, and there was morning," after the creation events of each day, also suggest that this theory is unlikely.

. . .

5) "Days" are days of revelation

The best-known exponent of this theory was Air-Commodore Percy J. Wiseman (1888 - 1948). He was an Assyriologist who wrote the book, *Creation Revealed in Six Days*.[26] Wiseman believed that days of creation were not days of creation but days of 'revelation'. His conviction was given further prominence by the Baptist theologian, Bernard Ramm (1916 - 1992) who wrote: "We believe ...that creation was *revealed* in six days, not performed in six days. We believe that the six days are pictorial revelatory days, not literal days, nor age-days. The days are means of communicating to man the great fact that *God is creator*, and that *He is Creator* of all" (italics his).[27]

This theory relies on an imaginative rewriting of scripture so that it reads: "In the beginning, God made *known* the heavens and the earth," rather than its correct reading: "In the beginning, God made the heavens and the earth."

It doesn't require a great biblical scholar to tell us that Wiseman's rewording is not a natural reading of the biblical text. An examination of the text makes no mention of any 'revelatory visions'.

6) A Synthesis of theories

Elements of 'Gap Creationism', 'Day-age creationism', and 'Days of revelation' have been combined together recently in a theory put forward by the Oxford mathematician and theologian, John Lennox.

Lennox is one of the finest apologists for the Christian faith, so his thinking on the first two chapters of Genesis is worth noting. He takes seriously the chronological sequence of the creative events, but notes that the word "day" can have a number of definitions.[28] A day of creation can simply be a period of creative activity.

Lennox believes that the initial act of creation (Genesis 1:1-2) is separated from the six days of creation that followed. The reason he gives for this is that the repeated phrases: "And God said," and "there was evening and there was morning," only begin in Genesis

1:3. By separating 'the beginning' from day 1, the universe is free to have an indeterminate age.[29]

Lennox also explains the creation of the sun and moon after the days of creation (in Genesis 1:16) by adopting the idea that the Hebrew word for 'create' used in this verse (*asah*) can mean 'to appoint', or 'to work in', something that is already there.[30]

7) Literary approach

The 'literary approach' treats Genesis 1 as a literary genre akin to poetry or song. The 7-day framework is, therefore, a literary device that addresses a readership familiar with the 7-day week. The opening chapter of the Bible is designed to be a logical, not a chronological approach. As such, no time-span should be read into it.

The second chapter of Genesis, (which speaks of Adam and Eve) is allegory. *Adham* is the Hebrew word for 'mankind'; he is the original 'everyman' figure. This creation account establishes key theological – not scientific – concepts. It speaks of the status of humans as God's vice-regents, who are given delegated responsibility to manage God's creation.

Taken together, Genesis 1 and 2 place no time constraints on the age of anything, and are not meant to be read as a science textbook.

What can we conclude?

How then are we meant to understand the first two chapters of Genesis that speak of God creating the world?

It is not easy to answer this question, as the writing we have in Genesis has few parallels. We are therefore unable to say that it is 'like' any particular form of writing.

What can be said is that these opening chapters of Genesis appear to be a tapestry of many styles of writing. It has poetic elements such as repeated phrases such as "and it was so," and, "it was good."

Other scholars see significance in the number of times key words are repeated. Therefore, numerology may be involved.

The first chapter of the Bible is certainly a carefully crafted piece of writing. It begins by speaking about three days in which the heavens, sea, and land are formed; and then it continues to the next three days when God populates each of these three environments.

Some of the early church fathers found significance in this ordered process. One of them was Gregory of Nyssa (335-394AD) who was Bishop of Cappadocia, in what is now central modern Turkey. (He was one of the Cappadocian 'Fathers' who played a key role in hammering out an understanding of the Trinity and the Nicene Creed.) Gregory picked up on the ordered structure of Genesis, chapter 1, and accorded biological significance to it: saying that God's act of creation, "proceeded by a sort of graduated and ordered advance to the creation of Man."[31] He suggests that when God made humankind, he made use of the biological features he first put into plants. God then incorporated these features into animals, where they were further developed, before they were used as a basis for God making humankind.

It can be tempting at this point to say, "Wow! Isn't this guy talking about evolution?" but, of course, he is not. The concept of evolution was something that had only been vaguely articulated by the Greek 'Atomists', Leucippus and Democritus. What it does show is that Gregory was keenly appreciative of the sequential, ordered process of God's creation.

It is fair to say that the creation accounts in the opening three chapters of the Bible were never intended to be a scientific textbook. They were intended to answer the questions "who" and "why" rather than "how" and "when." The early church fathers, Origen of Alexandria and Basil of Caesarea, understood this and therefore advocated an allegorical understanding of Genesis 1.[32] It is also worth noting that Galileo wrote a Letter to Madame Christine of Lorraine, Grand Duchess of Tuscany in 1615, in which he quoted St. Augustine's *De Genesi ad litteram*. This quote culminates in the statement: *Spiritus Dei noluisse ista docere homines nulli saluti profutura* ("The Spirit of God did not want to teach people things that would be of no help to their salvation"). Galileo wrote: "It is clear from a churchman who has been elevated to a very eminent position that the Holy Spirit's intention is to teach us how to go to heaven, and not how the heavens go".[33]

There is one other important significance to the first few chapters of Genesis. In a very real sense, the opening chapters of Genesis are a hymn of worship that celebrates the creative initiative of God. In peerless prose, they declare that:

- there is only one God.
- all that exists is created by God.
- God thinks his creation is "good."
- God seeks to have a loving relationship with us.
- evil is rebellion against God, and God has a zero tolerance for it.
- suffering is the result of humankind going down a path God never intended.
- God has not given up on us. He is rescuing his people, and his creation, back to himself.

These are the truths that *all* Christians can unite on with joy. And I hope you're one of them!

3

Jesus, Evidence, and Me

I learned to fly in the UK, courtesy of Southampton University Air Squadron. Tragically, other than a bit of 'outback' flying with a mate, I've hardly flown at all since. Because I've not had a current license, I've been content to fly with other people in command of the aircraft. One day, a guy I'd not met before offered to take me flying. As we were getting to know each other during a preliminary chat, he discovered that I was a pastor. He frowned and said, "Of course, you know that Jesus never said he was God, don't you?"

Now, I have to say: There are times and places for conversations – particularly just minutes before you place your life in a person's hands in a light aircraft. So, what did I say?

I said: "I have difficulty with that statement..." and then I gave a thirty-second summary of the gospel evidence for Jesus' divinity.

I'm pleased to report that he still took me flying, and that he got me back safely.

This conversation reminded me that many attacks on Christianity spring from a lack of knowledge.

In the fervent hope that it may help when someone says something similar to you, let's have a look at Jesus.

A Summary of Jesus' life

Before we begin, I can't assume everyone knows the story of Jesus' life, so here it is in summary. (Skip this bit and go to "Was Jesus God?" if you already know it well.)

Over the centuries in which the Old Testament was written, God's prophets foretold the coming of God to earth as the "Messiah" (Hebrew) or the "Christ" (Greek), both titles meaning 'the anointed one'. People had to contain their sense of anticipation and wait a long time before these prophecies were fulfilled. In fact, there was a four-hundred year wait between the last of these prophecies and the coming of Jesus.

Then, finally, something happened.

The Holy Spirit of God caused a virgin by the name of Mary to become pregnant with a baby boy. At the time, Mary was betrothed to Joseph, a carpenter from Nazareth in the northern region of Galilee.

Joseph had to journey south to the town of his ancestors, Bethlehem, in order to be registered in a census that was being undertaken by the Roman Empire for tax purposes. Whilst he and Mary were there, she gave birth to the Messiah. She gave birth in a stable because there was no room for them in the inn.

An angel instructed Mary and Joseph to call the child 'Jesus', which literally means: 'God saves'. God had come to earth as a vulnerable baby – a human being, to save us from our sins and rescue us back to himself.

Two groups of people were led by God to visit Jesus just after his birth. The first, was a band of lowly Palestinian shepherds. This was a clear indication that Jesus had come for ordinary people. The second, was a group of learned Zoroastrian mystics (magi), who journeyed all the way from Persia. Their invitation to attend Jesus' birth showed that Jesus had come for *all* people who earnestly seek God – regardless of their religious tradition.

Joseph, Mary, and Jesus then spent two years in Egypt as

refugees, fleeing the Jewish king, Herod, who was trying to kill Jesus. An ancient prophecy about a king being born in Bethlehem had caused Herod to feel that his kingdom was under threat. He therefore murdered all the baby boys born in Bethlehem.

After Herod died, Joseph, Mary and Jesus returned to Nazareth, where Jesus grew up.

Some time during the next 30 years, Joseph died, leaving Mary alone with her adult son Jesus and Jesus' younger brothers and sisters who had been born naturally from the union of Joseph and Mary.

When Jesus was thirty years old, he began his ministry as an itinerant preacher. He asked John the Baptist to baptize him. Jesus did this to indicate that he identified fully with ordinary human beings (who needed to have their sins washed away). Jesus then invited twelve men, (most of whom were from the local region of Galilee) to be his disciples. He traveled with them from town to town telling people that the kingdom of God was now available to everyone who repented and started living the way God wanted them to live. Jesus demonstrated the fact that the kingdom of God had come by healing people and driving out evil spirits from those who were possessed.

From time to time, Jesus traveled south to the capital city of Jerusalem in order to teach at the temple there. He often used to stay with friends in the village of Bethany a mile or so east of the city.

Jesus modeled a radical new intimacy with God, whom he called "Father."

For most of his ministry, Jesus tried to keep his identity a secret so as not to cause a riot, or result in him being mobbed. Only in the last few days of his ministry, when he entered Jerusalem for the last time, did he acknowledge his identity publicly.

The authority of Jesus' teaching and the miracles he performed soon caused the Jewish religious leaders to feel threatened, so they plotted to kill him. After three years of ministry, one of the disciples, Judas, betrayed Jesus into the hands of the authorities. Jesus was arrested, tried in a Jewish court, then taken to the Roman governor, Pontius Pilate. They did this because the Jewish leaders knew that only the Roman Empire could order a person to be executed.

Pilate knew that Jesus was innocent and did not deserve death, so he had him whipped and beaten in the hope that this would satisfy the Jewish leaders. However, the leaders still insisted that Jesus be crucified. To keep the peace, Pilate agreed. Jesus was then paraded through the city to the place of execution outside the city walls. There, he was impaled on a wooden cross and left to die. Two rebels were crucified, one on either side of him.

At the precise moment when Jesus died, the curtain that separated people from the presence of God in the temple was ripped from top to bottom. This was how God signified that the way was now open for people to come to him. Jesus had paid the price for everyone's sins on a cross.

Two influential men from the Jewish council then wrapped Jesus' body in strips of cloth and laid him in a freshly cut tomb. When they had finished, they rolled a heavy stone over the entrance. This occurred on a Friday evening.

Nothing happened during the next day, as the religious feast of Passover was being celebrated.

On Sunday morning, Mary Magdalene (a follower of Jesus) and some other women went to the tomb to anoint Jesus' body more thoroughly in preparation for his permanent burial. When they arrived, however, they found that the stone covering the tomb had been rolled away. An angel of God told Mary that Jesus had been raised from death!

She was amazed and ran back to tell the disciples. Very reasonably, they didn't believe her, but two of them (Peter and John) ran to the tomb and saw that it was empty – except for the folded grave clothes.

The disciples could hardly believe that Jesus was alive. Most of them returned north to Galilee with Peter to resume their profession as fishermen. One morning, Jesus, who had been resurrected from the dead, met them on the shore of the lake. Needless to say, the disciples were overjoyed.

Over the next forty days, Jesus appeared to his followers a number of times – on one occasion to over 500 of them! As he met with the disciples, he commissioned them to go into the world and tell people about him, so that everyone could put their faith in him and be saved. Before the disciples went on mission, however, Jesus asked them to remain in Jerusalem until they had been empowered by God's Holy Spirit. The Holy Spirit would remind them of everything Jesus had taught them, and give them the spiritual gifts (abilities) they needed to be effective missionaries.

Finally, the time came for Jesus to leave his disciples so that they could get on with their ministry. Jesus met with them just east of Jerusalem, not far from the village of Bethany where he used to stay with his friends. After reminding them of their mandate to be his missionaries, he was taken up from the earth before their very eyes – up into the sky until a cloud obscured him from their sight. The disciples didn't know what to make of this until two angels spoke to them. The angels assured them that Jesus would come back in a similar fashion at the end of time to inaugurate God's eternal kingdom.

Was Jesus God?

Let's now return to our question: Was Jesus God?

Quite a lot of people pat Jesus paternalistically on the head and say, "Nice fellow. You're a fine moral example," and will not believe that Jesus is anything more than that. Unfortunately, the four biographies of Jesus recorded in the New Testament will not allow anyone to get away with such a weak understanding of Jesus' significance. Here's why:

- Jesus accepted worship as God (John 9:35-38; 20:28).
- He claimed to be able to forgive sins (Mark 2:5).
- Jesus claimed that he would judge the world (Matthew 25:31-32).
- He claimed to raise people up to everlasting life (John 6:40; 10:28).

- Jesus claimed that to have seen him, is to have seen God (John 14:8-9).
- He claimed to have always existed (John 8:58).
- Jesus' morality was faultless, and he was without sin (1 Peter 2:22).
- Jesus fulfilled prophecy written about him hundreds of years before he came.
- The evidence that he overcame death is both unique and compelling.

It is also highly significant that even his enemies understood Jesus' claim to be God (John 10:31-33; 19:7).

I can think of no better way to end this section than with this popular quote from C.S. Lewis.

> *A man who was merely a man and said the sort of things Jesus said would not be a great moral teacher, he'd either be a lunatic – on a level with a man who says he's a poached egg – or else he'd be the devil of hell. You must make your choice. Either this man was and is the Son of God, or else a madman or something worse. You can shut him up for a fool, you can spit at him and kill him as a demon, or you can fall at his feet and call him Lord and God. But don't let us come up with any patronizing nonsense about his being a great human teacher. He has not left that open to us. He didn't intend to.*[1]

What was Jesus' mandate, goal, message, and task?

Jesus' mandate was to represent his Heavenly Father's authority, character and purpose, (John, chapters 4-12).

Jesus' goal was to carry out God's rescue plan for humankind and for all of creation.

Jesus' message was: "Get ready for the kingdom of God." The kingdom of God is God's 'end game', and he wants you to be part of it. It will be the occasion when God causes heaven and earth to be remade and combined. When this happens, God will be with his people in the fullest sense (2 Peter 3:13; Revelation 21:1-3).

It is worth noting that John the Baptist was sent by God to get people ready for the coming of Jesus. His message was, "Repent, because the Kingdom of God *is* coming." But when Jesus came, his message was, "Repent, because the Kingdom of God *has* come, and is now accessible to you." Jesus therefore *represented* the kingdom of God (Luke 17:21), *inaugurated* the kingdom of God (Mark 1:15), and *obtained* the kingdom of God...for us.

Jesus' task was to be a 'sacrificial lamb'. What does this mean?

God has one answer to the problem of evil: he kills it off. Jesus came to take on himself the evil of all of humankind. He was sacrificed for us like a lamb. Jesus epitomized our evil, and was rejected by God. That's why he said on the cross: "My God my God, why have you forsaken me?" (Matthew 27:46, quoting Psalm 22:1).

This is not a case of God the Father engaging in child brutality, as Richard Dawkins is so fond of claiming. (It's extraordinary, isn't it, that the greatest gift of love the world has ever seen should be so trashed and debased?) It should be remembered that Jesus is part of the Trinity of God that comprises Father, Son, and Holy Spirit (John 14:16-17; 1 Peter 1:2). Each member of it mutually indwells the others. Because each member of the Trinity perfectly represents the others, it can reasonably be said that *all* of the Trinity suffered on the cross.

Understanding the Trinity of God

In his book *The God Delusion*, Richard Dawkins also trashes the idea of the Trinity. His main beef is that he doesn't understand it. The poor chap wants to design a god that will fit into his intellect. It hasn't yet occurred to him that if a god were so small as to fit into his intellect, that god would be no god at all. Almost by definition, God has to be more than our intellect can conceive.

The Bible insists that there is only one true God (Deuteronomy 6:4). However, this one God lives in community within himself of Father, Son, and Holy Spirit. The church sought to describe this mystery by using the term 'the Trinity of God'. (Tertullian was the first to use this term in 210 AD.)

There are hints of the truth of the threefold nature of God even in the Old Testament:

Let us make humankind in our image (Genesis 1:26).
Man has now become like one of us (Genesis 3:22).
Whom shall I send? and who will go for us? (Isaiah 6:8).

It is also worth noting that one of the Old Testament words for God, *Elohim*, is a plural word.

Finally, there is a theological reason why 'the Trinity' makes sense. The Bible says that, "God is love" (1 John 4:8). But no one can love, or be loving, unless there is another object or person to love. God therefore needs to live in community within himself if he is to be loving. The doctrine of the trinity (or at least two persons) is therefore a logical necessity.

Let's now return to our main subject, Jesus, and explore why it was that Jesus died on the cross.

What did Jesus achieve by dying on the cross?

Here's a list of the main reasons Jesus died on the cross. These are sometimes referred to as the 'different theories of the atonement'. However, in reality, there is only one theory of the atonement – which has a number of facets. Different theologians come up with slightly different lists of these. Here's mine:

Jesus' death:

1. Was **an expression of love**
2. Was an act of **substitution** (Jesus swaps with us and suffers our punishment)
3. Was a **payment of debt** for our sins (ransom)
4. Was **atonement** (paying for our sins)
5. Signified **reconciliation** (appeased God's wrath at our sin and brought us peace)
6. Was a **moral example** of sacrificial love
7. Signified **transformation**. Jesus death makes us eligible to be filled with God's Holy Spirit. This means

we can understand the things of Christ, grow the character of Christ, and be raised to eternal life with Christ.
8. Signified **Christ as victorious king**. Sin and death are defeated, and Jesus rules with total authority, unchallenged by evil.

Some people waste a lot of time trying to decide which of the above is most correct. Rather foolishly, they set one factor against all the others. The truth is: *all* of them represent something that is significant about Jesus' death. They can be linked together logically in this way:

Because of God's love (*an expression of love*); Christ substitutes himself for us (*substitution*); so that he can pay the penalty for our sins (*ransom*); by atoning for them on our behalf (*atonement*); to appease God's anger at evil, and bring us peace with God (reconciliation); with an act of obedience (*moral example*); which results in us being filled with God's Spirit, so that we can grow the character of God (*transformation*). All of which results in evil being killed off, and Jesus being crowned king of all (*Christ, the victorious king*).

Jesus' attitude to Scripture

Jesus was steeped in Scripture (the Old Testament) and had the highest regard for it (Matthew 5:17-18). However, this did not stop Jesus amending some of the "halfway-to-the-truth" instructions God gave to his people, as a concession to their hard hearts, in the Old Testament (Mark 10:5).

Matthew lists of some of the 'concessional statements' that Jesus revised, e.g. "an eye for eye," in Matthew, chapter 5. This reminds us that Jesus is God's 'final word' (revelation) when it comes to scriptural truth.

You may wonder why the Old Testament is so important now that we have the New Testament. There are three reasons. Firstly: it is important because God did nothing significant in the New Testament that he didn't first prefigure in the Old Testament. In a very real sense: the Old Testament is the manger in which the New Testament is laid. Secondly: it is important because the Old Testament tells the story of how the New Testament events came to be. Thirdly: it is important because Jesus had the highest regard for it.

It is significant that Jesus expects us to see him in the prophecies of the Old Testament. He once said to some religious leaders: "You study the Scriptures diligently to learn about eternal life...but these are the scriptures that testify about me" (John 5:39). And when meeting two of his disciples on the road to Emmaus:

> (Jesus) *said to them, "How foolish you are, and how slow to believe all that the prophets have spoken! Did not the Messiah have to suffer these things and then enter his glory?" And beginning with Moses and all the Prophets, he explained to them what was said in all the Scriptures concerning himself* (Luke 24:25-27).

Jesus fulfilled Old Testament prophecies

It is spine tingling to read the numerous prophecies about Jesus that were written several hundred years before he was born. These include:

- His birth in Bethlehem (prophesied in Micah 5:2; fulfilled in Matthew 2:1)
- His birth to a virgin (prophesied in Isaiah 7:14; fulfilled in Matthew 1:18)
- His triumphal entry into Jerusalem (prophesied in Zechariah 9:9; fulfilled in John 12:12-15)
- His rejection by most people (prophesied in Isaiah 53:3; fulfilled in John 1:11)
- His betrayal for thirty pieces of silver (prophesied in Zechariah 11:12; fulfilled in Matthew 26:14-16)
- His crucifixion alongside sinners (prophesied in Isaiah 53:12; fulfilled in Matthew 27:38)

- His hands and feet being pierced (prophesied in Psalm 22:16; fulfilled in John 19:33-34)
- His legs weren't broken, unlike those who were crucified with him (prophesied in Psalm 34:20; fulfilled in John 19:31-33)
- Those around him gambled for his clothing (prophesied in Psalm 22:18; fulfilled in John 19:23-24)
- His resurrection (prophesied in Psalm 16:10; fulfilled in Acts 3:15)

There are also other very significant prophecies concerning the coming of Jesus as the Messiah. In Genesis, chapter 49, we read of Jacob, one of the great biblical patriarchs, who was old and dying. His last act was to bless his sons and let them know that he was fully aware of their character. He had twelve sons, the descendants of whom would become the twelve tribes of the Jews. One of his sons was Judah.

Up until that moment, Judah had not played a starring role in life. He wasn't the oldest son, or the most favored son. And yet, old man Jacob says to him: "The scepter will not depart from Judah, nor the ruler's staff from between his feet, until he comes to whom it belongs and the obedience of the nations is his" (Genesis 49:10).

This makes it plain that the eternal ruler (the Messiah) will come from the tribe of Judah, the tribe from which king David also came.

Old Testament prophecies about the Messiah sometimes refer to him as a "branch" of King David (Jeremiah 23:5; 33:15), or a branch of Jesse, (who was King David's father; see Isaiah 11:1). It will be of little surprise therefore to learn that Jesus was technically a descendant of King David (Luke 1:26-27,32).

It is worth noting, in passing, that the Bible also contains a number of thought provoking prophecies concerning nations and cities. For example: Ezekiel prophesied that the city of Tyre would be flattened and its stones and timbers thrown into the sea, never to be rebuilt (Ezekiel 26:3-14). This must have seemed a highly unlikely prophecy at the time. However, about 260 years later, Alexander the Great demolished the city to build a causeway to an offshore island in order to defeat the Phoenicians who were based there. The fulfillment of prophecies such as this should prompt us to take the Old Testament prophecies concerning Jesus seriously.

Have people changed the Bible in the last sixteen-hundred years?

The most useful ancient text of the Old Testament used to be the Masoretic text that was written by the Masoretic Jews between the 6th and 10th centuries AD. People wonder, fairly reasonably, if this text was the same that Jesus would have read a thousand years earlier.

The answer to this question came in 1947, when a young Bedouin shepherd boy discovered some pottery jars in a limestone cave whilst he was looking for a lost goat. (The cave was about one mile from the northwestern shore of the Dead Sea in Palestine.) Inside the jars were leather parchment scrolls wrapped in linen. These became known as the *Dead Sea Scrolls*.

Eventually, scrolls were found in eleven caves situated around the ancient ruins of the Qumran community. This community was a splinter group of pious, nationalistic Jews who chose to live an isolated monastic existence. They were particularly active between 130BC and 68AD which means they were active at the time of Jesus.

The community was eventually wiped out in 68AD by the Roman army bent on stamping out Jewish rebellion. Before they were killed, however, the community managed to hide their library in the surrounding caves.

About five-hundred documents, some just fragments, were found. About one-hundred of these were texts from the Old Testament. In fact, portions of every book in the Old Testament were found except the book of Esther. The remarkable thing was that when these texts were compared with the Masoretic text...they were nearly identical. This was despite them being up to a thousand years older! This gives us confidence that the Old Testament had not been changed in any significant way. What we read now in the Old Testament are the same scriptures Jesus read.

Jesus, the icon

Jesus is the 'icon' (the image) of God. In other words, Jesus is the 'photograph' of God. His full significance is described beautifully in the apostle Paul's letter to the church in Colossae.

> *The Son is the image of the invisible God, the firstborn over all creation. For in him all things were created: things in heaven and on earth, visible and invisible, whether thrones or powers or rulers or authorities; all things have been created through him and for him. He is before all things, and in him all things hold together. And he is the head of the body, the church; he is the beginning and the firstborn from among the dead, so that in everything he might have the supremacy. For God was pleased to have all his fullness dwell in him, and through him to reconcile to himself all things, whether things on earth or things in heaven, by making peace through his blood, shed on the cross.* (Colossians 1:15-20)

The relevance of Jesus being the icon of God is this: If you have ever wondered what God is like (amidst all the competing and confusing religions and philosophies that abound), simply look at Jesus.

A reflection

I invite you to pause for breath, at this point...and let me entertain you with a little muse.

In my research for this book, I've had to delve into the world of modern philosophy. I have to confess, I found the experience a bit like chewing my way through a haystack: it was hard to eat and not very nutritional. It was therefore a relief to come to the end of each day and spend a bit of time reading from the gospels. (This habit is part of my going-to-bed ritual.) I found myself marveling at the fact that I was reading the words of the greatest philosopher in history. Jesus spoke clearly about issues that are (or should be) at the heart of philosophy. He spoke of truth, meaning, and morality. Unlike the world of modern philosophy, his words were simple, understandable, yet profound – able to be understood by children...and me.

I like that!

Let's move on and tackle what is undoubtedly the most diagnostic feature of Christianity: Jesus' resurrection.

Jesus' resurrection

Is the resurrection of Jesus a reality we can hope in, or is it just a myth – something that has meaning only because we give it meaning? Is talk of resurrection just a projection of our need to feel that we have meaning after death?

What do you think?

It's worth giving the subject some serious thought. The American Episcopalian minister, John E. Large, wrote: "The entire character of a (person's) whole life depends on whether he (or she) answers 'Yes' or 'No' to the historic fact of the Resurrection." That's a bold statement. Whether or not you believe Rev. Large, it highlights the fact that how you respond to the resurrection is a key life decision.

There is little doubt that the subject of the resurrection has been central and definitive of Christianity from the very first (Acts 4:33; 13:30-33). All but the smallest New Testament writings testify to it. The apostle Paul spoke of it as being of "first importance" (1 Corinthians 15:3), and it was the subject central to his preaching. The apostle Luke reports that when Paul was in Athens, he "was preaching the good news about Jesus and the resurrection" (Acts 17:18).

The Anglican theologian, Michael Green says: "The Resurrection is therefore no tailpiece to Christian doctrine. It is the centerpiece."[2]

But can you believe it?

. . .

The gospel accounts of the resurrection

Let's remind ourselves of what the gospels actually say about the resurrection.

The accounts of Jesus resurrection in each of the four biographies of Jesus (gospels) are broadly similar, but they also contain differences that reflect the different theological emphases of the writers, and the different sources they had for their information. What is common to all the accounts is:

- The empty tomb. (Not even the Roman soldiers could find the body to disprove Jesus' resurrection.)
- A woman (Mary Magdalene) first discovered the empty tomb.
- The disciples' initial response was one of doubt and disbelief.
- Jesus' appearances to the eleven disciples.
- It was Jesus' appearances rather than the empty tomb that was decisive of the disciples' faith.
- He appeared only to those who were already his followers (Acts 10:40-42).
- Jesus' resurrected body had physical reality. He ate with his disciples, and his body could be handled (Luke 24:39-43, John 20:20,27). Therefore, he was no ghost. However, Jesus body had changed in that it was able to transcend physical limitations of space (John 20:19,26).
- Jesus commissioned his disciples to be his witnesses (Matthew 28:18-20; Luke 24:46-49; Acts 1:8; John 20:21).
- The early church used their witness of Jesus' bodily resurrection as proof of Jesus' divinity. Put simply: it was *the* event that motivated their mission (Acts 2:22-24,29-33; 10:39-42; 13:26-31; 17:31).

Different explanations for the resurrection

There can only be a few alternative explanations for Jesus' resurrection:

1) *The swoon theory. This suggests that Jesus didn't die but was in a coma from which he recovered.*

This claim is fanciful. Jesus was flogged savagely, crucified, speared in the side, wrapped from head to toe in embalming bandages, and left in a tomb for two days. It can't seriously be said that Jesus was fit enough to unwrap himself, pull back the heavy stone over the tomb entrance, dodge the soldiers who were on guard, and then persuade the disciples that he had risen from the dead! If he had swooned on the cross, he would have suffocated and had irreparable brain damage within nine minutes.

We can therefore safely conclude that the resurrection was not the survival of death but the overcoming of death.

2) *The disciples all had hallucinations or visions of Jesus.*

The fact that over five-hundred people (1 Corinthians 15:6) in different places should have had such simultaneous hallucinations or visions makes this highly unlikely.

3) *The disciples stole the body.*

This is not credible, as the disciples were as surprised about Jesus' resurrection as anyone.

Another key reason why this claim is not credible is that following the resurrection, Jesus' disciples exploded on to the world stage with missionary zeal. All of them had to overcome enormous odds, and all but one of them was martyred. No one can seriously believe that the disciples would be prepared to suffer martyrdom if they knew their message was based on a lie.

. . .

4) Jesus' resurrection was just a myth that developed in the first few years after Jesus' death.

C.S. Lewis doesn't think it was. He was one of the world's leading experts on myth literature, and he said that the New Testament records don't read like a myth. Rather, they read like eyewitness accounts. In fact, he says that they are one of the earliest existing eyewitness accounts in literature. He wrote: "I have been reading poems, romances, vision-literature, legends, and myths all my life. I know what they are like. I know that not one of them is like this."[3]

It is chronological arrogance to suggest that the disciples were a primitive people unable to tell the difference between myth and reality. The Apostle Peter said: "We did not follow cleverly invented stories when we told you about the power and coming of our Lord Jesus Christ, but we were eyewitnesses of his majesty" (2 Peter 1:16). Peter makes the point that Jesus was seen by: "witnesses who God had already chosen – by us who ate and drank with him after he rose from the dead" (Acts 10:41).

John (another of Jesus' disciples) writes similarly: "That ...which we have heard, which we have seen with our eyes, which we have touched – this we proclaim..." (1 John 1:1).

Paul's teaching on the resurrection

The apostle Paul was not one of Jesus' original disciples, but he was highly significant in the early history of the church. He was responsible for planting Christian churches amongst non-Jews living in modern day Turkey, Greece, and Italy. He made it clear that his teaching on the resurrection was not something he had worked out independently. It was something that he had "received" within just a few years of Jesus' death, and now "handed on" to others (1 Corinthians 15:3-5).

The resurrection of Jesus was the central theme of Paul's preaching, and Paul always insisted that it be correctly understood. The young church in the Greek city of Corinth contained some people who doubted the resurrection, so Paul wrote to them, saying:

> *But if it is preached that Christ has been raised from the dead, how can some of you say that there is no resurrection of the dead? If there is no resurrection of the dead, then not even Christ has been raised. And if Christ has not been raised, our preaching is useless and so is your faith. More than that, we are then found to be false witnesses about God, for we have testified about God that he raised Christ from the dead. But he did not raise him if in fact the dead are not raised. For if the dead are not raised, then Christ has not been raised either. And if Christ has not been raised, your faith is futile; you are still in your sins. Then those also who have fallen asleep in Christ are lost. If only for this life we have hope in Christ, we are of all people most to be pitied* (1 Corinthians 15:12-19).

…this needs no more explanation.

What is the significance of Jesus' ascension?

Finally, let's turn our attention to Jesus' ascension from the earth back to heaven.

Just before his ascension, Jesus was with his disciples outside the city wall on the east side of Jerusalem. They were meeting at a place that was very close to the olive grove where Jesus had prayed on the night he was arrested. It was now time for the resurrected Jesus to return to his Heavenly Father. After giving his disciples their final instructions, this is what happened:

> *After* (Jesus) *said this, he was taken up before their very eyes, and a cloud hid him from their sight.*
>
> *They were looking intently up into the sky as he was going, when suddenly two men dressed in white stood beside them. "Men of Galilee," they said, "why do you stand here looking into the sky? This same Jesus, who has been taken from you into heaven, will come back in the same way you have seen him go into heaven."* (Acts 1:9-11).

Wow! This seems to be a pretty strange exit. But I guess that any exit Jesus was going to make from planet Earth was going to be a bit extraordinary.

God and Me

Jesus' ascension was, in fact, full of significance, so let's examine it by using an octagon.

The question we need to circle with relevant biblical truths is: "What is the significance of Jesus' ascension?"

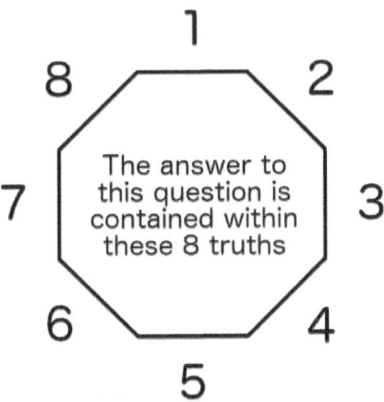

1. It proclaimed that Jesus' mission as a physical person on planet Earth was done.
2. It cleared the stage for the next part of God's initiative to be carried out; a work centered on the empowering presence of God's Holy Spirit.
3. It was proof of Jesus' divine identity.
4. It was visible evidence that God the Father had accepted the saving work of Jesus.
5. It was a demonstration of the manner in which Christ would return when he comes again.
6. It marked the start of the victorious resurrected life for God's people. Jesus was the first one resurrected (1 Corinthians 15:20).
7. It showed that Jesus' oneness with the Father was being fully restored.
8. It showed that Jesus is now with God and so is able to represent us to God.

I hope that explains it.

Can the New Testament accounts of Jesus be trusted?

The 'new atheists', such as Richard Dawkins, Sam Harris, and Christopher Hitchins, claim that the New Testament accounts of Jesus are nothing but unreliable ideas passed on like "Chinese whispers" [4] containing nothing but "hearsay upon hearsay." [5] As such, the New Testament accounts of Jesus are unreliable and fictitious.

In order for these New Atheists to perpetuate such falsehoods, they need to avoid scholarly research – and they have been remarkably successful at doing so. They give little evidence of having done more than paddle about in the shallow end of Google – re-quoting the anti-Christian rhetoric of their tribe.

The reality is: Christianity is not a culturally derived religious philosophy that evolved gradually over the years. Christianity is based on concrete historical events. This claim is hugely significant and very bold...for if it can be shown that the New Testament accounts of Jesus are nothing but myths and exaggerations formed incrementally over the years by overzealous adherents, Christianity disappears in a puff of smoke leaving nothing behind but moralistic platitudes.

So let's take a look at the historical integrity of the gospel stories of Jesus in the Bible.

Evidence from the New Testament

John, the disciple who was closest to Jesus, begins his epistles (letters) with these words:

> *That which was from the beginning, which we have heard, which we have seen with our eyes, which we have looked at, and our hands have touched – this we proclaim concerning the Word of Life. The life appeared, we have seen it and testify to it, and we proclaim to you the eternal life, which was with the Father and has appeared to us. We proclaim to you what we have seen and heard, so that you also may have fellowship with us* (1 John 1:1-3).

John is making it quite clear that he is writing from his first-hand experience of being with Jesus. He is not at all interested in teaching myths that might have developed about Jesus at a later stage.

Peter and the other apostles said similar things. Luke records them in Acts saying: "We are witnesses to these things" (Acts 5:32).

The apostle Paul was equally passionate about accurately transmitting Jesus' words and actions. He understood that the revelation he had of Jesus (and the truths handed to him by the apostles) were a sacred entrustment that he needed to pass on faithfully in an untainted way.

The gospel writer Luke, who wrote one of the gospel accounts of Jesus' life, says he took real pains to research all that happened in the life of Jesus using first-hand accounts of the apostles. He begins his gospel, saying:

Many have undertaken to draw up an account of the things that have been fulfilled among us, just as they were handed down to us by those who from the first were eyewitnesses and servants of the word. With this in mind, since I myself have carefully investigated everything from the beginning, I too decided to write an orderly account for you, most excellent Theophilus, so that you may know the certainty of the things you have been taught (Luke 1:1-4).

One of the extraordinary features of the New Testament is how soon the Scriptures were written after Jesus' death. There is no hint of the theology of Jesus gradually being fabricated by over-imaginative Christians in the years after his death. Far from it! The fully finished theological and historical record of Jesus exploded into being, fully formed, very quickly after Jesus' time on earth came to an end.

What is more: we have an incredible number of early New Testament manuscripts that give us the assurance that what was written within living memory of Jesus, is what we read today.

The earliest piece of New Testament manuscript found by archaeologists is a tiny piece of papyrus found in Egypt. It is known as P52, and it is thought to date between 90-150AD, possibly just thirty years after the apostle John wrote it.

Because so many early copies of the New Testament text have been found, the different texts can be crosschecked for accuracy. Remarkably, the texts have been found to retain an accuracy of over 99%. In archaeological terms, this level of accuracy is unheard of; it has no parallel.

So please don't dismiss the gospel accounts of Jesus in the New Testament as unreliable.

The historical credibility of the gospels

The late Christopher Hitchens, one of the most vociferous 'new atheists', made the claim that there is, "no firm evidence whatever that Jesus was a 'character in history.'"[6] He went on to say that, "The case for biblical consistency or authenticity or 'inspiration' has been in tatters for some time, and the rents and tears only become more obvious with better research."[7]

Hmmm!

In order for him to say such a thing, Hitchens has needed to ignore scholarly research, embrace slanderous rhetoric, and pass it off as informed comment. His assertions have less to do with scholasticism than Goebbels' craft of propaganda, obfuscation and deception. His claims are so mind-bogglingly inaccurate that they are shocking.

Here's why:

Christianity is a historical religion

As we've said earlier: Christianity is not a philosophy that developed over the years. Nor is it one that has depended on one person's claimed 'revelations' whilst meditating somewhere. Christianity is based on concrete historical events. This is Christianity's great strength: It is real, because it has a basis in history. This, of course, makes Christianity very vulnerable because if it can be shown to be factually incorrect historically – Christianity collapses like a pack of cards.

So, let's look at the historical evidence for Jesus' existence.

Josephus

The first evidence we have comes from Josephus.

Josephus was born c.37AD, just seven years after Jesus' death. He was a Jewish military leader who sought to defend Galilee from the invading Romans in 67AD. Unfortunately, General Vespasian (who later became emperor) captured Josephus. Josephus abruptly changed his allegiance and agreed to become an interpreter and advisor to the Romans. The Romans gave him a villa in Rome and supported him while he wrote a propagandist work, *Jewish War*, and a history of the Jewish people called *Jewish Antiquities*.

In this later work (written about 90AD) Josephus writes (and I'm careful here to exclude any controversial sections that some historians think were added later):

> *About this time there lived Jesus, a wise man ... for he was one who wrought surprising feats and was a teacher of such people who accept the truth gladly. He won over many Jews and many of the Greeks ... When Pilate, upon hearing him accused by men of the highest standing amongst us had condemned him to be crucified, those who had in the first place come to love him did not give up their affection for him (Jewish Antiquities, 18,63-64).*

Tacitus

Another person who wrote about Jesus was Cornelius Tacitus (c. 56-120AD). Tacitus was proconsul of Roman Asia. He wrote the *Annals of Imperial Rome*, which was a history of the emperors Tiberius, Gaius, Claudius, and Nero. Only some parts of the *Annals* have survived. One section of the surviving literature gives an account of the great fire of Rome that raged for six days, destroying 14 of the 18 city districts. Tacitus mentions that Nero tried to deflect the blame for the fire from himself to Christians. He wrote:

Therefore, to scotch the rumor, Nero substituted as culprits, and punished with the utmost refinements of cruelty, a class of man, loathed for their vices, who the crowd called Christians.

Christ, the founder of the name, had undergone the death penalty in the reign of Tiberius, by sentence of the procurator Pontius Pilate, and a pernicious superstition was checked for the moment, only to break out once more, not merely in Judea, the home of the disease, but in the capital itself, where all things horrible or shameful in the world collect and find a vogue (Tacitus, *Annals of Imperial Rome*, 15.44).

Pliny the Younger

Another near contemporary of Jesus was Pliny the Younger (c. 61-112AD). He was sent by Trajan to sort out the disorganized province of Bithynia, south of the Black Sea. Pliny wrote about the rapid spread of Christianity and the fact that he had interrogated some captured Christians to find out about their faith. The letter is significant because it takes the existence of Jesus Christ for granted. He wrote about Christians saying:

…they had been in the habit of meeting on an appointed day before daybreak and singing a hymn antiphonally to Christ as if to a god, and binding themselves with an oath – not to commit any crime but to abstain from theft, robbery, and adultery, from breach of faith, and from repudiating a trust when called upon to honor it. After this ceremony, it had been their custom to disperse and reassemble to take food of a harmless kind (Pliny, Letter 96).

The historical evidence of Jesus' existence is overwhelming, particularly when you add the very significant details recorded in the gospels. We need to remember that these gospel accounts of Jesus' life were written at a time when those who were eyewitnesses to Jesus' life could have challenged the truth of their contents.

There is no record of any challenge ever occurring.

. . .

Archaeological Evidence

Let's now turn our attention to the archaeological evidence for the gospel accounts of Jesus' life. It is fabulous stuff!

Nazareth

In 2008, the Atheist Press of America put out a book *The Myth of Nazareth – the invented town of Jesus*, written by amateur archaeologist, René Salm.

If René had taken a little more care he might have discovered that the modern-day town of Nazareth was, in all probability, a satellite hamlet of the main city of Nazareth that existed in Jesus' time. This main city (now known as *Tel Yafia*)[8] would have been 1.5 miles southwest of the hamlet of Nazareth where Mary lived. (Her hamlet was probably one of five contained within the city borders.)

It is reasonable to assume that Joseph had his workshop in Nazareth city because that's where the population center was. The city would also have been the place where the synagogue existed – later made famous by Jesus when he went there and read from the book of Isaiah at the start of his ministry (Luke 4:14-21). The little hamlet of Nazareth (where modern Nazareth now exists) would have been too small to have a synagogue – as archaeology has confirmed.

History gives us some clues about how Joseph happened to be living in Nazareth, 100 miles north of his hometown, Bethlehem.

For much of the period that existed between the time of the Old Testament and the New Testament, the Seleucid Empire occupied Galilee and Judea. The Seleucids imposed Greek culture on the region. However, the Jewish Maccabean revolution (167 to 160BC) freed the Jews from the Seleucids, and allowed Jewish colonists to move north into Galilee. Some of these colonists developed a city that they named 'Nazareth' in celebration of their Davidic ancestry. The Hebrew word *nazara* means "of Davidic ancestry."[9] Joseph, originally from Bethlehem (David's city), would therefore have been at home in Nazareth city, as he was a descendant of king David.

It is likely that the distinctive Jewish culture of Nazareth city was stamped out in 68AD when Vespasian's Roman army invaded the region. The city was then Romanized...and continued on through the centuries until it was obliterated by the Muslim invasion.

Final proof of Nazareth's existence came from a fragment of stonework found by archaeologists in 1962 at an ancient synagogue in Caesarea Maritima. The stone tablet contained a list of places where priests were sent to perform their duties.[10] One of the places it mentions is Nazareth. The inscription read: *"The eighteenth priestly course, Hapizzez,* [at] *Nazareth"* (line 18).

We therefore know that the city of Nazareth existed and that it was big enough to warrant the services of priests who were rostered on to minister there.[11]

Can I just pause here and vent a little exasperation? Do atheists seriously think that those writing the biographies of Jesus would have invented a mythical town (such as Atlantis) and written about it to people who had, or could have had access to, those with a living memory of Jesus...and expect it to be unchallenged?

Pontius Pilate

The gospels record Pontius Pilate as being the military leader who ordered the death of Jesus. However, references to Pilate in the writings of the Jewish historian, Josephus, suggested Pilate was civil, not a military leader. Who was right? Did the apparent mistake suggest that the gospel writings were later unreliable works?

Then, in 1961, an inscribed stone tablet was found, again in Cesarea Maritima. The stone appeared to come from a building built by Pilate to honour Tiberius Caesar. The inscription read (in part) "Pontius Pilatus, prefect of Judaea." The office of prefect was a military one, making it clear that the gospel accounts of Pilate's military authority were correct.

Galilee synagogues

For many years, contemporary scholars were troubled by a lack of synagogues. Prior to 2008, no archaeological evidence for any synagogue existing in Jesus' time could be found in the region of Galilee. As the gospels mention that *"Jesus went throughout Galilee, teaching in their synagogues"* (Mt 4:23), this was a bit of an embarrassment.

Some scholars concluded that the claim that Jesus preached in the synagogues of Galilee was an invention of the gospel writers. But then, in 2009, archaeologists discovered the remains of a pre-AD 70 synagogue in the Galilean town of Magdala (the town where Mary Magdalene came from). Later that year, they found another at Khirbet Wadi Hamam… and in 2016, yet another at Tel Rekhesh, near Mount Tabor.

These archaeological findings suggest that the gospel writers knew a great deal more than our modern scholars!

Jehohanan

Some historians attack the historical credibility of Jesus' being buried in the tomb of Joseph of Arimathea. They said that no person defiled by crucifixion would ever be put into a family tomb.

Then, in 1968, building contractors working in northeast Jerusalem uncovered a family grave. It contained an ossuary box, (a stone box containing the bones of someone who had died). The ossuary box had a Hebrew inscription on it saying that the bones were those of Jehohanan the son of Hagkol. Jehohanan had been crucified some time in the first century and his lower leg fractured – just like those of the two rebels who were crucified either side of Jesus. The end of the nail that had pierced Jehohanan's heel was bent, making it extremely difficult to withdraw, so it had remained imbedded in the bone.

So it seems that a crucified person could be buried in a family grave after all.

The pool of Bethesda

Liberal theologians (who cast doubt on a lot of biblical historicity) have claimed that the gospel of John contains fictitious accounts written to embellish the Jesus story. They used to cite the account of Jesus healing the lame man at the pool of Bethesda as one such example (John 5:1-9), as there was no archaeological evidence of such a pool existing.

And then...yes, you've guessed it...archaeologists working in the grounds of St. Anne's church, just north of the temple mount, confirmed the existence of an extensive pool complex that comprised the pools of Bethesda. Archaeologists had been working in the area for many decades, but it was only in 1964 that their excavations confirmed their existence.

John's gospel describes the pool in some detail. He speaks of the existence of five covered colonnades. These have all been found. One of the reasons excavations took so long to discover them was that so many buildings had been built over the top of the pools during the ages, including a pagan temple and a large Byzantine church.

Excavations showed the existence of two main pools separated by a dam wall. The depth of the pools is surprising. It is thought that these pools were used to water animals being taken through the sheep gate to the temple to be sacrificed. John's account of the water being "troubled" probably refers to the occasional earth tremors that occurred in the area. (Jerusalem is built over a geological fault line.)

Alexander, son of Simon

I've reserved the next archaeological find for last, as I find it particularly exciting.

In 1941, the Hebrew University professor, Eleazer Sukenick, and his assistant Nahman Avigad, were excavating the tombs of the Kidron Valley that runs along the eastern edge of the temple mount. They discovered a tomb that had been blocked by a large closing stone. When they entered the tomb, they found eleven ossuary boxes containing bones. The professor documented his findings, and the artifacts were stored away.

For some reason, the findings of the professor were not made public until 1962. When they were, it caused a sensation. On the side of one ossuary box facing the wall was inscribed "Simon Ale," the name "Simon," and the first three letters of "Alexander." [12] Realizing he didn't have enough room to carve "Alexander", the engraver started again on the second line, carving "Alexander." Then, on the third line, he inscribed "(son) of Simon."

The lid of the box was inscribed "of Alexander" in Greek...and below it, in smaller letters, "Alexander QRNYT." The most probable meaning of QRNYT is that it is a misspelling of *qrnyh* – Hebrew for "Cyrenian.

Archaeologists conclude that it is highly probable that these bones were those of the son of the man forced to carry the crossbeam of Jesus' cross. Mark writes:

> *A certain man from Cyrene, Simon, the father of Alexander and Rufus, was passing by on his way in from the country, and they forced him to carry the cross* (Mark 15:21).

Wow!

The fact that Mark gives details of both sons, suggests that their names were relevant to his readers. In other words, his readers would probably know of them because both men had become Christians. (It is possible that Alexander's brother, Rufus, is the Rufus mentioned by Paul in Romans 16:13.)

These are outstanding archaeological findings, and the consistent feature of these discoveries is that they back up the gospel accounts of Jesus. Christopher Hitchens' claim that biblical authenticity "has been in tatters for some time, and the rents and tears only become more obvious with better research" is so manifestly wrong and outrageous as to beggar belief.

Blame or believe

Jesus came to Earth with a truth claim...and that truth concerns your identity and mine. The tragedy is: many people have not listened to him. Sometimes, they haven't listened for rational reasons. Hopefully, these have been addressed. On other occasions, people haven't listened for emotional reasons. So, let's end this chapter by addressing some of them.

Should we blame God, or believe him?

Here's what can be said:

1. If God is distant and uninvolved with us; then blame God for being aloof. But if God has come to us to show us what he's like – then trust God.
2. If God is evil and is responsible for evil; blame God. But if God is good and has a plan to kill off evil – then trust God.
3. If God is powerless to change the character of a person on the inside; then blame God for being irrelevant. But if God has given us his transforming Spirit – then trust God.
4. If God has given us nothing to hope for beyond this life of suffering; blame God for being cruel. But if he has invited us to join his everlasting kingdom – then trust God.
5. If God is simply a theory, just one of many world-views competing for your allegiance; ignore him for being too vague. But if he is real and has come to us in history – then trust God.
6. If the idea of God has changed radically throughout history so that what is said about him is inconsistent; discard God for being confusing. But if the Bible has given a clear, consistent witness to God's character and purpose over the years – then trust God.
7. If God requires you to make yourself good enough to earn the right to be with him; then dismiss God for asking the impossible. But if he has died in your place to make it possible – then trust God

No other person in history has made such claims or done such extraordinary things as Jesus Christ. No one else in history has displayed such spiritual authority – and backed it up with miracles of healing. No one else in Jesus' time has been so well attested by historical records.

The big question, of course, is, "What does this mean for you?"

4

History, Morality, and Me

There is an ideological battle going on between world-views in the Western world. It is a battle for your heart. One of the central issues in this battle is this question: Does the universe have meaning because God made it, or does it have no meaning? It is a question of 'origins'.

Having a right understanding of origins is important because what you believe about it will determine the 'world-view' you live by. The Christian world-view is grounded in the Bible's doctrine of creation being a deliberate act. This is in contrast to atheism's world-view, which believes the universe is both non-rational and meaningless.

It is no accident that the story of origins is placed right at the start of the Bible. It sits there, as if to say: "If you don't get this locked into place, don't bother reading any further." Certainly, if you don't build on the truth of the opening few chapters of the Bible, your life will be adrift; un-tethered to an ultimate grounding for morality, meaning, truth, and hope.

The first three chapters of the Bible state unambiguously that there is only one God, and that this one God has created all that exists. It makes it clear that God thought his creation was precious.

(The Hebrew word used to describe this is *towb*, which means 'good/lovely/precious'.) They also make it clear that God is not apathetic toward humankind, but seeks to have a relationship with us.

These are the central truths upon which the rest of the Bible is predicated. The Bible is the record of God rescuing us back to himself, along with the rest of creation – and it is an amazing story.

So, tell me: What is it you believe about your 'origins'? Why do you exist? Are you a meaningless accident, or are you really meant to be here? What evidence is there of you being a meaningless by-product of an absurd and inexplicable phenomenon of existence? Or does the extraordinary, finely tuned order of the cosmos, its mathematical beauty, and its ability to form humanity, indicate purpose?

What is the truth about you?

Is it all about my happiness?

The concept of truth has taken a bit of a battering in recent decades. Evidently, people are less inclined to seek it these days, preferring instead to pursue those things that make them 'happy'. Happiness is now the measure of what is 'good'.

This sort of thinking is similar to the Epicurean philosophy that existed twenty-three hundred years ago. And now here it is again, bobbing up in history. Epicurus lived in the 3rd century BC. He was a rationalist who advocated prudence and aimed at the ideal of developing happy, equalitarian communities, without any thought of God. Death was simply the dissolving of a bag of atoms. Sadly, it didn't take long for his thinking to degenerate into a philosophy of self-focused happiness. *My* happiness became the ultimate good. *My* happiness became the ultimate goal. The ultimate significance was therefore *self*. And – dare I say it – the ultimate god I serve, became *self*.

I once listened to the Australian politician, Kevin Andrews, talk about his book on marriage. It was called, rather sadly, *Maybe I do*. When introducing his book to us, he said that a few decades ago, marriage was considered to be a morally good thing to do...and it was morally good to do all you could to make your marriage last. However, in recent years, this has been overtaken by a new morality. Now the focus is not on doing the right moral thing in marriage. Now the measure of all things is 'does it make me happy?' Something is only morally good if it makes me happy.

It is little wonder that narcissism has become one of the diagnostic features of our age. The term 'narcissism' comes from the Greek myth of Narcissus, a young man who fell in love with his own reflection in a pool of water. It is important to note that narcissism is different from self-esteem. Narcissism is having an inflated and untrue image of self. Self-esteem is having a true image of yourself, and knowing your worth.

People with self-esteem value personal achievement and personal relationships. This is in contrast to Narcissists who lack empathy and have poor relationship skills. So, here's a hint: Don't marry one.

Professor Jean Twenge and Keith Campbell, have been investigating whether people born in more recent generations are more narcissistic than previous generations. It turns out that they are, and they have documented their findings in their book *The Narcissism Epidemic: Living in the Age of Entitlement.*[1] Evidently, plastic surgery rates have increased, and there is a greater drive to be 'unique', to stand out rather than fit in. This is even evident in the names people are choosing for their children. Crucially, they show that relationships are not as stable as they once were. More children are being born to unmarried couples, and people don't stay married for as long.

Into the midst of this self-worship and self-obsession comes Jesus. He comes as a servant to wash the feet of his disciples and die on a cross for us to pay the price for our sins. The difference between his attitude and that of the world today is monumental.

The story of atheism

Let's return to the ideological fight over you. Who will win your heart – God or atheism?

To help you decide, let's have a look at atheism.

The oldest and most pervasive sin of humankind is the first sin mentioned in the Bible. It was the desire of Adam and Eve to have the authority of God when it came to their opinion about right and wrong (Genesis 3:1-6). This has expressed itself in history either by humanity inventing religions that they can use to control God...or deciding they didn't need God at all. In recent years, Western civilization has largely chosen the latter.

The early Greek philosophers Leucippus (5th century BC) and Democritus (4th century BC) promoted 'atomism'. This was the idea that all matter (including gods) was made of indivisible tiny particles. Whilst gods may exist, they were not interested in humanity. It was therefore better to concentrate on what could be rationally understood. This philosophy became formative of the materialist thinking of Epicurus, whom we have already mentioned. His radical materialist thinking said that we should focus on building caring, inclusive communities and not look at creation and ask why it exists or who is responsible for it. Rather, we should only ask *how* the natural sciences work. We need to get on and try and make the best of things without thought of God.

This radical materialist thinking effectively shut people down from asking the really interesting questions regarding identity and meaning. It promoted a very shallow, two-dimensional way of thinking that resulted in communities living without purpose, and without a moral bedrock. It is significant that Plato was dismissive of such philosophy, saying that no atheist could be trusted because they had no god to whom they were accountable.[2]

Epicurean thinking went on to influence the Roman philosopher, Lucretius who popularized atheism through his famous poem *De rerum natura* in 55BC. The poem became lost to history until Poggio Bracchiolini, a papal secretary, rediscovered it in the library of a German monastery in 1417. Lucretius' work was quickly disseminated, largely due to the newly invented printing press (which aided the dispersal of atheistic literature some years before it aided the spread of Reformation literature, including the Bible).[3]

Philosophers were hungry for this sort of thinking during the Enlightenment and spread atheism throughout Europe under the banner of 'rationalism'. The Irish freethinker, John Toland (1670 - 1722) took the thinking to Germany where he tutored Caroline of Ansbach, the teenage princess who went on to marry George II of England.

America's contribution to the spread of atheism came from fueling into flame the idea that religion was 'at war' with science. The educationalist and diplomat, Andrew White, and the philosopher and physician, John Draper, both used a misinterpretation of the Galileo trial to promote the myth that Christianity was inherently antagonistic to science.

And now this atheism has trickled down through history to you...and is being preached by the likes of Richard Dawkins.

So, what are you going to do with it?

Atheism is a fabulous tool for giving yourself a philosophic mandate to 'do your own thing', to 'do what you like', to 'be your own king'. This mandate for self-obsessed autonomy is, of course, particularly attractive to the young. Only later do they discover that it turns to ashes in their mouths, leaving them with the taste of meaninglessness and lack of hope. Their suicide rates have risen alarmingly.

So, be careful with atheism. God has revealed his glory in the cosmos, and revealed his love in Jesus. I therefore confess to getting grumpy when people stand in the way of our children hearing about this good news. So, let me direct some fairly blunt talk to the self-styled urban literati – the deistic priests of our time – who tell us what is, and is not, permissible to believe. It is a message for trendy libertines who have a monopoly on our media, who huff and puff their political correctness and atheistic convictions. My message is this:

> *Hands off our children! Don't you dare damage them by imposing atheistic meaninglessness in the guise of secularism. Don't rip their value and their*

sacred identity from them. Don't rip away their 'ground of truth' and leave them floundering in shallow, hedonistic, self-obsession. Your legacy to them is one of meaninglessness and lack of identity — both of which help fuel the statistics of their suicide.

Don't you dare damage our children with your atheistic, values-free convictions, and claim you are being rational. You are <u>not</u> being rational. To claim that everything came from nothing as a result of nothing, takes a staggering level of faith. It certainly fractures the laws of 'cause and effect', the basic principle that undergirds all of science.

God came in history as Jesus — a verifiable fact. He came to die for our sins and rescue us back to God. This is a life-giving, hope-giving, value-imputing act that stands in stark contrast to the illogical meaninglessness you are seeking to impose on our children.

Whew! Just felt I needed to say that.

Who's leading social change?

This brings me to the subject of who it is that is leading Western civilization down the path of atheism.

The media have certainly played a big part in this. They are increasingly moving their emphasis from reporting news to imposing social engineering agendas on society. Media personnel seem to have become today's self-appointed 'Gnostic priests' possessed of secret wisdom the rest of us don't have. We are simply "useful idiots," (to borrow a term used by Communist leaders to describe non-Communists during the Cold War).

The scorning of Christianity and the deification of self (a habit we picked up during the Enlightenment) is a culture that is fostered particularly by the humanities departments of our universities. These, of course, have provided most of our media personnel.

It is a wonder to me that much sense comes from the warring interests of competing minority groups at our universities. The university culture that currently exists seems united in only two things: the denigration of Western civilization, and the ridicule of Christianity. As such, the path they point to for the future looks both bleak and poorly defined. Very little thought seems to have been given to what our meaning is; what the basis of morality is; and what destiny we can hope for. Our humanities departments seem unable to teach anything other than a resentment philosophy that leaves people floundering in a sea of self-obsessed meaninglessness. This is a dangerous place to be...which brings me to a story:

Guarding the philosophical climate of a nation

I once lived just a few kilometers from a place of mass murder.

At the time, my father was a chaplain to the NATO forces that were stationed at Hohne in northern Germany. I spent my holidays there when term ended at boarding school. The infamous Nazi concentration camp, Belsen, was just a couple of miles away.

I remember it clearly. A straight concrete road ran to Belsen from Hohne. I visited it once when I was sixteen years of age, but being so young, I was not able to understand the full horror of what I was seeing in the photographs on display there. What I did notice, however, was that I couldn't hear the sound of any birds singing. It was as if nature itself was holding its breath, appalled at the evil that had taken place there.

What little I was able to absorb caused me to wonder how the country I lived in and admired, could be capable of such evil. Somehow, the most civilized nation in the world; a nation of exquisite culture and scientific excellence, had walked away from its Christian heritage – and produced the extermination camps of Belsen, Auschwitz, Treblinka, and Majdanek.

General William Donovan, a member of the US prosecution team at the Nuremburg war trials, kept records of all that was learned at the war trials conducted there. These records were organized into 150 volumes, and are now kept at Cornell University. They make sobering reading as they reveal that the Nazis understood that Bible-believing, evangelical churches would have to be neutralized by infiltration, extermination and indoctrination. Only those churches that compromised their Christian values would be spared. Donovan reported: "National Socialism, by its very nature, was hostile to Christianity ...The purpose of the National Socialist movement was to convert the German people into a homogeneous racial group united in ...aggressive warfare." Donovan's reports make it clear that, notwithstanding public rhetoric, the Nazi party planned to eliminate authentic Christianity completely.[4]

It would seem that atheism, whether it be in the form of Hitler's National Socialism, Communism, or the neo-Marxist ideologies that are becoming the vogue in the West – cannot help but remove all that is sacred from what it means to be human...and this paves the way for the vilest abuses that humankind can perpetrate. Tragically, it seems that without God, humanity reverts to the law of the animal kingdom, where it makes perfect sense for the strong to enslave, predate, and abuse the weak.

The Austrian psychologist, Viktor Frankl, survived the horrors of no less than four Nazi concentration camps. When he reflected on his experience, he wrote: "I am absolutely convinced that the gas chambers of Auschwitz, Treblinka, and Majdanek were ultimately prepared not in some ministry or other in Berlin but rather at the desks and lecture halls of nihilistic scientists and philosophers."[5]

Abuses by any military regime cannot occur unless its nation's opinion leaders first establish a philosophic climate that removes both the sacredness of humankind and godly moral boundaries. Sadly, the West is now doing both. The humanities departments in our universities have been allowed to develop an intolerant anti-Christian, Neo-Marxist culture that is oppressive. The justification for this is that they are 'enlightened rationalists.' In reality, they neither understand the scientific wonders and mysteries of the cosmos, nor the historical and theological underpinnings of Christianity. They just re-quote tired anti-Christian clichés which they have failed to examine thoroughly for truth. It seems as if the wisdom of millennia accumulated by the world's cultures is being trashed, and the lessons of history ignored. No one remembers that Communism once tried to dismiss the concept of family, but had to reverse their decision when they saw its ruinous effect on society.

Today's liberal ideas have been smuggled into our society under the banner of 'compassion', 'justice' and 'diversity'. These emotive words have been used to shut down rational debate. I sometimes wonder whether I've woken up in some sort of parallel universe. It's hard to believe what's happening.

With some surprise, I discover that I am now a grandfather. This lovely reality brings with it some disquieting fears. I confess to being deeply concerned for my grandchildren's future. My generation had the choice of passing on to them a blessing or a curse. Sadly, I fear we have passed on the latter. Our children have been brought up with a state-sanctioned secular world-view. As a result, they don't know anything about why they exist, what their meaning is, what their moral boundaries are, or what destiny they can hope for. As a result, they believe themselves to be meaningless...and are committing suicide in record numbers.

So, what of the future?

History has taught us that the lifecycle of a civilization is inexorable and inevitable – almost. Only one thing has ever reversed a civilization's decline and injected new life into it, and that one thing is Christianity. John Wesley's Methodism is one such example. It is widely credited with preventing England's poor from descending into total gin-sodden depravity, and it introduced a moral climate that probably prevented England from suffering the bloody uprisings and revolutions that were occurring in Europe. The poor and the desperate encountered the gospel.

And so can you.

Truth and heritage

It can fairly be said that we are currently living in the twilight of truth. We live in a world of half-truths, manipulation, and deceit that has made truth hard to find. This is interesting given that our Christian heritage once provided a culture that valued truth. Fortunately, some in society have retained enough memory of Christian morality to not abandon the concept of truth entirely. In fact, it can be said that our current secular society is parasitic on its Christian heritage for its claims of tolerance and justice...whilst simultaneously undermining these ideals by promoting meaninglessness, moral laxity, and lack of absolutes. This is a pity because the best that secularism can offer society is a list of rubbery rules that lack any foundation that might give confidence that they were 'right'.

As the West free-falls away from its Christian heritage, it is beginning to forget the ideals that have underpinned its medical, educational, legal, and political systems. Whilst Christian culture remains vaguely present in people's psyche, it is all but invisible to them because they have swum in it for so many centuries. Just like a fish swimming in water doesn't know it is wet, people today don't know what a world with apparently 'self-evident' morality looks like. They can't conceive of truth, or good, without instinctively drawing on their Christian heritage to some degree. Despite their excursion into postmodern ideals of relativism and the scorning of meta-narratives such as the Bible, most people in the West do not fully appreciate the level to which they are still influenced by Christian values.

But now, society is marching into a future without Christianity, and they don't know what it's going to be like. From the evidence we have so far, (garnered from historical precedent), Western civilization's prospects are not promising.

A pertinent question to ask is: What is the end-point to the West's foray into atheism? Is it to become drunk with the promise of unrestraint; to become slaves to untutored stupidity and self-destructive immorality? Is it the freedom to be mad, bad and sad? If history has taught us anything, it is this: It is fiction to believe we don't need God to form a civilized, just society. Many philosophers have tried. Even non-atheistic philosophers such as Immanuel Kant and Søren Kierkegaard have fallen into this trap. Both attempted to come up with a philosophy for morality that didn't require God...and both failed.

Could this mean that the 18th century Scottish philosopher, David Hume, is right in believing that moral decisions are made intuitively in response to our emotions...and nothing is inherently right or wrong?

What can history teach us?

As the Enlightenment unfolded, Hume's 'emotional self' came

to be seen as nothing more than a cultural construct. For the libertines, this meant relocating the source of authority about good to 'the self'. And for those wanting to reform society, it meant relocating the source of authority about good to a governing system (an idea encouraged by the thinking of the German philosopher, Hegel).

The tension between these two ideologies has resulted in the bun-fight we see going on in society today. On one hand, we have libertarians seeking personal freedom – as per Hume; and on the other, we have minority groups (post-modernists) who want to reform society so they can have power – as per Marx. Neo-Marxists do, however, make use of liberal-thinking libertines. They need advocates of liberal thinking to help rid society of Christian values...which then leaves the stage clear for new governing systems to be put in place.

Significantly, both groups don't know what to do about 'morality' and have left it undefined and undervalued. Sadly, with no God to guarantee what good is, society is losing its cohesion and has become terribly vulnerable.

Historical evidence indicates that when God is dismissed, society loses the cultural antibodies it needs to protect itself from totalitarianism – where truth becomes meaningless, justice is trashed, high control is exercised, and humans are reduced to being useful automatons – and if not useful, expunged. Societies that have cast off Christian values inevitably collapse into some sort of totalitarianism that dehumanizes and devalues people. It consigned millions to starve to death in its pursuit of communist collective ideology. It murdered people in gas chambers, and littered the 'killing fields' of Cambodia with bones. At a societal level, history teaches us that humanism inevitably transmutes to in-humanism despite the ideals of its philosophers.

Notwithstanding this, the West is blindly stumbling toward an atheistic future, banning Jesus from its schools, its politics, its moral laws, and marriage. Forgive me if I am not optimistic about this. It is difficult not to feel a little bleak as a new generation emerges that doesn't know its identity, or what it is that guarantees worth and hope.

So, what does this mean?

It means this: There is an urgent need for our nation to repent, to discover its true purpose, true value, true meaning, and true hope. In other words, it is time to look seriously at the claims of Jesus.

It is highly significant that we can check them out. Why? Because Christianity is evidence based, as we said earlier. This means that Christian hope is not just wishful thinking. It is not a philosophical analgesic someone dreamed up to make them feel better in the face of the inevitability of death. It has at its heart, the love of God, the initiative of God, and the presence of God amongst us as Jesus.

Christian hope is therefore a future certainty, grounded in the reality of Jesus.

There is not much hope without the truth of God, is there? The German philosopher, Friedrich Nietzsche popularized the idea that "God is dead" and attacked all doctrines that he considered to be a drain on life's "expansive energies." (This probably helped explain why he went mad and died, probably of syphilis, in 1900.) Without God, his "life expanding" comments didn't amount to much. He said, "In reality, hope is the worst of all evils, because it prolongs man's torments."[6]

Oh dear!

Let me give you an invitation. When you are tired of the deceits of humankind and feel ready to embrace truth, explore the reality of God.

Personally, I believe God hangs his business card in the cosmos; teaches us his character in Scripture; and comes seeking us in person as Jesus. In other words, he invites us to share in a divine friendship that is as large as the cosmos, as intimate as a child in a manger, and as committed as a man on a cross.

True atheists can't allow moral outrage

Some evil is so shocking that it defies belief. A Nazi guard asking a mother to choose which of her two children will be taken to the gas chamber; the rape and mutilation of women in war; tossing babies in the air and catching them on bayonets; the bombing of children in a school…

How do you respond to this?

This sort of raw evil causes moral outrage in most of us. Only the depraved and those who are evilly deluded could think otherwise. We somehow know instinctively that these things are wrong.

This prompts the question: How do people become evil, and what world-views encourage it?

Hitler adapted Nietzsche's atheistic philosophy and used it to underpin his Nazi ideology. Without the constraints of God, it was perfectly okay for Hitler to dominate, enslave and kill the weak. His abiding ambition was for the Aryan race to take over Europe through savage warfare, and establish itself as the crowning power of Europe, indeed: of history.

In doing this, Hitler was simply imitating the perceived brutal reality of the animal and plant world. It was therefore 'natural'. But whilst there is some sort of perverse logic to this thinking, most of us recoil at the evil it sanctioned…and we do so at a deep, visceral level.

The same is true for Communism. It too has stripped humanity of its sacredness and subsumed everything to the well-being of 'The Party'. When discussing the terrible consequences of its policies on the starving peasants of the Ukraine, Stalin is reputed to have said, "If only one man dies of hunger, that is a tragedy. If millions die, that is only statistics."

This de-humanizing philosophy also explains the evils committed by Pol Pot and his army. (They did the bayonet thing with the babies in Cambodia.)

But here's the question: If there is no God to guarantee what is morally good or morally evil, how can we know what 'good' actually is? At best, all we can say is that evolution has taught us that things are more 'efficient' for our species if we co-operate and are nice. But that doesn't really satisfy. After all, evolution has taught many animals to kill off rivals from other species, and even from within their own species.

So, the big question is: Where do atheists get their 'visceral' moral code from? If they hold true to their atheistic tenets, they can't have moral outrage. They can only talk in terms of what is efficient for the wellbeing of their DNA.

From this, I can only conclude that most atheists actually make very bad atheists. Put simply: their world-view is not consistent with what they experience in reality.

Some atheists speak of 'good' as something that is self-evident, and therefore we don't need God to be moral. There are two answers to this.

The first is that for many atheists, morality is self-evident only because they have, as we said earlier, a folk-memory of the Christian culture that was instilled in their lives by their grandparents. The sad reality is that many atheists are leaning on the Christian heritage of their forbears...whilst simultaneously whittling these values away. Quite how long these values will last in their hands, who knows?

The second thing worth mentioning is that Christian morality is not self-evident in many non-Christian civilizations. In some cultures, trickery and deceit is lauded (e.g. by the Sawi tribe in Irian Jaya, pre-1960). In others, strength and dominance over others was lauded above all else (e.g. the early Roman Empire).

What we can say, however, is that most humans are instinctively moral beings. The Bible suggests this is because we are made in the image of God – who is the preeminent moral being.

So, what can we conclude?

Simply this: If you want to be authentically and consistently moral, you need to acknowledge God. Otherwise, there is no reason, value, or purpose in the 'good' you define for yourself. And what happens when the 'good' of *my* happiness is threatened by *your* good? Whose good wins?

Without God, morality falls into a heap.

This reality has even percolated through to Richard Dawkins. He admitted that if God were eliminated from society, people would behave poorly. Dawkins cited an experiment carried out by Professor Melissa Bateson of the University of Newcastle, UK. It entailed setting up a coffee station with an 'honesty box' system of payment. Evidently, when a picture of a large pair of eyes was displayed near the honesty box, customers were three times more likely to pay. It instilled the idea that someone was watching.

The Jewish agnostic, David Belinski, picked up this idea when he wrote:

> *What Hitler did not believe, and what Stalin did not believe, and what Mao did not believe, and what the SS did not believe, and what the Gestapo did not believe, and what the NKVD did not believe, and what the commissars, functionaries, swaggering executioners, Nazi doctors, Communist Party theoreticians, intellectuals, Brown Shirts, Black Shirts, gauleiters, and a thousand party hacks did not believe, was that God was watching what they were doing.*[7]

So, if morality is important to you, seek out the God who both encourages it and guarantees it.

A warning from Russia

Aleksandr Solzhenitsyn (1918 - 2008) was a Russian philosopher and a political prisoner of the Communist Party. He was eventually released from the *Gulag* he was in, and came to America, where he watched, with deep sorrow, as Western democracies slowly became the sort of amoral society he'd just escaped from. In a speech given at Harvard's 327th anniversary in 1978, he said:

> *The defense of individual rights has reached such extremes as to make society as a whole defenseless against certain individuals. It is time, in the West, to defend not so much human rights as human obligations.*
>
> *Destructive and irresponsible freedom has been granted boundless space. Society appears to have little defense against the abyss of human decadence, such as, for example, misuse of liberty for moral violence against young people* (and) *motion pictures full of pornography, crime, and horror.*[8]

Solzhenitsyn sounds a warning bell, but he laments the fact that the West is not listening. The reason for this, he said, is because change in societal value has come about gradually. This has resulted in society sliding lazily into a *laissez faire*, benevolent humanism. He says that the driving philosophy behind this move is social Marxism, the erroneous idea that, "there is no evil inherent in human nature. All the defects of life are caused by wrong social systems, which must be corrected."[9]

Solzhenitsyn gives a stark warning. He says that liberalism inevitably morphs into radicalism, and radicalism morphs into totalitarianism.

If Solzhenitsyn is right, then it is a frightening snapshot of the future for Western society...unless we re-discover our spiritual identity.

It should therefore be of concern that the Australian media reported that socialism is booming in popularity among young people.[10] It is booming, evidently, because they have no knowledge of how the socialist world-view has played out as Communism in world history. No one has ever tapped them on the shoulder and pointed out that refugees are not flocking to seek out the civility and culture of any Communist or neo-Marxist state. Communism, in the form of Lenin, Stalin and Mao was responsible for killing tens of millions of people. Many were murdered and many others were starved to death because of the enforced ideology of collective farming. Pol Pot was less subtle: he simply engaged in blatant genocide. By any measure: Marxism's heritage is blood red.

But it seems that many young adults don't know their world history. This is ironic because in their lust for unbridled liberty, they are, in fact, laying themselves open to a repressive ideology that will enforce conformity...and lack any form of Christian civility.

At a conference on Marxism in Melbourne in 2015, the British academic, Roz Ward, spoke about why she developed the *Safe Schools* program (designed to create safer and more inclusive environments for same-sex-attracted, and intersex students in primary and secondary schools). She did so, she said, for the express purpose of implementing Marxism in the classroom. Roz Ward provides a good example of a neo-Marxist using the libertine wing of society to further her own ideological cause.

Such behavior gives me no reason to be confident about the future. Such things have even caused the columnist and activist, Jonathon Van Maren, concern. He wrote an article entitled, "Atheists sound the alarm: Decline of Christianity is seriously hurting society."[11] In his article, he cites the British journalist, Douglas Murray, who calls himself a 'Christian atheist' i.e. someone who is an atheist but who has Christian morals. Murray says:

> ...*our modern concept of human rights, based as it is on a Judeo-Christian foundation, may very well outlive Christianity by only a few short years. Cut off from the source, our conception of human rights may shrivel and die very quickly, leaving us fumbling about in a thick and impenetrable darkness.*

This should give us cause for thought.

The American philosopher, David Bentley Hart, reminds us:

> *Among all the many great transitions that have marked the evolution of Western civilization ...there has been only one – the triumph of Christianity – that can be called in the fullest sense a 'revolution': a truly massive and epochal revision of humanity's prevailing vision of reality, so pervasive in its influence and so vast in its consequences as to actually have created a new conception of the world, of history, of human nature, of time, and of the moral good.*[12]

It would be a pity to see all this disappear.

Both reason and intuition are pointers to the need for morality, but it is only God who can give that morality its foundation and guarantee of what is 'good'. Without God's parameters and values, morality collapses into expediency...and expediency will always trash truth. When that happens, you have moral freefall that only a totalitarian state can survive...for a while.

Put simply: history has shown that the idea that a nation can have a healthy morality without religion is a fiction.

Satisfaction and fulfillment

Humankind has to face one of two great disappointments. The

first: is never being able to achieve one's goals. The second: is to have achieved them.

Why do I tell you this?

You may remember the American Rock band, Imagine Dragons? The band gained notoriety in 2012 when it shot to fame with its debut album *Night Visions*. It sold over 2 million copies in the US and went platinum in twelve countries. They were named "The Breakthrough Band of 2013," and *Rolling Stone* magazine named their single *Radioactive* "the biggest rock hit of the year."

They went on to win a Grammy Award for Best Rock Performance, and a World Music Award. In May 2014, the band was nominated for a total of fourteen different Billboard Music Awards, including Top Artist of the Year and a Milestone Award. They had reached the top...and experienced the goal they had worked toward all their life.

However, the things that went along with fame disturbed the band's lead singer, Daniel Reynolds. He found himself growing increasingly disconnected from his family and from life in general as the band's success grew. He stated: "That's a scary thing when you get everything that you could have wanted but yet you still feel an emptiness, because at that point you think, *Oh man, if this doesn't fill it, then I don't know where to look anymore.*"

Daniel had achieved the goal he had dreamed of and pursued his whole life...but when he reached it, he found that it left him empty

So tell me: How's your sense of emptiness? What has not yet been fulfilled in your life? What are you still hungering for concerning hope, identity, and meaning?

The Australian Aboriginals have a saying: "A man will remain a child until he knows his story." So tell me: Do you know your story? Do you know who you are, why you exist on this planet, and what your intended destiny is?

If you listen to the current bevy of strident atheists, life is pretty bleak. There is only darkness. The twentieth century French biologist, Jacques Monod, said: "The ancient covenant is in pieces: man at last knows that he is alone in the unfeeling immensity of the universe, out of which he has emerged only by chance. Neither his destiny nor his duty have been written down." [13]

The danger in remaining "a child" and not knowing your identity or purpose is that you collapse back into the behavior of the animal kingdom, and things can become pretty ugly.

It is therefore crucial that you know who you are, what your purpose is, and how much God values you.

5

Philosophy, Truth, and Me

From where does today's society get its sense of identity? From where does it get its values?

Personally, I don't think that society gets either from anything very academic. Society seems to lazily absorb its values from films, media opinion leaders, and songs. I have always felt that songs are where the soul of a civilization comes out into the open. I'm reminded of Simon and Garfunkel's wistful ballad, *Sounds of Silence*, in which they sing: "the words of the prophets are written on the subway walls..."

Is that where we have to go to get our identity – to the nihilism and rebellion graffitied onto subway walls...and if so, should this be of concern?

Yes and no.

I say "no" because I am very glad that society does not go to our universities' philosophy departments for answers about meaning and values. Many Western philosophers have closed their minds to the idea of God, and can only see life through the filter of atheism. As a result of this, the art of philosophy has largely died...and philosophy departments have closed in many universities. Hardly anyone in our nation can name a current philosopher who is making a significant impact on the culture of our time.

Why is this?

I've had a little peek into the world of modern philosophy, and I don't like much of what I see. It is a world that has invented its own vocabulary – a secret language that is unintelligible to most other people. But whilst modern philosophy's inability to communicate itself in common language is a major failing, it is not its main failing. Its main failing is that philosophers in the last century or so have chosen to put on blinkers that stop them seeing the rational evidence for God. They give little evidence of looking at any philosophy earlier than René Descartes (1596 - 1650) and so ignore all non-materialist philosophies. (Descartes, a French philosopher, is considered to be the father of modern philosophy. Though touted as a champion of rationalism and atheism, René Descartes was actually a devout Christian. For him, faith and reason were intimately bound together.)

Having relegated God to the sidelines, philosophy today has been unable to give humankind any grounds for knowing its identity, meaning, truth, or hope. It can only offer silence when it comes to the 'big' questions of life. As a result, today's philosophy is in retreat, and can only do two things:

First: it has stopped asking questions about the big issues of identity, meaning and values...and has concentrated on bickering about the rules of logical thought. In other words, today's philosophers have turned philosophy into a sterile academic mind game. And nobody cares much about that!

Second: as modern philosophy has journeyed down the atheistic rabbit hole, it has lost sight of the basic question: "If this is the way the world is, what is the best way to live?" It has simply concluded that life is meaningless, and that there is no such thing as truth. Nothing is inherently good or sacred.

Well...thanks very much, you modern philosophers. You are not only incomprehensible, but you are so blinkered that you are completely unable to offer anything to humanity other than meaninglessness, and a philosophy of living that is as mournful as it is destructive.

It is destructive because this thinking boils down to 'do your own thing'; 'be your own god'. This, of course, opens the doors to unbridled, self-centered, hedonism. This philosophy really got under way in the 1960s with the thinking of Jean-Paul Sartre (1905 - 1980). With his existentialism, 'nothingness' replaced God; hopelessness replaced hope; and truth became something you invented in the moment.

Sartre spoke of humans being trapped in a permanent state of frustration because we can choose what we are but we can never become what we really want to be. (His is the angst-cry of a typical existentialist who makes no room for God.) Sartre says that the only relevant values are the ones you create in moments you encounter other people. Essentially, it is all about 'you'. You create your own values in reaction to others. This gives you the freedom to choose whatever you want to believe, because there is no reality beyond the self.

His relevance for us today is that his existentialism has given birth to the 'wild-child' we know today as 'post-modernism'. It is a way of thinking that has significantly influenced today's culture, often unconsciously. Post-modernism scorns institutional establishments and traditional moralities, examining both forensically for their systemic repression of minority groups. It calls for the old order and their meta-narratives (such as the Bible) to be supplanted by the new order – minority groups. It demands that old truths be trashed. There is now no such thing as truth. Truth is simply what works for you at the time. You are free to change it tomorrow.

Sartre advocated polygamy and had, at one time, four mistresses on the go. His philosophy of loose-living and revolutionary ideas perfectly suited the climate of the 60s.

Then eventually, all the revolutionaries woke up sexually dissipated, without knowing who they were. And when they grew up a bit more, they couldn't pass on any meaning or values to their children. Some of the better informed also noticed Jean-Paul's revolutionary Marxist ideals being played out by Pol Pot's murderous regime in Cambodia.

So...if that's the best modern philosophy can offer – good riddance.

But there is a part of me that knows that notionally, philosophy *should* be concerned with ideas of truth, meaning, and sound reasoning – and that, surely, is a good thing. I, for one, would welcome truth that was a little more than what is written on a subway wall. But if you are to do philosophy well, you will need to take off the blinkers and consider the rational, social, historical and moral evidences that exist for God.

Anti-theism removes reason from existence, and removes what's sacred from humanity. This has led to scientific absurdity and the most horrific evils of history. Put simply: The madness of anti-theism has delivered hell on earth.

In contrast, authentic Christianity has been civilization's greatest blessing.

Where are the atheists?

Some in the science departments of our universities have begun to notice that the philosophy departments are becoming clubhouses for atheists. The American physicist, Robert Griffiths (winner of the Heinemann Prize in mathematical physics in 1984) said: "If we need an atheist for a debate, we go to the philosophy department. The physics department isn't much use."[1]

It is extraordinary, isn't it, that you don't go to the science department (the place of things empirical and rational) to find an atheist; you go to the philosophy department. Now, I know Griffiths' comment is a generalization, but it nonetheless makes you think.

The geneticist, Baruch Shalev, documented the religious views of all 719 Nobel Prize winners from 1901 to 2000, noting the percentage who were atheists, agnostics or freethinkers.

Surprisingly, only 10.5% fell into that godless category. Very significantly, this figure dropped to only 4.7% for physicists, and rose to 35.2% for winners in literature.[2] It would seem that those who really 'know' the empirical reality of the universe are those who believe in God.

Christian Anfinsen, Nobel Laureate in chemistry said the same thing with rather less grace: "I think only an idiot can be an atheist. We must admit that there exists an incomprehensible power or force with limitless foresight and knowledge that started the whole universe going in the first place."[3]

If this is true, it rather suggests that our atheistic philosophers don't know enough.

Philosophers don't know enough

The extraordinary order scientists see in the universe demands some sort of explanation. The American astrophysicist, Gregory Benford, writes: "The overwhelming impression is one of order. The more we discover about the universe, the more we find that it is governed by rational laws ...You still have the question: why does the universe bother to exist?"[4]

Whilst science can lay bare the workings of the universe, it can't tell us *why* it exists. As such, it is silent on the really big questions of life. Erwin Schrödinger (1887 - 1961), a Nobel Prize-winning physicist, put it well when he said: "The scientific picture of the world around me is very deficient. It gives me a lot of factual information, puts all our experience in a magnificently consistent order, but is ghastly silent about all that is really near to our heart, that really matters to us."[5]

The idea that truth is only that which can be scientifically verified (or which is capable of logical or mathematical proof) is a way of thinking, called 'positivism'. I'll let Einstein tell you what it means. He said: "I am not a positivist. Positivism states that what cannot be observed does not exist. This conception is scientifically indefensible, for it is impossible to make valid affirmations of what people 'can' or 'cannot' observe. One would have to say, 'only what we observe exists', which is obviously false." [6]

Three cheers for Einstein!

Anthony Flew, who as we said earlier, was atheism's preeminent philosopher in the late twentieth century, came to believe in God's existence through examining the evidence. He talks about the "endemic evil" of dogmatic atheism that says, "We should not ask for an explanation of how it is that the world exists; it is here and that's all."[7]

I think Flew is right to draw this "endemic evil" to our attention.

The renowned physicist, Stephen Hawking, ends his book, *A Brief History of Time*, with a question. Why is it "that we and the universe exist? If we find the answer to that, it would be the ultimate triumph of human reason – for then we should know the mind of God."[8] It is tragic, but perhaps unsurprising, that many modern philosophers do not want to know the mind of God, and so fail to understand the purpose of creation.

I can't help but reflect that such determined atheism, adhered to despite the facts, must be hard to live with. What would you dare let yourself think about? What would you do with the prodding of your heart to search out the reasons for your existence? Would you ever let yourself look up into the night sky?

As I said in chapter 1, Bertrand Russell, (arguably the leading academic atheist in the early twentieth century) would not let himself look at the cosmos and ponder why it had come into being. He wrote a book called, *Why I am Not a Christian*. Sadly, Russell succumbed to the habit of building grotesque caricatures of Christianity – which he found easy to destroy. His daughter, Katherine (who became a Christian) wrote about this flaw, saying: "When [father] wanted to attack religion, he sought out its most egregious errors and held them up to ridicule, while avoiding serious discussion of the basic message."[9]

Russell was determined to hold on to his atheism in defiance of the Presbyterian strictures of his grandmother. He saw them as an impediment to his sexual appetite. Bertie wanted to be a freethinker like his father who, sadly, had died when he was a child. However, his atheism came at some cost to his peace of mind. His daughter, Katherine, wrote:

> *I believe myself that his whole life was a search for God ... Indeed, he had first*

taken up philosophy in hope of finding proof of the evidence of the existence of God ... Somewhere at the back of my father's mind, at the bottom of his heart, in the depths of his soul [which he did not believe he had] there was an empty space that had once been filled by God, and he never found anything else to put in it ... (He had the) *ghostlike feeling of not belonging, of having no home in this world.*"[10]

Russell's lack of peace was well expressed in a poem he wrote to Edith, his fourth wife. The first stanza of the poem reads:

> *Through the long years*
> *I have sought peace,*
> *I found ecstasy,*
> *I found anguish,*
> *I found madness,*
> *I found loneliness.*
> *I found the solitary pain*
> *that gnaws the heart,*
> *But peace I did not find.*[11]

What a terribly sad epitaph!

The Christian philosopher, David Bentley Hart, begins his book *The Experience of God*, by saying, "An absolutely convinced atheist, it often seems to me, is simply someone who has failed to notice something very obvious."[12] He continues this thought at the very end of his book, *The Experience of God*, saying:

Those who have entirely lost the ability to see the transcendent reality that shows itself in all things, and who refuse to seek it out or even to believe the search a meaningful one, have confined themselves for now within an illusory world, and wander in a labyrinth of dreams. Those others, however, who are still able to see the truth that shines in and through and beyond the world of ordinary experience, and who know that nature is in its every aspect the gift of the supernatural, and who understand that God is that absolute reality in whom, in every moment, they live and move and have their being – they are awake.[13]

To encourage 'wakefulness,' let me make this bold statement: Atheism is the religion of the busy. Busyness stops people thinking deeply and exploring the truth of things. Busy people only have time to adsorb the culture of 'the norm' – a culture defined by commercialism and society's opinion leaders.

Indigenous Australians have sometimes reminded us of a discipline that has been lost to the Western world. Miriam-Rose Ungunmerr-Baumann, an indigenous artist and writer from Daly River said at the 1988 International Liturgy Assembly in Hobart:

> *What I want to talk about is another special quality of my people. I believe it is the most important. It is our unique gift. It is perhaps the greatest gift we can give to our fellow Australians. In our language this quality is called 'dadirri' ...It is inner, deep listening and quiet, still awareness ...It is something like what you call 'contemplation' ...It renews us and brings us peace.*

God says to us: "Be still and know that I am God" (Psalm 46:10). Why? Because he wants to be known.

So, I invite you to free yourself of 'hurry sickness' and be still.

I have dared to suggest that atheism is fueled by a dreadful cocktail of ignorance and willfulness. Anthony Walsh is an American criminologist and professor at Boise State University. He wrote a book called *A Nation Divided*, in which he said:

> *For a great many philosophers and scientists, the problem with those whose science and philosophy have led them to reject God is that they have not learned enough. They have succumbed to 'God of the gaps' thinking whereby God was the placeholder waiting for science to fill the gaps. More science and more philosophy is the cure for such thinking.*[14]

Francis Bacon (1561 - 1626) developed the rules underpinning 'scientific method' and was therefore a huge influence on science. It is significant that he too made the claim that a hunger for great knowledge in philosophy will lead you to God. He said, "A little philosophy inclineth man's mind to atheism, but depth in philosophy bringeth men's minds about to religion."[15]

This brings to mind Jesus' teaching: "Ask and it will be given to you; seek and you will find; knock and the door will be opened to you" (Matthew 7:7).

Let's not be frightened of seeking.

Philosophers respond to Richard Dawkins

The English biologist, Richard Dawkins, has written a number of books seeking to prove that the complexity and order we see in nature has a perfectly rational explanation, and that belief in God is not necessary.[16] Dawkins argues that evolution works at the level of the gene. The survival and replication of genes is the true purpose of life. Genes occupy and then discard bodies.

This, of course, raises the question of how and why the DNA in genes became so clever. How did the codes get encoded in the DNA of genes? As such, Dawkins may not have identified genes as being the basic agent responsible for change, so much as pointed to genes being the tools God uses to allow change. Dawkins also fails to answer why it is that we can rebel against our genetic tendencies and make real choices. Similarly, he needs to explain why it is that evolution has not only molded our bodies but also human consciousness, a consciousness that leads most of us to seek God.

Anthony Flew also criticizes Dawkins for attributing to genes characteristics that can only be attributed to persons.[17] He makes reference to Dawkins' book, *The Selfish Gene* and says, "Genes, of course, can be neither selfish or unselfish anymore than they, or any other non-conscious entities, can engage in competition or make selections."[18]

Flew picks up the claim Dawkins made that: "we, and all other animals, are machines created by our genes," and says that if this were true, it would be no use Dawkins going on to say: "Let us try to teach generosity and altruism, because we are born selfish." Flew says that, "No eloquence can move programmed robots."[19] He goes on to remind us that, "Natural selection is not inherently creative; it does not positively produce anything."[20] Flew's comment is correct in that natural selection cannot produce anything from nothing.

However, the environment is able to select which randomly generated mutation in a species will cause that species to thrive.

David Bentley Hart, with his sharp philosophical mind, is appalled at the populist, distortions of fact and logical thought exhibited by the new breed of militant atheist. He speaks of their thinking as:

> ...*vacuous arguments afloat on oceans of historical ignorance, made turbulent by storms of strident self-righteousness, is as contemptible as any other form of dreary fundamentalism. And it is sometimes difficult, frankly, to be perfectly generous in one's response to the sort of invective currently fashionable among the devoutly undevout, or to the sort of historical misrepresentations it typically involves.*[21]

Hart singles out Richard Dawkins in particular, saying, "His embarrassing incapacity for philosophical reasoning – never fails to entrance his eager readers with his rhetorical recklessness."[22] Elsewhere, Hart says:

> ...*it seems obvious that among the innumerable evidences of late modern culture's lack of spiritual depths one must include its manifest impotence to produce profound atheists. Instead, the best it seems we can hope for today are dreary purveyors of historical illiteracy, theatrical indignation, subfusc moralizing, and the sort of logical confusions that Richard Dawkins has brought to a level of almost transcendent perfection.*[23]

One can't help but wonder how the 'new atheists' (Sam Harris, Richard Dawkins, Daniel Dennett, and Christopher Hitchens) can attract such adoring fans? Perhaps the apostle Paul gives us a clue when he warns us, "For the time will come when people will not put up with sound doctrine. Instead, to suit their own desires, they will gather around them a great number of teachers to say what their itching ears want to hear" (2 Timothy 4:3).

The fact that Dawkins *et al.* can be applauded, lauded, and made into very rich men by those who mindlessly cheer them on says something quite distressing about Western society. We seem to have entered a cultural dark age where ignorance and obfuscation masquerade as intelligent thought.

Certainly, there seems to be a bewildering willfulness to atheism these days, spurred on by an inability to remember what has happened in history. This point was brought home to me when I was walking outside the University of Adelaide during "Orientation Week," a time when all the university's clubs were advertising themselves to new students. The Marxists had a trestle table, so I wandered over for a chat. I asked them what their 'pin-up' nation was that showcased Marxism to its best advantage, either currently, or in past history. They couldn't answer. I inquired whether it was Stalin (who killed about 12 million people), or Mao (he killed 42 million) or Pol Pot (who murdered about 2 million)?

I was asked to leave.

It seemed to me as if today's neo-Marxists suffer from a particularly debilitating case of amnesia.

Bentley Hart also makes this point saying: "The reason the very concept of God has become at once so impoverished, so thoroughly mythical, and ultimately so incredible for so many modern persons is not because of all the interesting things we have learned over the past few centuries, but because of all the vital things we have forgotten."[24]

If you want to hear David Bentley Hart in full flight, expressing his scorn at the thinking of the new atheists, you can't go past his appraisal of Daniel Dennett's book *Breaking the Spell*. Hart writes:

> *Dennett's argument consists in little more than the persistent misapplication of quantitative and empirical terms to unquantifiable and intrinsically non-empirical realities, sustained by classifications that are entirely arbitrary and fortified by arguments that any attentive reader should notice are wholly circular.*[25]

– which is about as thorough a destruction you will ever read of someone's book!

. . .

What you think, matters

Here's an interesting tit-bit for you: the word 'cosmos' comes from a Greek word meaning 'orderly system'. The philosopher, Pythagoras (570 - 490BC) was the first to use the term in relation to our ordered universe. Cosmos is therefore the opposite of chaos, and this is significant, because our universe is not just any sort of universe; it is highly ordered.

All beliefs, including atheism, are belief systems based on presuppositions that cannot be proved. As such, *all* belief systems are held by faith. The big question, of course, is how reasonable is that faith. If it has not taken adequate account of the extraordinary order and 'fine tuning' of the physical forces in the universe that have allowed life to develop—then, I submit, that faith is poorly founded.

Taking care with truth, certainly as it pertains to modern philosophy, is not in vogue at the moment. Modern philosophers have trashed the idea of truth. I confess that when reading the life of philosophers from Nietzsche to Sartre, it was difficult to escape the conclusion that their Nihilistic or neo-Marxist ideas were designed to support their sexual addictions. Their verbosity masked venality and their sophistry supplanted science.

The French 20th century philosopher, Paul-Michel Foucault, is lionized in many of today's university philosophy departments. Foucault's philosophy formed the basis for postmodernism and its trashing of all forms of truth. It brought him no joy, however, as Foucault's mental landscape was characterized by the macabre, sado-masochism, homosexuality and rather distressingly, pedophilia. He often contemplated suicide. His sado-masochistic and homosexual escapades resulted in him dying of AIDs in 1984 at the age of 57.

Foucault's story highlights the suspicion that libertine modern philosophers didn't so much get their thinking *from* philosophy, as bolster their addictions *with* philosophy. And it's not hard for these radical ideas to become attractive if you can offer unbridled hedonism or greater personal power in a new world order.

Many modern philosophers inherited their radical ideas from

the 'Frankfurt School' of philosophy that flourished in Goethe University between the two world wars. Hitler's persecution of such thinking resulted in some of its proponents fleeing to America. This began the long march of revolutionary philosophy through the academia of the West, which reached fever pitch during the university occupations of 1968. The Frankfurt School is still a major influence in many humanities departments of the West today.

Significantly, the big three Greek philosophers: Socrates, Plato and Aristotle, did not follow the atheistic thinking of the atomist philosophers who preceded them. All three of them saw evidence of 'mind' in the cosmos and the necessity of 'mind' in ethics.

Centuries later, the Roman Stoic philosopher, Seneca, examined the atheistic thinking in Lucretius' highly influential poem *De Rerum Natura* (that sidelined God and advocated a purely materialistic understanding of truth). Seneca argued against the sentiments of the poem and also spoke of the evidence of 'mind'.

The thirteenth century Dominican philosopher, Thomas Aquinas, went further. He put the case for the existence of God into a logical argument that he called his "Five Ways." Aquinas' thinking has been attacked through the centuries but despite this, his teaching continues to provide an important basis for Christian philosophical thinking today.

So, may I ask: What are you going to do with the philosophic influences that have made their way through history to you? I suggest it is important to be alert to them and not absorb their culture uncritically. Truth matters.

Nihilism

The defining ideology of today's atheistic culture is nihilism, the belief that nothing has meaning. As nihilism doesn't stand for anything, it wants to allow everything in all its perversity – pornography, late term abortions, and more. The battle cry for nihilists is 'personal freedom', nothing must infringe it.

This loss of faith in the old certainties that held society together has, according to the British historian, Arnold Toynbee, been the consistent symptom of civilizations in decline – civilizations that commit cultural suicide.[26]

Today's strident demands for personal freedom are being smuggled into society under the banner of 'tolerance'. But as G.K. Chesterton pointed out in one of his pithy aphorisms: "Tolerance is the virtue of someone who doesn't actually believe anything." So, it's worth asking, isn't it: Should everything be tolerated? If not, who decides what's 'in' and what's 'out'? Who has the power…and by what means do they choose?

Tolerance, as it pertains to civility and gracious behavior, is a good thing; but, when tolerance is a trick used by those in power to erase traditional truth from society, it should be of huge concern.

The truth is: if everything must be tolerated, then nothing can be said to be true. And if Christianity, with its claims about God, can be said to be untrue, then it can be relegated to a place of insignificance. The reality is, of course, if Christianity is not allowed a place in society – society has not become tolerant; it has become intolerant. It has reversed the centuries of good work done by people who fought for religious freedom and civility.

This growing repression of Christianity should be of great concern, for no other world-view has ever produced civilizations that have been so fruitful, fair, and emancipated. Bentley Hart says that only Christianity "constituted a rejection of and alternative to nihilism's despair, violence, and idolatry of power; as such, Christianity shattered the imposing and enchanting facade behind which nihilism once hid."[27]

Nihilism does not look very attractive when compared to the wisdom and civility of Christianity. So, please don't choose it.

Of greater concern is the fact that people today don't so much choose nihilism (or neo-Marxism) so much as lazily fall into it because they lack the inclination to engage in good critical thinking. The American philosopher and theologian, Bruce Gore, says that the sort of intellectual rigor demonstrated by the 13th century philosopher Thomas Aquinas, which so impacted his generation, could not achieve the same result today. The current generation exists "in a culture of sound bites; not sustained rational thought but impressions." He goes on to lament: "This isn't sustained rational discourse." It is just verbal potshots that don't necessarily connect to anything that is a reliable frame of reference. He warns that this trend is heading society toward "intellectual collapse."[28]

Real reasons for atheism

Social researchers tell us that the percentage of people who are atheists is increasing in the West. It is interesting that most atheists claim rational reasons for their non-belief in God. However, research conducted by the American Psychological Association suggests this is not so. They conducted studies in which they interviewed atheists, and graded the extent to which their atheism was influenced by experiences of disappointment, anger, hurt, or alienation.

What is fascinating is that 54% reported that they had relational and emotional reasons for non-belief. Another study of 429 Americans put the number higher at 72%. In other words, people were atheists for emotional reasons. Their non-belief had nothing, or very little, to do with being rational.[29] Nonetheless, the twentieth century saw a marked rise in the incidence of atheism in the West in the 1940s and 50s. The 1970s however bucked the trend in some Western philosophy departments. *Time* magazine reported that there was a revival of belief in God amongst many of the world's top philosophers. It said:

> *God? Wasn't he chased out of heaven by Marx, banished to the unconscious by Freud and announced by Nietzsche to be deceased? Did not Darwin drive him out of the empirical world? Well, not entirely. In a quiet revolution in thought and arguments that hardly anyone could have foreseen only two decades ago, God is making a comeback. Most intriguingly, this is happening not among theologians or ordinary believers ...but in the crisp, intellectual circles of academic philosophers.*[30]

Notwithstanding the advent of the *Society of Christian Philosophers* in 1978, the interest in God by Western university philosophy departments has not been maintained. Atheism is usually the only world-view allowed now, and this is a pity.

Despite the fact that atheists claim their world-view is based on rationalism, it is a world-view with gaping holes in its logic. Atheism requires people to have a very blinkered view of reality, and it requires a person to hold scientific convictions that are irrational. Specifically, it requires:

1. the belief that everything in the universe (or universes) came from nothing, as a result of nothing.
2. the belief that the absurd level of order and fine-tuning of the universe which has allowed life is the result of chance…and to claim this when the only factor known that has ever explained such a thing is 'intelligence'.
3. an ignorance of world history and of world-views that have been responsible for the best when it comes to civility and justice.
4. the belief that the deep-seated moral code within us is simply a product of evolution, which has taught us that things are more 'efficient' for individuals if we co-operate and are nice. It requires you to believe this, even when evolution has taught most other animals to kill off rivals from other species, and from within their own species.
5. an ignorance of Jesus Christ and the historical evidence surrounding the gospel claims of his life, death and resurrection.

Put simply: the empiricist prison of atheism doesn't match most people's experience of life.

So, what can we conclude?

Atheism may hide behind the coattails of rationality, but when you sweep the coattails away, it is difficult to see anything other than wounded people…or those who are willful atheists, i.e. those who *want* to not believe because they want to 'do their own thing'.

Evidence suggests that there is a mind behind the universe…and if this is so, we'd do well to find out about that 'Mind'...and cooperate with the big plan.

Nietzsche and the legacy of atheism

Friedrich Nietzsche (1844 - 1900) was a German philosopher who exerted a profound influence on modern intellectual history. It's worth having a look at him as he brings into sharp focus what atheist philosophy looks like.

Nietzsche argued that there were two fundamental types of morality: 'master morality' and 'slave morality'. Master morality values pride, strong will, nobility, and power. Slave morality values kindness, empathy, and sympathy – characteristics that are to be scorned.

Master morality makes judgments about whether an action is 'good' or 'bad' depending solely on whether it suits a current situation. It is the noble 'self' that determines value, and this 'self' does not seek or require anyone else's approval. In contrast to this, 'slave morality' lives by values that have proved most useful for a community, that have been handed down to him or her by history or convention.

Nietzsche, with his masterful command of pithy sayings and irony, says we should throw off the shackles of convention, scorn what is weak, and work to become a "superman," (literally: "overman") i.e. give rein to our unconscious "will for power."

Wow! No wonder the rebellious youth of the twentieth century loved it!

It is not hard to see why Hitler also loved it and used Nietzsche's philosophy to formulate his Nazi ideology of dominance and power.

In the cold reality of history's morning, it is easy to see Nietzsche's philosophy for what it is: an elitist imprimatur for selfishness and ego. It is a philosophy that offers hubris and takes away meaning. It is also a philosophy that provides no anchor for morality – a fact that frightened Nietzsche, but not enough to prevent him from the sexual liaisons responsible for the syphilis that probably sent him mad and ended his life prematurely.

Nietzsche popularized the phrase, "God is dead."

The reality is: Nietzsche is dead, and Christianity is still alive – even if it is waning in the Western world. The reason his philosophy couldn't kill Christianity is simple: It was because Nietzsche's existentialism crashed against the existential experience of Christians who knew God as *Abba*, (Father). Nietzsche's philosophy may well have sloughed off the merely religious (with their rituals and bureaucracies), but it did not bother the true Christian who has experienced God personally.

It is significant that Nietzsche couldn't cope with the moral vacuum and meaninglessness inherent in his own philosophy. He felt a deep sense of connectedness (rather than meaninglessness) with a horse when he saw it being flogged. He observed this at the time he began to go mad. It would seem that Nietzsche's heart argued with his head.

Nietzsche, as I said, railed against anything he considered to be weak or lacking passion. He deplored 'slave mentality' which abhorred strength in order to make virtues of empathy and kindness. Nietzsche was scornful of those who needed to invent or adopt Christianity in order to justify their weakness.

However, just as the optimism of humanism bled to death on the bloody fields of Flanders in World War I, Nietzsche's philosophy became bloodied by the brutalities of every despot that used it to seek their own empowerment. Nietzsche's "superman," and the selfish tyrant, turned out to be terrible twins – impossible to tell apart.

Atheism and death

One of the things atheism is deafeningly silent about is death. The reason is simple: it offers no hope beyond death. Occasionally, atheism tries its hand at bravado and says that those who are truly mature don't need any concept of life after death.[31] It was not, however, a concept that gave Stalin any comfort when he was dying. His daughter, Svetlana, wrote that his last act before death was to shake his fist in rage against God.[32] So, in a perverse way, he

God and Me

acknowledged God at his death, albeit not in a way that did him much good!

So...may I ask: How well does the world-view you live by, handle death?

If you are (very reasonably) wondering what I mean by 'world-view': it is what you believe about your meaning, morality, and destiny. How well does your world-view address the reality of death and suffering which you will inevitably face? I ask it because I'm not sure atheism handles it very well.

When faced with death or suffering, the atheist can do one of two things: He or she can rail, as Stalin did, in moral outrage against God. The problem with this, of course, is that if there is no God, it is a senseless exercise...and oxymoronic.

The alternative is to simply say that death and suffering are just symptoms of the meaninglessness of existence. As such, neither should evoke any emotion at all.

In the face of this meaninglessness, there can only be one of five responses:

1. The first option is to live a life that gives as much pleasure as possible, i.e. a life of self-centered hedonism. But a note of warning: If this option is chosen, it has been the experience of history that it will not satisfy. You will be left with a withered soul that aches for more. The soul seeks inexorably for meaning, as a compass needle seeks North Pole.
2. You have the option of being very depressed. Some people are asking whether one factor causing an increase in suicide numbers is a sense of meaninglessness in an increasingly atheistic culture.[33]
3. Another option is to borrow some of Christianity's principles and live a life that is relationally rich and full of acts of service. In other words, an atheist can elect to live a 'good' life and thereby force a meaning on a meaningless life – even if it is only self-delusion. Of course, the atheist can't really call what they do 'good'

because there is no God to guarantee what 'good' is. Good is simply what leaves them feeling...well, good. And isn't that interesting? When the atheist lives the Christian way, they feel fulfilled and happy, despite knowing that everything they do has no ultimate meaning.
4. Give way to a lust for power and kill anyone who disagrees (as happened in the French Revolution and in Hitler's Germany).
5. The other alternative, of course, is to stop being an atheist and believe that God exists!

And so we leave the bewildered atheists with their conundrum. Their soul wants to point north, whilst their head wants to point south.

The reality is, atheism is not kind to the soul. Atheists need to be very careful not to dwell too much on the logical outcome of their concept of truth. Truth is a beautiful thing when it shines a light on hope, but it is a terrible thing when it shines a light on meaninglessness.

So, what can we say to conclude?

Most of us have a sense that we were created for something more than this life. We feel we have loved too much, and meant too much, for us to have no significance after death. There is a persistent suspicion that we are designed to have some sort of relationship with eternity.

The Old Testament writers understood this. One of them (probably King Solomon) wrote: "(God) has...set eternity in the human heart; yet no one can fathom what God has done from beginning to end" (Ecclesiastes 3:11). In other words, the notion of eternity burns in our hearts, but we can't work out what God is up to.

Eternity

Arthur Malcolm Stace (1885 – 1967) was an Australian soldier. He gained fame as a reformed alcoholic who converted to Christianity, and spread his message by writing the word 'Eternity' in chalk on the footpaths of Sydney. He did this from 1932 to 1967 – thirty-five years!

This word has since become part of Sydney's folklaw. It was the word Sydney's civic leaders chose to have emblazoned in lights across the Harbor Bridge in the first minutes of 2000. It is a disturbing and powerful word. It is one that challenges society's pursuit of meaninglessness, lack of boundaries, self-obsession, and hedonism.

As I reflect on the Bible's teaching on eternity, the one thing it gives, more than anything else, is hope. It gives hope when we are faced with the obscenity and finality of death.

The existence of eternity also gives us dignity. Its existence means that we are created for more than collecting toys and T-shirts from your favorite holiday island. To simply be content with doing that is a woefully shallow way of living.

Why atheist intellectuals become Christians

It is enlightening to read the testimonies of eminent academics who were once atheists, and learn what it was that caused them to do a U-turn and embrace belief in God.

One of them was the British writer and intellectual, Francis Spufford, professor of creative writing at Goldsmiths College, London. His is an interesting case because he came to faith partly as a result of observing the difference in moral behavior between atheists and Christians. He said that he lost his faith in atheism partly as a result of feeling that his secular circle was more judgmental and unforgiving than the church he and his atheist friends had mocked. It dawned on him that despite not consistently living up to their ideals, Christians at least held the key to human acceptance and community. Christians were under no illusions; they had a profound belief in each other's imperfection and guilt. However, they had an even deeper trust in God's forgiveness. In this "league of the guilty," as Spufford put it, no one had grounds for looking down on anyone else, and no one had any bragging rights. This highly attractive aspect of Christianity helped him become a practicing Christian.

The other intellectual who became a Christian is, of course, Anthony Flew. We have talked about his conversion earlier, so we won't dwell on it, other than to note again the reason he came to believe in God.

It is difficult to do justice to the shock his conversion caused the atheistic world. In the late twentieth century, Flew was *the* front-runner making the philosophic case for atheism. He was their thinker. So when he came to believe in the existence of God, it caused dismay and disbelief amongst atheists.

What I love about Flew's story is the courage he displayed in seeking truth. He did not withdraw from debate with leading Christians, but sought out their thinking with the objective of understanding it. So it was that in 2004, Flew became a theist.

The reason he gave for believing in God was, as we've already said: the extraordinary 'fine tuning' of our universe that enabled it to develop sentient life. He said, "I now believe that the universe was brought into existence by an infinite Intelligence. I believe that this universe's intricate laws manifest what scientists have called the Mind of God. I believe that life and reproduction originate in a divine Source."[34] Flew made it quite clear that he had come to his position, not because of fear of death in his advancing age, or because he had lost his intellectual faculties. Quite the reverse: he said that, "the journey to my discovery of the Divine has thus far been a pilgrimage of reason. I have followed the argument where it has led me. And it has led me to accept the existence of a self-existent, immutable, immaterial, omnipotent, and omniscient Being."[35] Flew went on to say: "Science spotlights three dimensions of nature that point to God. The first is the fact that nature obeys laws. The second is the dimension of life, of intelligently organized and purpose-driven beings, which arose from matter. The third is the very existence of nature."[36]

So, there we have it: observations of morality and observations of scientific reality have caused intellectual atheists to believe in the existence of God.

Neither Spufford nor Flew were scientists. If we venture into the world of science, the incidence of theism (belief in God) increases. This does not surprise the cosmologist, Paul Davies. He makes the point that there is no evidence to suggest that the universe is logically necessary. As such, its existence needs explanation. He says that the atheist's claim that the laws of nature exist without reason is absurd. Davies goes on to say: "As a scientist, I find this hard to accept. There must be an unchanging rational ground in which the logical, orderly nature of the universe is rooted."[37]

It is important to note that 'order' is not something scientists impose on the universe, order is the 'nature' of the universe...and it is this order that requires a better explanation than atheism.

Truth

Authentic intellectual investigation centers on the notion of truth, so it is a concept worth exploring.

I think it's fair to say that the notion of truth has not fared well outside of Christianity. Some religions allow people to lie and deceive if it benefits their religious cause. The result of this is that you can never tell if such people are telling the truth. Leaders of totalitarian secular regimes also lie – so much so, that everyone expects it. These leaders lie about atrocities, civil abuses, and the malicious activities they are engaged in. As such, they have long since used up the capital of trust people have invested in them. No one believes them anymore.

In the animal world, where there is no morality, it makes perfect sense to deceive, enslave and predate in order to thrive. And that's where a society's morality must inevitably end up if you think you are just another animal, and ignore God.

It might be pertinent at this point to look objectively at what truth is, because its very concept is under attack these days. I'll mention just three rules for defining truth.

1. The first is, the 'law of non-contradiction'. This states that if something is true, it cannot be something else. For

example: Michael cannot be my son, and not be my son. (People who claim that all religions are the same often fracture this law.)
2. The second requirement is that a truth must be universally true. The truth about my cat being black must be true in Nigeria, as well as in Alaska. If it is not true, I must work on my truth claim and add some qualifications.
3. The third requirement for a truth statement is that it needs to be logical. In other words, it needs obey the rules of the syllogism: e.g.

All men are mortal.
Aristotle is a man.
Therefore, Aristotle is mortal.

Truth is a precious thing, and authentic Christians are passionate about it. They have to be, because they know that God requires it, defines it, and embodies it. Christianity, more than any other religion, is preoccupied with truth. Certainly, Jesus was. He said, "I tell you the truth" about eighty times in the gospels – which is a pretty fair indication of the importance he placed on it.

The primacy of truth is not easily found in other religions. Hinduism is essentially based on mythology, Buddhism on mysticism, and Islam on a private revelation that others can't verify. The new, syncretistic religions of today, such as New Age, are fairly careless about truth, whilst secular Postmodernism goes even further and has given up on the idea of truth altogether.

In contrast to this, Christianity makes a feature of truth.

Christianity, you see, is not just one faith among many: it is faith based on truth. In other words, Christianity is evidence-based (as we said earlier). If it can be shown that any of the essential truths about Jesus are false, Christianity becomes invalid. Notwithstanding the cancerous invasion of 'deism' into Christian institutions in the guise of liberal theology, Christianity remains a religion that is founded on the historical life, death, and resurrection of Jesus.[38] Wherever the institutional church has forgotten this, it has emptied its churches, lost its passion for mission, and found itself unable to offer anything in the way of hope. It has simply preached moralism.

Truth matters. Instinctively, we know this is so. There is something good about truth. Truth seems to be something outside of us, beyond us – something that measures us and invites us to climb up to it. Most of us are glad that truth is there, even if we can't always reach it.

To act in a way that is true and right is to live out a concept of truth that is unique to humans. Simply to act in a way that is merely expedient (or programmed by evolution) is to be sub-human – it is to be less than we have been called to be. To engage in this sort of behavior is to collapse back into nature's "red in tooth and claw" where it makes perfect sense to enslave, kill, and exploit in order to thrive.

Please don't be sub-human.

The American journalist and satirist, Henry Louis Mencken (1888–1956), wrote:

God is the immemorial refuge of the incompetent, the helpless, the miserable. They find not only sanctuary in his arms, but also a kind of superiority, soothing to their macerated egos; he will set them above their betters.[39]

Is he right, or is this yet another example of atheistic rhetoric running ahead of truth? Is it true that Christianity is simply a crutch for ineffectual people with an anxiety complex?

I hope I have said enough to indicate this is not the case. The Christian faith is historically, morally and scientifically reasonable – and is held to be true by millions of people across many nations and centuries. While that doesn't prove anything, it should at least suggest that we not dismiss Christianity carelessly. The fact that anything bothers to exist at all demands more from us than a shrug of the shoulders. To believe the universe came from nothing, and that its incredible mathematical order is meaningless, requires an extraordinary leap of faith.

Frankly, it is not a faith I share. Neither is it one shared by thousands of the world's most eminent scientists. There are very good reasons for taking the existence of God seriously. But I think it is important to understand that whilst people of faith know that what they believe is rational, they also know that their faith in God is *more* than rational. This makes logical sense. The truth about God necessarily has to be more than that which our rational brains can conceive – if God is to be more than something our brains have conceived.

Science points to a mind behind the universe. And since time, matter and space came into being at the time the universe came into being, God must exist outside of space and time. God therefore doesn't need a physical body. (This is why the ancient writers of Scripture described God as an eternal Spirit.

This fact might usefully have been whispered into the ear of Yuri Gagarin who was reputed to have said, "I see no God" when orbiting Earth aboard Vostok 1 in 1961. Christians, of course, were not surprised he didn't see God. No Christian thought he would literally be there in space. The laws of physics teach us that time and space are inseparably linked. (Scientists refer to the substance of the cosmos as 'spacetime'.) This means that if God exists, and is not physically there in space, he's also not physically constrained by time. In other words, if he exists, he must logically live in eternity.

Brian Leftow is the Nolloth Professor of the Philosophy of the Christian Religion at Oriel College, Oxford. He reminds us that: "The condition for a creative agent to exist is not for it to have a body...rather to have the capability of intentional action."[40]

As we draw this chapter to an end, one question requires an explanation: Why does the universe exist? Anthony Flew reminds us: "If there is to be a plausible law to explain the beginning of the universe, then it would have to say something like: 'empty space necessarily gives rise to matter-energy'" – which is ridiculous."[41]

The Oxford philosopher, Richard Swinburne, says simply, "It is very unlikely that a universe would exist uncaused, but rather more likely that God would exist uncaused."[42] So, the existence of the universe, and the laws that govern it, make belief in a higher mind reasonable.

Even Charles Darwin spoke of "the laws impressed on matter by the Creator."[43]

The big question is: Where do these laws come from?

For the Christian, the answer is found in Jeremiah 33:25, where God says that he has "established the laws of heaven and earth."

I invite you to seek out that law giver.

6

Quantum Physics, Atheism, and Me

I have a friend who is a professor. (I sometimes move in exalted circles!) The relevance of this is that I'd been doing some reading in the area of quantum physics, and I came up with a question that had relevance to my existence...and, incidentally, yours. So I emailed him the question.

He didn't know the answer. So he passed the question on to the Institute for Photonics and Advanced Sensing at the University of Adelaide. Evidently, the question got passed around the faculty and none of them were very sure how to answer it, so they sent a quantum physicist out in a taxi to talk to me.

Let me tell you, I was staggered – both at the grace of the brilliant young man who came to visit me, and that anyone should take me, a theologian, seriously.

Centuries ago, theology was known as 'the queen of the sciences'. This was because people believed that all science relied on God, and that the greatest science was exploring the truth of God. Science was therefore the craft of uncovering God's order.

Alas, theology's crown has long since been cast aside. Talk of God is now seen to be irrational and unscientific, something to be spurned and derided. Many universities don't even have a theology department now.

But here's the thing: If God exists, and is rightly described in the Bible, then scientists and theologians could well benefit from looking at each other's work. Of course, neither discipline should be controlled, or bullied, by the other. Humankind largely got over that sort of silliness centuries ago.

Both disciplines are concerned with uncovering truth, and as such, both have something to contribute. Put bluntly, science can stop theology from making stupid claims; and theology can help free science from its narrow, empiricist prison.

I was a bit hesitant to put this chapter in the book, because it invites you, dear reader, to travel down the crazy rabbit hole of quantum physics, which, believe me, is weird. So, here's my promise: I will keep it simple, and it will be relevant. In fact, understanding it may be the key to your very existence.

If you're ready, let's begin.

If Christianity is right, God has drawn progressively closer to us in four steps. First, he shows us the probability of his existence in the wonders of creation (Romans 1:20; Acts 17:24-27). The order, beauty, and rational accessibility of the universe can be appreciated by anyone, but scientists uncover the details of its workings.

God then came closer, and revealed something of his nature to his chosen prophets in the Old Testament. They recorded their experiences in documents that later became Scripture.

Then, God came even closer – and came to us in person, as Christ Jesus. Jesus is the perfect 'icon' (representation) of God.

Finally, God came closer still: He came *within* his people by his Spirit – both to empower his followers for mission, and to build God's character within them.

The thing is: if this is true, then Christianity is well positioned to put science into a bigger picture. As we've said before, theology is able to frame science's 'how' with theology's 'why'. As such, the two disciplines should at least be civil enough to raise their hats to each other.

Sometimes they can do more. The recent discoveries of

quantum physics are very exciting, and should be of great interest to theologians – not least because they show that atheism is a worldview that is scientifically unlikely.

Two things are worth exploring. Firstly: how theology can point out issues relevant to science, (which would help scientists understand the order they see in the universe). Secondly: how science can enrich theology by showing how quantum physics makes atheism highly implausible.

Let's now turn to a remarkable feature of the universe – its extraordinary order; and explore how theology can point out a significant truth concerning this order to science.

Order

The Judeo-Christian scriptures teach that God has chosen to reveal himself – at least in part – in creation. This idea was given prominence in 17th century England by the concept of there being 'two books', which were able to point people to God. These 'books' were: 1) The Bible; and, 2) the wonders of creation. The idea was that something of God's nature could be understood through the study of the natural world. The famous 17th century scientist, Robert Boyle, wrote:

> *When with bold telescopes I survey the old and newly discovered stars and planets ...when with excellent microscopes I discern nature's curious workmanship, when with the help of anatomical knives and the light of chemical furnaces I study the book of nature ...I find myself exclaiming with the psalmist, "How manifold are thy works, O God, in wisdom hast thou made them all!"*[1]

Boyle was able to celebrate the two disciplines of science and theology, declaring, "as the two great books of nature and scripture have the same author, so the study of the latter does not at all hinder the inquisitive man's delight in the study of the former."[2]

The physician and author, Thomas Browne (1605–1682), was another who was convinced of the validity of both the Bible and nature in revealing God. He wrote: "Thus are there two books from whence I collect my divinity: besides that written one of God, another of his servant nature, that universal and publick (sic) manuscript, that lies expansed to the eyes of all. Those that never saw him in the one have discovered him in the other."[3]

This seventeenth century sentiment continues to be voiced today. Francis Collins, who directed the thirteen-year project that identified the 3.1 billion letters of the human genome, says: "I have found there is a wonderful harmony in the complementary truths of science and faith. The God of the Bible is also the God of the genome. God can be found in the cathedral or in the laboratory. By investigating God's majestic and awesome creation, science can actually be a means of worship."[4]

Mathematics has been another tool used by scientists to lay bare the order of the universe. This leads me back to the young quantum physicist who visited me, for we spent some time chatting about mathematics – specifically, mathematical philosophy.

Mathematical philosophers have wearied themselves for many centuries trying to determine what mathematics actually is. An atheistic approach to this question cannot help but be human-centric. It suggests that mathematics is simply a language humans have invented to help them quantify things such as the number of eggs in an egg carton.

However, other mathematicians disagree with this human-centric view and point out that mathematics is not so much a language, but a mysterious land that sits waiting for us to explore and make great discoveries. They point out that math delivers surprises that mathematicians never asked of it, e.g. the Mandelbrot set.

The Mandelbrot set is based on a fairly simple equation that was expected to draw a fuzzy white dot. Instead, it drew beautiful, intricate, organic-looking, pictures that were infinitely magnifiable – limited only by the computing power of the computer doing the calculations. Look them up on the Internet. They are beautiful.

Atheists who think we are just a meaningless bag of sub-atomic particles are 'materialist reductionists'. They reduce humanity to 'materials' and say there is nothing more that makes humans significant. Needless to say, such atheists don't cope well with the sort of surprises posed by the Mandelbrot set.

All this talk about mathematical philosophy and materialist reductionism makes me sound very clever. Let me assure you, I'm not. I've learned, however, that ignorance is sometimes very handy. The great advantage of ignorance is that it can sometimes result in asking questions and seeing things from a totally new point of view. This occurred when I was talking to my brilliant quantum physicist friend. I had been thinking about how mathematics could be both: 1) a language we invent to quantify things, and: 2) a strange unexplored land. I was bold enough to suggest it could be both.

My clue for this came from quantum physics.

The quantum world is one in which a sub-atomic particle can exist as a non-physical 'cloud of probability', or as a discrete particle – depending on what you are doing with it. So, why couldn't mathematics be the same? After all, both mathematics and quantum physics define the universe at a very elemental level. They could therefore be expected to have similar properties. Math could be like a strange unexplored land, until scientists look at it and handle it. Then it collapses into the physical language of mathematics that we have defined.

I asked my physicist friend what correlations he saw between math and quantum physics. He didn't know. But he did say that whilst the quantum world was weird and non-intuitive, mathematics describes it beautifully. He then wondered, somewhat wistfully, whether mathematics would always be able to define quantum physics – as scientists continued to drill down into its murky waters.

As a theologian, I was emboldened enough to say, "I can't give you a scientific answer to your question, but I can give you a theological one."

He looked at me quizzically.

"Yes," I said. "If God exists, then the 'fingerprints' of his order will always be seen at every level of creation. You will always find mathematical order in your quantum explorations."

The significance of this conversation is that it was a fruitful discussion between a scientist and a theologian. (It even resulted in my writing a paper about the dualistic nature of mathematics.)[5]

I'm therefore bold enough to suggest that good things can happen when the two disciplines of science and theology chat to each other.

The power of math

Quantum physics seeks to understand the world of sub-atomic particles. The scientific laws of this branch of physics are very different from those that operate in Einstein's world of 'special relativity'. Whilst quantum physics looks at very small objects; special relativity looks at objects that are very fast. The discontinuity between these two branches of physics caused the English physicist, Paul Dirac, to wonder what would happen if the two sets of laws were brought together, and a tiny electron was accelerated so that it went very fast. He worked out from mathematics that the only way the two branches of physics could be resolved, is if a totally new object existed – a positively charged, mirror image of the electron. He called this theoretical particle a 'positron'.

The positron was the anti-matter counterpart of an electron.

Four years later, the American Physicist, Carl Anderson, discovered the positron using a cloud chamber.

The significant thing about all this is that a particle was hypothesized by mathematics – before it was discovered in reality.

Paul Dirac later reflected on the power of mathematics, and why the universe was constructed along beautiful mathematical lines. He said: "God is a mathematician of a very high order, and he used very advanced mathematics in constructing the universe." [6]

The Hungarian-American theoretical physicist, Eugene Wigner, expressed a similar thought. He spoke about the "unreasonable effectiveness of mathematics in the natural sciences."[7] In saying this, he was echoing a conviction of Galileo who said:

Philosophy is written in the grand book, the universe, which stands continually open to our gaze. But the book cannot be understood unless one first learns to comprehend the language and read the letters in which it is composed. It is written in the language of mathematics.[8]

A more recent example of the faith scientists have in the power of mathematics occurred when their calculations persuaded a research team to spend US$4.75 billion to build the Large Hadron Collider near Geneva! Their faith in mathematics was rewarded in 2012 when they found the Higgs boson, a sub-atomic particle they reasoned must exist as a result of math.

It seems that mathematics is the scientific language of the universe – and this is only possible because the universe is ordered. Quite simply: order is the big surprise of the universe.

Order in chaos

Scientists are starting to discover that order can sometimes even be found in chaos. It seems that some chaotic systems can behave in non-chaotic ways. Weird, but true.

If you plot the successive events of a chaotic system on a three-dimensional graph, you would expect to end up with a chaotic mess. Often, you do. However, sometimes you end up with a beautiful pattern in which the sequence of events seems to circle around one particular point for a long time. These favored possibilities have been dubbed 'strange attractors'. In other words, there appears to be orderly disorder in some chaotic systems.[9] It's even possible for a chaotic system to have more than one strange attractor. Others don't seem to have any.

A conversation

Imagine that a mathematical physicist studying strange attractors is having coffee with a Christian theologian.

What might the theologian say on hearing about strange attractors?

The theologian might nod their head and say: "As a theologian, what you say doesn't surprise me at all. God is the one who brings order out of nothing and creates. I suspect you will never find perfect disorder in any physical system that God has been responsible for. If you've not found strange attractors in some chaotic systems, perhaps you've not run the experiment for long enough. After all, long periods of time are no problem to God, who exists both within and beyond time."

The theologian might pause for a moment, before adding: "The only place where theologians would expect to find chaos, would be where there is evil. All Satan can do is destroy. He can only kick down God's sandcastles. He can never build them."

That might make for a mutually enriching discussion!

The theological question prompted by the order we see in creation is this: Does this order tell us anything about God? In other words: Is the order of creation a language God has used to point to his essential nature?

If God is whispering something about his nature through his creation, then perhaps theologians and scientists might benefit from having an occasional cup of coffee together. Of course, scientists must be careful to maintain the integrity of scientific method, but this doesn't mean they can't let theologians look over their shoulder, and hear them say: "Yes. That makes sense."

This brings to mind the closing comments of the astronomer and physicist, Robert Jastrow, in his book, *God and the Astronomers*. He writes:

> *At this moment, it seems as though science will never be able to raise the curtain on the mystery of creation. For the scientist who has lived by his faith in the power of reason, the story ends like a bad dream. He has scaled the mountains of ignorance; he is about to conquer the highest peak; as he pulls himself over the final rock, he is greeted by a band of theologians who have been sitting there for centuries.*[10]

Understanding God in science

Christian theologians fully expect that something of God's

nature will be understood from science – and are therefore able to rejoice at new scientific discoveries.

However, theologians also have to look beyond the order they see in the cosmos, and make sense of suffering, chaos and evil. They understand that whilst the universe is God-breathed, it is also something which has been corrupted by sin and suffering (Genesis 3:1-19; Romans 8:20-21). Theologians understand that this universe is not God's end game. They speak of a fulfillment that lies beyond it – which each of us is invited to participate in.

It must also be said that God is infinitely more than that which can be determined simply by the order of creation. Nonetheless, the order of the cosmos does say something about the character of God. At the very least, it tells us that God is rational.

Theologians understand that God is not a fraudster. By this, they mean that God reveals himself as he actually is. God does not wear a mask to misrepresent himself because we can't cope with the reality of who he is. So, when God reveals himself through the order of the universe, he is revealing himself as he actually is. God's strategy is to reveal as much of himself as we can comprehend. But he does not overpower us with so much self-revelation that it squashes our free choice and removes our need for faith.

This honesty of God in his self-revelation is a consistent feature. For example: God allows us to see his essential reality in Jesus (Colossians 1:15-20). Similarly, when God showed us that he lives in community within himself as Father, Son, and Holy Spirit, this was not a mask. God was allowing us to see his essential being.

If this self-revelation of God is difficult to comprehend – good. It has to have aspects of mystery. God must logically be beyond our understanding if (as you've heard me say before) he is more than something created by our imaginings.

'Order' as the fingerprint of God

Theologians understand that God is inherently creative. God brings order from nothing. This means that wherever we see order in created systems, we see the fingerprint of God. The order we see in creation therefore suggests that faith in God is reasonable.

Physicist and cosmologist, Paul Davies, says that scientists also have to share this faith. They have to have faith "that the universe is governed by dependable, immutable, absolute, universal, mathematical laws of an unspecified origin ...(To) think that such laws exist without reason is anti-rational."[11]

These understandings suggest that there is room for theologians to talk to scientists about the order they see.

Atheism and quantum physics

The universe is made up of tiny sub-atomic particles that are governed by physical laws quite unlike the normal Newtonian physics that operate in the macro world. Quantum physics is the field of physics that studies this strange sub-atomic world – and believe me, it is strange. The Danish physicist, Niels Bohr, says that those who are not shocked when they first come across quantum physics cannot possibly have understood it.[12] The American physicist, Richard Feynman, agrees. He says, "I think I can safely say that nobody understands quantum mechanics."[13]

So let's retreat back to the safety of theology for a moment.

The Bible speaks of God as the one who brings order out of nothing. The theological stories that teach this truth are contained in the creation accounts at the beginning of the Bible. They speak of God seeing something in his mind's eye – and of him then calling creation into being, out of nothing.

Please remember that phrase: "...God seeing something in his mind's eye"...

...Now let's go back to the world of quantum physics.

Imagine that a ray gun (shooting sub-atomic particles, such as electrons) is aimed at a barrier. This barrier has two vertical slits cut into it.

There is a back wall some distance behind the barrier that stops those particles that pass through the slits. This back wall has the ability to measure where these particles hit.

When all this was in place, the scientists fired the gun.

The result amazed them.

Scientists discovered that the electrons didn't behave like tiny marbles, but behaved like waves. When the electrons passed through the slits, they fanned out in semi-circular ripples. The two sets of curving ripples (from the two slits) interfered with each other, before hitting the back wall in a wave pattern.

Scientists then wondered what would happen if they fired the particles one at a time. Doing this meant there was no chance of particles being able to interfere with each other.

However, a wave pattern still formed on the back wall.

The scientists were stunned. Each particle had apparently split itself into two, gone through two slits simultaneously, and interfered with each other, before hitting the back wall. As particles don't do this, it was concluded that each particle must exist as a 'wave of probability' that allowed it to pass through both slits, yet still be physical enough to interfere with itself.

If that wasn't strange enough, things soon became even more complicated.

Scientists then placed a measuring device near the slits so they could observe which slit an individual electron actually passed through. They then fired the electron gun, shooting one particle at a time toward the two slits for a period of one hour.

The result of this was stranger than anyone could have imagined. When the electrons were being observed, they stopped behaving like a wave and began behaving like tiny marbles. The electrons now hit the wall behind the slits in two vertical lines.

So there we have it: Sub-atomic particles, such as electrons, don't actually exist as physical particles until they are observed.

…Which brings us back to God.

The first three verses of the Bible say: "In the beginning God created the heavens and the earth. Now the earth was formless and empty, darkness was over the surface of the deep, and the Spirit of God was hovering over the waters. And God said, Let there be…'" (Genesis 1:1-3).

In other words, God saw something in his mind's eye – and that caused what he saw to come into being. This is consistent with quantum physics. The act of God observing caused something that was once just a wave of probability to become physical reality.

This truth should be of some interest to us because you and I exist within physical reality. We are composed of sub-atomic particles that someone has observed, causing us to become a physical reality.

This truth calls to mind the words God spoke to Jeremiah in the Old Testament: "Before I formed you in the womb I knew you" (Jeremiah 1:5). Perhaps these words have a significance we've not been able to appreciate until now!

The idea that sub-atomic particles need to be observed before they become a tiny ball of matter is a discovery that leaves the atheist in a difficult position. Quantum physics makes it clear that the sub-atomic particles that comprise an atheist should not exist, except as waves of probability that are in superposition with itself – because no God has observed them into physical reality.

Quantum physics seems to suggest that your existence requires someone to observe your component sub-atomic particles into being. In other words, your existence needs someone *outside* of you who is capable of intent.

The quantum 'double slit' experiment raises a number of questions:

- What would happen if you switched off the instrument that was doing the observing?
- What would you see if you dismantled the observing instrument and just put its component bits in place?
- How far away would you need to put the observing instrument before the image on the back wall changed from two vertical lines back to a wave pattern?

Intriguingly, we now know the answer to some of these questions. This is because physicists have discovered the 'quantum erasing'. In simple terms, this is how it works.

The instrument set up to measure which slit the quantum

particle went through was linked to a computer. Whilst the computer stored the information, the quantum particles behaved like tiny marbles. However, the moment the information was erased from the computer, the quantum particles stopped behaving like tiny marbles and turned into waves of probability that produced a wave pattern on the back wall.

This says something extraordinary about the role of consciousness in quantum physics.

Questions about 'consciousness' also arise when we consider what it means to 'observe'. Here are a few definitions:

- To observe means to view with the expectation of understanding the reality of something.
- To observe is to bring something into significance in the consciousness of the observer.
- To observe is to establish a cognitive relationship with something.

These definitions conjure an image of something that is conscious enough to be relational.

It is worth noting, at this point, the convictions of the American theoretical physicist, John Archibald Wheeler (1911-2008).

Wheeler was the chap who popularised the term 'black hole.' He also coined the term "participatory anthropic principle." Now, before your brain has conniptions, let me explain. The "strong anthropic principle" is the conviction that the universe has been designed to allow intelligent life to develop. (As I've said earlier, the apparent 'fine tuning' of the universe that allows us to exist, has convinced many scientists this is the case.) The extra perspective that Wheeler adds is this: Because a divine consciousness wanted humankind to develop, there is a sense in which we have become participants in the overall plan – hence the term, "participatory anthropic principle."

This, of course, fits beautifully into Christian thinking.

. . .

What is matter?

Some leading scientists working in the field of quantum physics are now beginning to speak of matter itself being a "content of consciousness." One of the scientists making this claim is the Nobel prize-winning physicist, Eugene Wigner. He says: "Study of the external world leads to the conclusion that contents of consciousness are the ultimate reality."[14] John von Neumann (also a Nobel prize-winning physicist) shares this view. He says: "All real things are contents of consciousness."[15]

It has to be said that not all quantum physicists agree with these scientists.

The issue at stake is this: Is it the electron that is conscious and observing the instrument watching it? Or is it the reverse? Is it the consciousness of intelligent observers, metered through the observing instrument, which is exerting power over the electron?

It is difficult to imagine how an electron could be conscious, for it would not be enough for it to simply be conscious; it would also need to be intelligent. The electron would need to be intelligent enough to recognize that a measuring instrument was in place, and that it was working.

It therefore seems more likely that it is the cognitive intent of the observer that collapses the electron from being a wave of probability...into being a tiny particle of matter.

Whilst this conclusion seems reasonable, it is not an 'open and shut' case – particularly given the existence of another strange feature of the quantum world: the phenomenon of 'entanglement'.

Physicists have discovered that if two sub-atomic particles have connected with each other – and then fly off to different parts of the universe, the particles will still act as if they are connected. What you do to one particle will instantly be mirrored in the other. (The Irish physicist, John Bell records Einstein's disparaging reference to quantum entanglement when Einstein described it as "spooky action at a distance.")[16]

This feature of the quantum world suggests a level of connectedness between sub-atomic particles that is independent of the physical strictures imposed by the speed of light. Perhaps this could be 'consciousness'.

So let's digress and consider what it might mean if it was the consciousness of the sub-atomic particles, and not the observer, that caused the particles to collapse into tiny bits of matter.

It would suggest that all matter is imbued with consciousness. That conclusion would sit well with the convictions of Eugene Wigner and John von Neumann. If it were true, such a finding would have enormous impact, as it would break science out of its empiricist prison, and force it to consider a wider reality. It would certainly present a challenge to atheism. Conversely, it would make perfect sense to theologians, for it would suggest that all creation exhibits, in part, the consciousness of God.

It might reasonably be pointed out that the fact that atoms and molecules exist as tiny particles doesn't mean that their electrons are behaving as tiny particles. They may still be behaving as 'waves of probability'. This is true – to a point. The fact remains that if anything physical is to exist in the universe, sub-atomic particles need to build it. Nothing physical can be built just by collecting a whole bunch of waves of probabilities together. An unbound particle existing as a wave of probability somehow needs to transition into being a 'bound' particle, i.e. one that links with other particles – if it is to build an atom.

An unbound particle will allow itself to become bound when it can exist in a lower energy state. (All matter rolls downhill when it comes to energy.) However, energetics cannot explain why a cloud of probability collapses into a physical particle that can co-operate with others. The only mechanism physicists are currently aware of that causes anything like this to happen is 'consciousness'.

The fact that sub-atomic particles only exist as a physical reality when observed is a phenomenon that intersects with the thinking of George Berkeley, the brilliant early 18th century Anglo/Irish philosopher. He said that things exist only insofar as they are perceived. (In philosophic terms, this understanding is called "idealism".) This non-instinctive, even jarring, thinking is softened by

Berkeley's corollary: that created things are always perceived by the infinite mind, God, and therefore, they exist.

This brings to mind a limerick by the early 20th century Catholic theologian, Ronald Knox:

> There was a young man who said, 'God
> Must think it exceedingly odd
> If he finds that this tree
> Continues to be
> When there's no-one about in the Quad.'

To which, came the reply (from an unknown author):

> Dear Sir:
> Your astonishment's odd;
> I am always about in the Quad.
> And that's why the tree
> Will continue to be,
> Since observed by
> Yours faithfully
> God.[17]

One way or another, it seems that consciousness lies behind the existence of all physical things. Sub-atomic particles in the quantum world only collapse into physical bits of matter when observed. This phenomenon, of course, does not occur in the larger world of biology. There is no evidence that a person collapses into a physical form only when another person observes them...and this is significant. It appears that all the sub-atomic particles that constitute physical things in the universe have *already* been observed – and so exist as physical realities.

And this poses a very real problem for atheists.

The Atheist's dilemma

Atheists generally fall into two camps when asked the question: Why does anything exist?

Some say that the universe has always existed. The great English, atheist physicist, Fred Hoyle, desperately tried to believe this for many years, until evidence for the Big Bang, i.e. a beginning, became overwhelming.

The idea that the universe has always existed, has recently been resurrected by those positing the idea that there are an infinite number of universes that collapse and give rise to new ones. As we saw earlier, this doesn't actually solve the question. It just shifts it to another level. Where did the infinite number of universes come from? No scientist of any worth will lazily invoke the term 'infinite' to magically make anything they want into a reality.

Fundamentally, the idea that the universe has always existed falls foul of the second law of thermodynamics, which says, in essence, that everything that exists is slowly sliding down an energy slope into disorder.

Other atheists believe that the universe has come from nothing. One of these is, as we mentioned earlier, Lawrence Krauss.[18] His book *A Universe from Nothing* evoked a sharp response from the American Orthodox philosopher, David Bentley Hart, who wrote: "…it would be a very poorly trained theologian indeed who produced anything as philosophically confused or as engorged with category errors as Lawrence Krauss's, *A Universe from Nothing*."[19]

This calls to mind a wry comment made by Einstein, who said: "the man of science makes a very bad philosopher."[20] A look at the diatribes against religion emanating from the English biologist, Richard Dawkins, would also bear this out.

The essential difficulty with believing that the universe came from nothing is this: It requires you to believe, as I've said before: that everything came from nothing, as a result of nothing, via a mechanism that has never been discovered, and for which there is no precedent – and which fractures the law of 'cause and effect' that underpins all science.

As such, it is not believable.

. . .

Consciousness

If math provides the software program for building the universe, how do its instructions cross over to quantum physics, which provides the elemental building blocks of the universe? What is the controlling link between math and the quantum world?

It is reasonable to believe the clue to the answer is provided both by the quantum double slit experiment and by the ridiculous level of fine-tuning of the basic forces that have allowed life to develop in the universe. I want to suggest that the link between mathematics and quantum physics is 'consciousness'.

In postulating this, I am not simply engaging in ungrounded theological speculation. The theory is grounded in empirical reality.

Scientists are discovering that there is a two-way conversation between math and quantum physics. Not only is mathematics effective in quantum physics, but quantum physics is increasingly being seen to be effective in modern mathematics. The Dutch theoretical physicist, Robbert Dijkgraaf, writes:

> *Ideas that originate in particle physics have an uncanny tendency to appear in the most diverse mathematical fields. This is especially true for string theory. Its stimulating influence in mathematics will have a lasting and rewarding impact, whatever its final role in fundamental physics turns out to be. The number of disciplines that it touches is dizzying: analysis, geometry, algebra, topology, representation theory, combinatorics, probability – the list goes on and on.*[21]

Zhengfeng Ji (a Chinese quantum and information scientist, currently a professor at the University of Technology in Sydney, Australia) has shown how almost infinitely complex mathematical problems can be solved with the help of quantum physics. Ji and his team of co-workers have discovered that quantum 'entanglement' (Einstein's "spooky action at a distance") massively boosts the power of a mathematical system to verify a truth.[22] It would seem that quantum physics helps out math; and math helps out quantum physics.

Here's another thing that caused a frisson of excitement in the quantum world:

In 1655, the English mathematician and cleric, John Wallis, produced a formula for pi (π) that was the product of an infinite number of ratios.[23]

$$\frac{2 \times 2}{1 \times 3} \times \frac{4 \times 4}{3 \times 5} \times \frac{6 \times 6}{5 \times 7} \times \frac{8 \times 8}{7 \times 9} \ldots \text{(repeat multiplying the next ratios } ad\ infinitum\text{)}$$

= 1.570796 (to six decimal places) = the "Wallis Product"

The Wallis Product = $\frac{\pi}{2}$

Scientists were amazed when the same formula was discovered in quantum physics – in their calculations of the energy levels of a hydrogen atom!

What these recent discoveries point to is an extraordinary level of connectedness in everything. The big question is: What is it that seems to connect and hold things together?

Consciousness is one possibility. In fact, at this moment, it is hard to identify another contender. The existence of an overarching consciousness makes sense of what scientists are observing...and it also makes sense of those things that are causing scientists to wonder.

When the late Stephen Hawking wrote in the penultimate page of his book, *A Brief History of Time*:

> *What is it that breathes fire into the equations and makes a universe for them to describe? The usual approach of science of constructing a mathematical model cannot answer the questions of why there should be a universe for the model to describe. Why does the universe go to all the bother of existing?*[24]

...the only answer that matches logic and human experience is 'consciousness'.

When Richard Dawkins mistakenly attributes to our genes qualities and motives that can only rightly be ascribed to intelligent beings,[25] he is, in fact, unconsciously pointing to the need to factor in an overarching consciousness.

Similarly: Paul Davies talks about the need for scientists to have faith that the universe is ordered if they are to do science...and have faith that humankind has the necessary mental ability to unlock its secrets, he is saying something very profound about the universe. [26] He also reminds us that life is not just about "chemical reactions," it is about information. [27] In saying this, Davies is pointing to the need for something to exist that looks very much like intentional purpose, i.e. consciousness.

Francis Crick, (who with his colleague, James Watson, discovered the double helix structure of DNA in 1953) wondered how it was possible that nature had invented highly complex nucleic acids such as DNA and RNA, as well as enzymes made of protein that govern their function. He was faced with a classic chicken-and-egg problem. One couldn't exist without the function of the other. In the end, he and his colleague, Leslie Orgel, reasoned that life could have arisen elsewhere in the universe (where a compound capable of replacing the function of the enzymes occurred), which was disseminated to other planets like Earth by the deliberate activity of an extraterrestrial society, (something which is called "directed panspermia").[28]

It's extraordinary, isn't it? Crick, an ardent atheist, cannot fathom how life came to be without positing consciousness. But in his case, he has simply swapped the consciousness of God for the consciousness of alien life forms! One has to ask: Is this the best that our most brilliant atheists can come up with?

Crick was to spend the last few decades of his life exploring the nature of consciousness – one of the most profound mysteries. At the end of his career, he considered that he had failed to get any understanding of it. One can't help but be impressed that he had the courage to investigate such a big issue. One also can't avoid a sneaking suspicion that his atheism may have put blinkers on his thinking.

It needs to be said that in putting forward the theory that consciousness is what puts math to work in the quantum world so that it builds a universe, we are not simply smuggling a 'God of the gaps' into science. God of the gaps is the lamentable practice of seeing a seemingly impossible complex phenomenon in nature (or the cosmos) that science can't yet explain – and lazily saying, "God did it." Then, as science advances and explains how the phenomenon occurred through natural processes, the need to invoke God is overturned and Christians are made to look stupid.

'God of the gaps' is not what is being proposed here – although I have little doubt that what is being proposed will cause an angry emotional response from atheists who feel that their world-view and autonomy is under threat.

In proposing consciousness as the link between math and the quantum world, we do so for empirical reasons. It is a theory that fits best with the facts of quantum's double slit experiment, and with the facts surrounding the fine-tuning of the elementary forces of the universe.

If this 'consciousness theory' becomes one that is widely held, the implications are huge. It will cut to the very nature, purpose, and dignity of humankind.

Why?

Basically because if you add 'consciousness' to the reality of linear time, the result looks a lot like purpose.

Scientists were amazed when the same formula was discovered in quantum physics – in their calculations of the energy levels of a hydrogen atom!

What these recent discoveries point to is an extraordinary level of connectedness in everything. The big question is: What is it that seems to connect and hold things together?

Consciousness is one possibility. In fact, at this moment, it is hard to identify another contender. The existence of an overarching consciousness makes sense of what scientists are observing...and it also makes sense of those things that are causing scientists to wonder.

When the late Stephen Hawking wrote in the penultimate page of his book, *A Brief History of Time*:

> *What is it that breathes fire into the equations and makes a universe for them to describe? The usual approach of science of constructing a mathematical model*

cannot answer the questions of why there should be a universe for the model to describe. Why does the universe go to all the bother of existing?[29]

...the only answer that matches logic and human experience is 'consciousness'.

When Richard Dawkins mistakenly attributes to our genes qualities and motives that can only rightly be ascribed to intelligent beings,[30] he is, in fact, unconsciously pointing to the need to factor in an overarching consciousness.

Similarly: Paul Davies talks about the need for scientists to have faith that the universe is ordered if they are to do science...and have faith that humankind has the necessary mental ability to unlock its secrets, he is saying something very profound about the universe. [31] He also reminds us that life is not just about "chemical reactions," it is about information. [32] In saying this, Davies is pointing to the need for something to exist that looks very much like intentional purpose, i.e. consciousness.

Francis Crick, (who with his colleague, James Watson, discovered the double helix structure of DNA in 1953) wondered how it was possible that nature had invented highly complex nucleic acids such as DNA and RNA, as well as enzymes made of protein that govern their function. He was faced with a classic chicken-and-egg problem. One couldn't exist without the function of the other. In the end, he and his colleague, Leslie Orgel, reasoned that life could have arisen elsewhere in the universe (where a compound capable of replacing the function of the enzymes occurred), which was disseminated to other planets like Earth by the deliberate activity of an extraterrestrial society, (something which is called "directed panspermia").[33]

It's extraordinary, isn't it? Crick, an ardent atheist, cannot fathom how life came to be without positing consciousness. But in his case, he has simply swapped the consciousness of God for the consciousness of alien life forms! One has to ask: Is this the best that our most brilliant atheists can come up with?

Crick was to spend the last few decades of his life exploring the nature of consciousness – one of the most profound mysteries. At the end of his career, he considered that he had failed to get any understanding of it. One can't help but be impressed that he had the courage to investigate such a big issue. One also can't avoid a sneaking suspicion that his atheism may have put blinkers on his thinking.

It needs to be said that in putting forward the theory that consciousness is what puts math to work in the quantum world so that it builds a universe, we are not simply smuggling a 'God of the gaps' into science. God of the gaps is the lamentable practice of seeing a seemingly impossible complex phenomenon in nature (or the cosmos) that science can't yet explain – and lazily saying, "God did it." Then, as science advances and explains how the phenomenon occurred through natural processes, the need to invoke God is overturned and Christians are made to look stupid.

'God of the gaps' is not what is being proposed here – although I have little doubt that what is being proposed will cause an angry emotional response from atheists who feel that their world-view and autonomy is under threat.

In proposing consciousness as the link between math and the quantum world, we do so for empirical reasons. It is a theory that fits best with the facts of quantum's double slit experiment, and with the facts surrounding the fine-tuning of the elementary forces of the universe.

If this 'consciousness theory' becomes one that is widely held, the implications are huge. It will cut to the very nature, purpose, and dignity of humankind.

Why?

Basically because if you add 'consciousness' to the reality of linear time, the result looks a lot like purpose.

Conclusion

So what can we conclude?

Science and faith have important things to say to each other and can be mutually enriching.

It is also fair to say that the findings of quantum physics raise big issues for atheism—and Christian apologists would do well to understand these issues. Until very recently, atheists have claimed to be the ones standing on the high ground of rationalism and have looked down at theologians with barely concealed derision. Now it seems it is the theologian who is standing on the high ground of rationalism.

Rationalism no longer provides a safe haven for atheism. However, there are many reasons for atheism—and most of them, as has been discussed earlier, don't have much to do with truth. So, whether or not the findings of quantum physics present a mortal blow to atheism...is something only history will decide.

If you're wondering what the main question was that I asked of my quantum physicist friend, it was simply this: "Who (or what) has 'observed' the subatomic particles of the universe, causing them to collapse into a physical universe...and produced you?"

I'm still waiting for an answer.

7

Suffering, Grief, and Me

The last thing anyone wants to hear at a time of grief is a theological treatise. If you are in deep grief, then I invite you to just read this opening section, then come back to the theological section when you feel you are ready to explore the issue of suffering more.

Let me also say, that I am writing this chapter as much as a pastor as an academic.

A Personal note from me to you in your grief.

Suffering is a vexing subject and, for all of us, a deeply personal one. It is impossible to give quick, trite answers. I will therefore mention just two things. The first is that God shares your grief. He grieves with you because he loves you. The shortest verse in the Bible is: "Jesus wept." He did so when he saw the grief of two sisters caused by the death of their brother Lazarus.

God understands your grief...and shares it. Because he loves you, he is wounded when he sees you grieve.

The second thing is this: If you have suffered from grief, abuse or injustice, know that God is angry. He hates it. That's why he has set a time when the imperfections of this world will be identified, judged, and killed off. God's eternal kingdom is his 'end game', and God wants you to be part of it. That's the place where every tear will be wiped dry (Revelation 21:4) and all the things that once bewildered you will become clear...although I very much suspect that you won't even remember your questions when you're there!

The Theological Section

I was once invited to do some preaching in America by a friend. As I was still relatively young in those days, I found myself playing a game of flag American football, where you have to snatch a flag velcroed onto the belt of an opponent, instead of tackling him. Somewhat predictably, the game deteriorated and things got more physical. It was fun. I remember the leader of the local church youth group who organized it, John, very well. He impressed me greatly with his love for God, and his love for the young adults he cared for.

I mention this only because two years later, John got called to New York to attend a finance meeting at the World Trade Center. He died when Islamic terrorists flew a plane into the building where his meeting was being held.

The question is: Where was God in all of this?

None of us will get through life without encountering significant grief. Life, with all its imperfections, is a bruising business. It is therefore perfectly understandable for someone who is experiencing suffering to ask: Why did it happen? What is the meaning of it all? And crucially: Why did God allow it?

I think it can be safely said that the incidence and severity of suffering constitutes one of the biggest obstacles that prevents people reaching out to God. A South Australian study conducted amongst 311 tertiary-trained people revealed that 41% of them agreed with the statement: "The incidence of suffering in the world suggests that no loving God is in control." About 12% were undecided.[1]

So, what can we say in response?

First, as I have already said: God loves you and cares for you more deeply than you will ever know. The love God has for you means that he shares your pain, and the fact that he endured it himself as Jesus means he understands your pain. Secondly, know that God excels at bringing hope from ruins, life from the ashes, and resurrection from death.

There are no easy answers to the vexing question of suffering. Some things will always remain a mystery. However, the Bible does give us some guidance on the subject. In fact, as I look at the different philosophies and religions around the world, nothing gives such a complete, sensible, and hope-engendering explanation of suffering as Christianity.

The atheist simply says that suffering is a fact of life in an unfeeling universe. When it is pointed out to him that some suffering comes from wicked gratuitous evil, the atheist simply says that it is an "education problem." In other words, the atheist doesn't take evil seriously.

The adequacy of a Christian understanding was brought into sharp focus when I had the privilege of visiting the great nation of India.

You can't be in India very long before you encounter a beggar – some obviously suffering. My understanding of Hindu culture told me that people believed they could gain merit from God if they were generous to a beggar. However, it also told me that a Hindu priest could say three things to the beggar (let's say the beggar was a man). The priest could say that his pain was an illusion and not real, for that is what the Vedas teach. Secondly: He could say that the beggar's low estate was caused by his sinfulness in an earlier life (reincarnation). Thirdly, the priest might tell the beggar to live out his station in life and not improve it, in order to faithfully live out his karma.

The Christian, however, would say three very different things. Firstly, the Christian would say that the beggar's pain was real. Secondly, the Christian might say that the beggar's suffering was the result of a broken, sinful world, which we all should take responsibility for. Thirdly, The Christian might feel the Spirit of God within him or her prompt them to help the beggar improve his station in life.

The reality of how Christianity played out in India was not difficult to see. Time and again, I came across Christian initiatives designed to help the poor, offering them free medical care and micro-business loans.

Christianity has something very significant to say about the vexing issue of suffering. The real skill is to steer a course between theological poverty (being ignorant of the things the Bible teaches about suffering), and theological arrogance (believing we can know everything about suffering).

Care needs to be taken when using verses from the Bible to teach about suffering. Giving simplistic answers about suffering by quoting just one or two verses of Scripture will not be helpful in most cases. If, for example, you quote James 1:2-4 and tell the mother of a dying child that God allows suffering in order to bring about a 'greater good', you will justifiably earn her scorn.

An examination of Scripture shows us that there are many aspects concerning suffering that need to be appreciated and held in balance if we are to know all the truth that can be known. Like a diamond with many facets, we need to understand each face if we are to appreciate the whole diamond.

What then does the Bible teach about suffering?

Where does suffering come from?

Suffering is one of the sad features of a world that is 'off the rails', i.e. which has been corrupted by our sin (Genesis 3:1-19; Galatians 6:7-8); our lack of wisdom, i.e. our bad choices (Proverbs 10:14; 22:3); and Satan (Luke 13:16).

At an elemental level, suffering is caused by humankind's rejection of God. This is one of the key truths taught in the story of Adam and Eve (Genesis, chapter 3). However, whilst suffering does not come from God, he does allow it (Job 1:8-22, 2:1-7). The big question is: Why?

When God created humankind, he was prepared to take a

terrible risk. He risked giving humankind the freewill to accept or reject his love and lordship. The risk was that we would choose to reject God, and bring on ourselves the consequences of sin – which is suffering (Genesis 3:11-19).

The imperfections of a suffering creation are seen in two ways. The first is through suffering caused by moral evil.

As any parent knows who has had to let their children embrace adulthood and leave home, true love allows freedom – however much anxiety it causes the parent. Love requires freedom and freedom has its risks. So God gives us freedom, and risks. God risks that we will make bad choices and suffer the consequences. So, whilst the will of God is perfect, the will of humanity is not. Hitler, for example, made bad choices and caused a lot of suffering.

The second way we experience suffering is through physical calamity. No moral evil is involved. When talking about physical calamity, I am talking about the suffering brought about by physical acts of nature.

It is a fact that some children die of cancer. It is a fact that fifteen thousand people were killed during an earthquake on All Saints Day in Lisbon in 1755. Many were killed in churches when they collapsed upon them. Surely God could have organized things so that this didn't happen! You get the uncomfortable feeling that God would be declared culpable in almost any court of law.

As we are talking about 'laws of nature', let's return to the eminent particle physicist, John Polkinghorne. In his writing about suffering, he seeks to steer a middle line between the idea that God has love without power (an impotent spectator), and the idea that God has power without love (a cosmic tyrant).

Polkinghorne suggests that God interacts with creation, but chooses not to overrule its divinely granted freedom to be itself. Created order is a 'package deal' that includes creativity, change and risk. For example, mutations can occur spontaneously in the reproductive cells of living organisms that may either be lethal to them or cause them to be better adapted to their environment. The same biochemical processes that enable cells to mutate (making evolution possible) are those which enable cells to become cancerous and generate tumors. You cannot have one without the other. We are part of a physical universe with all its inherent creativity and danger. God is neither following a rigid blueprint nor abandoning existence to look after itself. Rather, he has encoded the universe to develop itself, and evolve self-conscious, worshiping beings. Physical suffering and evolutionary blind alleys are the necessary cost of this fruitful complexity.[2]

To some extent, this is true. But there is a chilly empiricism to this sort of thinking that does not satisfy. Not only that; there seems to be too much apparently senseless suffering for it to be explained away as the necessary cost of having a creative universe. There is a sense in which the universe itself seems flawed in its operations. Why is this?

I want to propose a theory about suffering that joins the biblical teaching of Genesis 3 and Romans 8 to the rationalism of John Polkinghorne. My theory is based on three convictions:

1. God exists outside of time.
2. Suffering, extinctions, and predation occurred before the existence of humankind.
3. Sin is an offense against God...and will ultimately be judged and killed off by him.

If we take seriously the fact that something of God's ideal plan for us was spoiled by the sin of humanity, we must ask: Why did dinosaurs get osteoarthritis?[3] Why did suffering exist *before* humans were around to ruin things? Was the horrible suffering that existed before humanity the 'good' that God wanted (expressed in Genesis 1:3-31), or was it also the product of something imperfect and spoiled? How can we allow for this theologically? Is there a model of thinking that might explain why dinosaurs got osteoarthritis?

Here's my thesis:

As God stands outside of time, any offense against God by humanity *at any point in time* can have implications for *all* of time. In other words, God's judgment on sin can go backward in time as well as forward.

At first blush, this might seem absurd. However, we see an exact parallel to this in those things Jesus accomplished for us on the cross. The benefits to humanity from Jesus' death on the cross reach both backward in history and forward. He died for the sins committed by humankind through all of time. In a similar way, the consequences of sin can reach backward and forward in time...which explains why dinosaurs got osteoarthritis.

Suffering caused by physical evil is a temporary expression of a broken universe that is driven by laws that have been corrupted by sin. Nature, as well as humankind, is waiting to be made new. (The apostle Paul teaches this quite clearly in Romans 8:18-22.) This corruption of the laws of nature explains the natural calamity caused by tsunamis and diseases.

Do bad things happen to bad people?

The belief that all suffering is caused by the victim living a bad life is a cruel and unjust one. Jesus crashed against this simplistic thinking in his teaching in Luke 13:1-5. Let me tell you the story.

Some people (who were probably aware of Jesus' Galilean accent) had told Jesus of a time when Pontius Pilate killed some Galileans in the temple court. Perhaps those telling Jesus about this were trying to warn Jesus to be careful. Alternatively, they might have been implying that since Galileans were notorious for causing political trouble, it served them right. (Galilee was located north of the political and religious center in Jerusalem, and Galileans often resented its control.)

Jesus reminded those with whom he was speaking of the eighteen people who died when a tower fell on them. As this occurred near the pool of Siloam in their own sacred city of Jerusalem, the victims could in no way be considered troublemakers.

So, how did Jesus make sense of this needless death − a tragic accident that had nothing to do with people's poor choices?

Jesus made it plain that those who died were not necessarily more evil than anyone else. He taught that their suffering was one of the sad consequences of the rejection of God by *all* people, and of the world's choice to go down a path that God never intended. As such, suffering points to the need for all of us to turn to God and seek his forgiveness.

This teaching makes sense. It in no way supports the silly idea that only evil people suffer. Jesus' teaching points to the reality that life is inherently spoiled. He highlights the responsibility we all have to co-operate with God so that things can be restored.

Christians understand that suffering is a temporary expression of a broken universe. God will bring its imperfection to an end when he makes all things new (Matthew 19:28) and wipes away every tear (Revelation 21:1-4). They also understand that even in the midst of suffering, God is not absent. He knows the number of hairs on our head (Matthew 10:30) and every detail of our circumstances. God cares because he loves, and is able to identify fully with us because he himself has suffered as Jesus. This means that while we might not be saved from hardships, we will never have to face the trials of life alone. Jesus has promised that he will never forsake us and, if invited, will walk with us through life, lending us his strength (Matthew 28:18-20; Hebrews 13:5).

Putting God on trial

Some people suggest that God should be rejected because he is responsible for suffering and has done nothing to change it. They ask how anyone can be expected to believe in a just, all-powerful God who is unmoved by Nazi extermination camps. Because Auschwitz took place in full view of God, God failed the test.

Certainly, horrific events like the Nazi extermination camps test the worth and credibility of faith. In the Nuremburg War crimes trials, a Polish guard at Auschwitz described how children were thrown straight into the furnaces without first being gassed. He said that their screams could be heard throughout the camp. The Jewish scholar, Irving Greenberg, says, "No statement, theological or otherwise, should be made that would not be credible in the presence of burning children."[4]

Elie Wiesel was a Nobel-Prize winning writer and activist. He wrote an autobiography called *Night*, in which he recounted his experiences surviving the Holocaust. Wiesel wrote:

> *Never shall I forget that smoke. Never shall I forget the little faces of the children, whose bodies I saw turned into wreaths of smoke beneath a silent blue sky. Never shall I forget those flames which consumed my faith forever. Never shall I forget the nocturnal silence which deprived me, for all eternity, of the desire to live. Never shall I forget those moments which murdered my God and my soul and turned my dreams to dust. Never shall I forget these things, even if I am condemned to live as long as God himself. Never.*[5]

The atheist philosopher, Camus, was another who could not find God in suffering. In his novel *The Plague*, Dr. Rieux watches the torturous death of a child and says, "Until my dying day I shall refuse to love a scheme of things in which children are put to torture."[6]

In a similar vein, C.S. Lewis also asked, whilst in grief and anguish over the death of his wife, whether God is like a surgeon who remorselessly cuts into us for our later good, whilst we scream in protest at the hurt.[7]

These accounts are powerful reminders that any attempt to explain suffering by pointing to a higher purpose is not enough to explain suffering fully.

Basic questions

Let's revisit some questions that often get asked in times of suffering. The first is: Does God care or is he distant, and uninvolved?

No! God is not above us in our misery but alongside us in our darkness, sharing our pain.

The second question is: Does God understand?

Yes, he does. God shared our suffering as Jesus (Isaiah 53:3-5 [a prophecy about Jesus], Hebrews 2:18; 4:15). God is therefore no distant uninvolved God. He came to live with us. Jesus was born a suspected illegitimate child, had no home of his own, he wept, got tired, was betrayed by a friend, and was executed in the most humiliating and painful way devised by humankind. That's how much God identified with us. He is the fellow sufferer who understands.

The third question is: Is God just a compassionate spectator?

No, he is not. God works actively against suffering, evil, and oppression through his church. Christianity does not simply give a facile response to the problem of suffering based only on some future hope. On the contrary, God directs his people to work at overcoming suffering and injustice wherever they see it today. Jesus came in history to bring concrete liberation now, not just in some projected future. And we must do the same.

If you are tempted to say that the church is not doing a very good job, then let me suggest that you give it a hand.

Learning from the Trinity

As I was pondering the subject of suffering, it occurred to me that the Trinity of God gives us some useful insight. It works like this:

When we cried out against God in our suffering, and despaired of there ever being a final solution; God introduced himself to us as the Father, the one who will have the last word, and who has set a time when this present age will be replaced by a new order uncorrupted by sin and suffering.

When we cried out that God did not understand how it felt to be the victim of suffering; God introduced himself to us as the Son, i.e. as one who has experienced the agonies of life, and so understands.

When we cried out against God because, although he understood our suffering, we were still helpless to address it; God introduced himself to us as the Holy Spirit, the empowering presence of God. The Holy Spirit is the one who compels us to address suffering practically wherever it is found. Therefore, whilst bad things happen to good people, God ensures that good people happen to bad things.

When God revealed himself as Father, Son, and Holy Spirit, God gave us a beautiful assurance and perspective on suffering.

. . .

God's response to suffering

Jesus combated suffering and sickness wherever he came across it, and saw it as an enemy to be overcome. He was vitally concerned with breaking people free from all that oppressed them (Luke 4:17-21). That's why he performed miracles of healing (Matthew 8:16-17). Today, Jesus invites us to continue his work, and to pray for people to be healed, using his authority and name (Matthew 10:1).

Remember, however, that healing occurs sometimes through miraculous ways, and sometimes through God-instituted 'natural' ways, i.e. through prayers, pills and pillows.

If you are wondering why God doesn't do more miracles, one needs to appreciate that God chooses never to be so obvious through miraculous acts of healing as to compel faith, (otherwise choosing a relationship with God would not be a free choice). This is why none of God's miracles are so compelling that they can be believed without faith. Miracles, (God superimposing his further authority on the laws of nature he instituted), are by definition, rare.

It is my experience that the incidence of miracles seems to increase with people's faith and faithfulness. God seems to garnish the faithful work of his people with miracles now and then. Normally, however, God has ordained that the universe operates according to the laws of nature. If fire did not always burn, and water always drown, the results would be chaotic.

It is important to remember that God will not let his authority be entirely absent from any situation of suffering. Even in the most vile cases of suffering, the voice of God, however small, will be heard by God's people to give strength, to reform, to bring renewal, to allow new beginnings, and to bring a spirit of forgiveness.

This is what we can throw in the face of evil when we experience it.

The positive side of pain

Whilst God does not cause suffering, God can sometimes use it for his purpose. Examples of this include God allowing a man to be blind so that Jesus could do a work of healing that would glorify God's name (John 9:1-3).

On another occasion, suffering helped spread the gospel. The apostle Paul's first imprisonment in Rome resulted in Paul's military jailers learning about Jesus (Philippians 1:12-13).

It is important to remember, however, that although God can use suffering for his higher purpose, this does not excuse the evil that caused the suffering. God is in a battle with evil and has a program to kill it off (1 John 3:8). But in the meantime, he chooses to use some suffering to bring about things that are good.

Life without pain is neither possible nor desirable. Some pain is necessary as it is the way our body tells us it is damaged. Psychological pain is also necessary as it tells us that lack of love and selfish individualism are not good for us. God can speak to us in our pain. C.S. Lewis put it well when he said: "God whispers to us in our pleasures, speaks in our conscience, but shouts in our pains. Pain is God's megaphone to arouse a deaf world."[8]

All of us need the risks of life to help us mature. The Australian social activist, Stephanie Dowrick writes: "We long for a trouble-free Eden, for ourselves, and even more for our children. But they will learn courage after they leave Eden, not before, and they will learn it through their engagement with living, not through avoidance."[9]

Without wishing to sanitize or sanctify all pain, it is a truism that there are some things that are only taught through pain. The Bible often speaks of times of suffering being occasions that refine people's faith.

We were under great pressure, far beyond our ability to endure, so that we despaired even of life ... But this happened that we might not rely on ourselves but on God. (2 Corinthians 1:8-9)

Consider it pure joy, my brothers, whenever you face trials of many kinds, because you know that the testing of your faith develops perseverance. Perseverance must finish its work so that you may be mature and complete, not lacking anything. (James 1:2-4)

> *...you may have had to suffer grief in all kinds of trials. These have come so that your faith ...may be proved genuine and may result in praise, glory, and honor when Jesus Christ is revealed.* (1 Peter 1:6-7)

God may therefore allow suffering in order to bring about a greater good. As we do not have the mind of God, we cannot always appreciate how this can be. To us, it may just look dreadful. But the American pastor, Rick Warren, reminds us:

> *God is far more concerned with our character than he is with our comfort. His plan is to perfect us, not to pamper us. For this reason he allows all kinds of character-building circumstances: conflict, disappointment, difficulty, temptation, times of dryness and delays.*[10]

God can also allow sickness or disabilities in order to display his authority over these things and bring healing (John 9:1-3). Therefore, learn to seek God in prayer, and try to discern whether you should, or should not, pray for someone to be healed when an occasion presents.

It seems to be the case that God allows cracks in an otherwise perfect mold, so that God's love can shine out. There are many wonderful stories of people who have encouraged others by their faith in the face of suffering.

Remember too that whilst (for example) being born deformed is not God's best will for anyone, God's perception of deformity is not the same as ours. We are preoccupied with economic output and external appearances. But is someone with no legs any more deformed than someone who is too selfish to give, too hurt to love, or too self-absorbed to concern themselves with God? God doesn't see as we see. God looks on the inside (1 Samuel 16:7).

Remember too: we always have the option of responding to suffering with love. When this happens, it can be a very powerful witness to those who are observing how we live. The apostle Paul reminds us that God's comfort of us in our suffering teaches us to comfort others in their suffering (2 Corinthians 1:3-4).

• • •

Managing suffering as a Christian

When we yield to Christ and allow Christ's character to grow within us, the concerns of our heart become widened to embrace those things God cares about. This makes Christians particularly vulnerable to suffering. Because we share God's heart, we become particularly sensitized to injustice and sin.

Christians also suffer because they dare to put these things right. They engaged in a spiritual battle in which they seek to build God's kingdom, in God's power, to God's glory (Ephesians 6:12). But doing this can be costly. Christ's injunction to take up our cross daily is a very real challenge (Mark 8:34).

It's important to remember that Christians are not immune to suffering. If they were, people would become Christians just to stop bad things happening to them, and Christianity would not then be the free choice God wants. Christians are therefore subject to the same rhythms and vagaries of life as non-Christians (Matthew 5:45). Jesus said: "In this world, you will have trouble. But take heart! I have overcome the world." (John 16:33)

Medical professionals tell us that 'self-focused' people find it harder to manage their pain than 'other-focused' people. So, the lesson is simple: Be other-focused. Perhaps this was something that helped Jesus to manage his appalling agony on the cross.

Suffering is inevitable but we can always choose how we respond to it. It can make us selfish or saintly, believers or cynics. It's very much our choice.

How we respond to suffering will largely depend on how deep our spiritual roots go down into God. As you know, trees with shallow roots will die in times of drought. Therefore, allow testing times to cause you to put your spiritual roots down even deeper into God (Jeremiah 17:7-8; Luke 8:11-13; Ephesians 3:17-19).

Is it worth praying?

As I write this, the world is in the midst of the COVID-19 pandemic. The Internet is showing pictures of people prostrating themselves in prayer before God in city squares, beseeching God to have mercy on them. The big question, of course, is whether prayer changes anything.

According to research done by Jeanet Bentzen at the University of Copenhagen, the number of Google searches for "prayer" increased by forty percent during the COVID-19 pandemic. This phenomenon was not seen in the global financial crisis of 2007 – 2009...and that is probably understandable. The GFC might make you broke, but it didn't kill you.

COVID-19 is a pandemic, a plague of truly biblical proportions...and people have responded differently to it depending on their character and what they believe. Generally speaking, it appears that the pandemic has pricked the atheistic/self-worshiping hubris of many in the West. We have been reminded that we are not gods; we can't do everything 'my way', and center everything on 'my' pleasures. COVID-19 has brought us all face to face with our mortality. It has forced us to think about what is good, worthwhile, and what it is that gives us meaning.

But this is avoiding the issue we began with: Does prayer change anything?

The answer depends, in part, on the type of prayer. I suspect that some of the increased interest in prayer is a reflection of people's desperate search for relief in the face of crisis. For some, it will be little more than superstition – loading the odds in your favor. This sort of prayer is a bit like not walking on the cracks of a pavement, or not walking under a ladder. Whilst God, in his grace, may hear such prayer, I'm not convinced of its efficacy.

But what about prayer that is truly relational? What about prayer that seeks the reality of God; prayer in which the petitioner sees the holiness of God, and in that light, sees the state of their own sinfulness and the sinfulness of their nation? What about prayer in which there is true humility and repentance? Wow! If the testimony of biblical history is true, this type of prayer is powerful. God says in the Old Testament:

If my people who are called by my name will humble themselves and pray and seek my face and turn from their wicked ways, then will I hear from heaven and will forgive their sin and will heal their land (2 Chronicles 7:14).

God holds his hands out to us and invites us to pray, i.e. to talk with him honestly. Why? Because he is relational. The relevance of this is fairly obvious. If prayer didn't change anything, God wouldn't ask us to pray. It would be a futile exercise. But God loves doing life with us...and prayer is his chosen language of communication.

And that is why people of humility and conviction pray.

It has been the testimony of history that prayer changes things. This doesn't mean that bad things never happen to Christians. They do. As we said earlier, the Bible says that the "rain falls on the just and the unjust" (Matthew 5:45). It also says that God has chosen never to be so obvious as to compel belief. He always leaves room for the need for faith if we are to know him.

Christians know that the best is yet to come...but in the meantime, they pray – for they know that prayer changes things.

Did God send COVID-19?

Did God send COVID-19? That's a very unsettling question isn't it? What can we say?

Let's define the biblical truths that are relevant to the question, and build another octagon. The question we need to ring with biblical truths is: "Did God send COVID-19?"

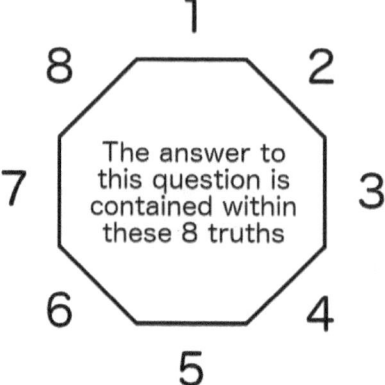

1. God is loving and is the perfect definition of love.
2. Times of crisis are times of opportunity when we can show God's love, generosity and self-sacrifice.
3. God has the right to bring judgment on us in this life as a consequence of us choosing evil. He has warned us of this reality. But God's judgment is always aimed at bringing about our repentance so that new beginnings and blessings can follow.
4. God is just and is the perfect definition of justice.
5. We all live in a broken and fallen world, and we all share in its dangers.
6. God sometimes uses a situation of sickness to show his glory by bringing healing (John 9:2-3).
7. Times of difficulty can help us grow godly character (James 1:2-4).
8. This life is not all there is. Christians can view it from the perspective of eternity. God, and his goodness will ultimately triumph. Evil will be judged and killed off (Romans 8:35; Revelation 21:1-4).

Having identified these truths, where do you think the answer lies?

. . .

Suffering through persecution.

Christians will be persecuted so don't be surprised when it happens (John 15:20; 1 Thessalonians 3:2-4). The early disciples coped with this by having an eternal perspective that put suffering in its right place (2 Corinthians 4:16-17). As such, they weren't crushed under it, but viewed it from above – from the perspective of eternity.

Stay faithful

God is honored when you remain faithful in times of suffering (Job 1:8-12; 2:3-6; Ephesians 3:10). Doing so demonstrates to the rulers of the "spiritual realm" that your faith in God has not caused you to be defeated (Ephesians 6:12). Trusting God in the face of suffering is the greatest compliment you can give to God (Job 13:15).

For some people, it is enough to know that their situation is in God's hands. In situations like this, God may elect to tell them the reason for their suffering and by doing so, bring them into partnership with his plans. That's exactly what he did with the apostle Paul (2 Corinthians 12:7-10).

The apostles Peter and Paul were both familiar with suffering. Their attitude to it is enlightening. They spoke of it as "sharing" in Christ's suffering – which they considered to be a privilege (Philippians 1:29; 3:10; 1 Peter 4:12-14).

Wow!

Paul also made this thought provoking statement: "Now I rejoice in what was suffered for you, and I fill up in my flesh what is still lacking in regard to Christ's afflictions for the sake of his body, which is the church" (Colossians 1:24). In saying this, Paul is not suggesting that there is a deficiency in Jesus' atoning sacrifice for our sins, rather, there is an amount of hardship and persecution Christians must inevitably suffer if they are going to engage in the battle of winning people to God's kingdom. Christians must bear their share of this, and consider it a privilege to do so.

However, because we are 'in Christ', we need to appreciate that when we suffer, Christ suffers. This is why Jesus said to Saul (when

Saul was persecuting Christians) *"Saul, Saul, why do you persecute me?"* (Acts 9:4)

Everything that happens to us, whether good or bad, can contribute to life if we know how to use it (Luke 21:12-13). Therefore, think beyond your pain and choose to love, choose to forgive, and choose to show others the hope of God.

In summary

A right understanding of suffering requires us to take into account many facets of truth. This calls for another octagon.

The question we want to ring with biblical truths is: "If God loves us, why is there suffering?"

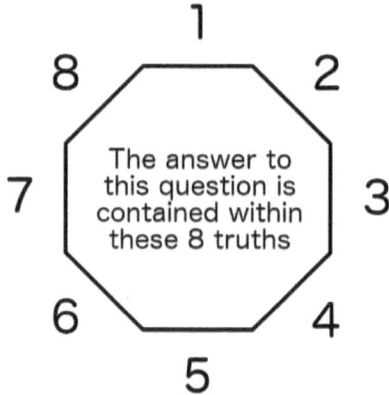

1. God understands our suffering and has experienced it as Jesus. He also promises to be with us in it.
2. Suffering that comes from natural causes is the result of God's creation having been corrupted by sin.
3. Some suffering is caused by bad moral choices and unwise actions.
4. Staying faithful during suffering puts Satan in his place and honors God. It is an action that will be rewarded.
5. Suffering can allow the development of maturity, character, and reliance on God.

6. God will ultimately defeat suffering. He will wipe away every tear.
7. God's Holy Spirit constrains and empowers us to address suffering whenever we see it.
8. Satan seeks to kill and destroy those things God loves. Christians, in particular, are engaged in a spiritual battle. They will be persecuted.

One thing gives Christians perspective and hope amidst their suffering: it is their conviction that even if God has not yet chosen to bring about complete victory over their suffering now, there will come a time when God will establish his new kingdom, and victory over suffering will be complete (Revelation 21:1-4). As such, the imperfections of life today point to the perfect that is to come. So be encouraged! Don't lose heart (2 Corinthians 4:16).

God hates evil, suffering and injustice just as much as you do. That's why he has a plan locked in place to overcome it. We can look forward to sharing in that victory in the future. Jesus taught that the suffering we experience in this life would be completely swallowed up by the joy that is to come. He likened it to the pain of childbirth being forgotten in the joy of the birth of a child (John 16:20-22).

Christians do not have to give suffering the ultimate authority to determine their feelings. They are called to be a people who do not let suffering have ultimate power over them. They are those who can give thanks to God 'in' all situations, (although not, necessarily 'for' all situations). This truth is beautifully expressed in the Old Testament book of Habakkuk.

> *Though the fig tree does not bud*
> *and there are no grapes on the vines,*
> *though the olive crop fails*
> *and the fields produce no food,*
> *though there are no sheep in the pen*
> *and no cattle in the stalls,*
> *yet I will rejoice in the Lord,*

I will be joyful in God my Savior. (Habakkuk 3:17-18)

In the end, we don't fully know everything about suffering. Being mortal, there are things we don't understand. However, we can know that God cares, and that God loves. Not only that: God promises to be *with* us to help us in all our trials (Psalms 10:14). We can also know that he will work all things out in the end. God will have the last word.

Hooray!

8

Other Faiths, Christianity, and Me

One of the difficulties people have with Christianity is the perceived arrogance Christians have in claiming that Jesus Christ is the only person through whom we can reach God. How dare Christians think like that!

But before we allow our umbrage to boil over, it's worth mentioning a couple of things. The first is: Christianity is not the only faith that claims an exclusive handle on truth. Many others do too, including Islam. So why is Christianity so often the one singled out for scorn over its exclusivist claim?

The reason is this: Most other religions are tied to the culture of a people-group, e.g. Hinduism, Islam and Buddhism. To suggest that any of these religions is inadequate is therefore seen to be a slur on the culture and identity of a people – and that is not to be countenanced. Tourists like to see the locals practice their 'interesting' religion. It's very quaint – and it provides occasions for endless photo opportunities.

Christianity, however, is trans-cultural, and so its detractors don't feel they are being disrespectful to any people-group when criticizing it. If it is associated with any particular people-group, it is associated (quite erroneously) with the over-privileged West. With the current penchant for Western universities to scorn Western culture, Christianity is seen as fair game.

We live in an age where tolerance has supplanted truth as a moral virtue. Christianity therefore does not fare well, because it does not compromise. Authentic Christianity doesn't pretend to be just a cultural badge people put on their internal sense of spirituality. Other religions, such as Sikhism, Baha'i, New Age, Unitarianism, and, I would have to add, the revisionist Christianity espoused by the likes of the American Episcopalian, John Spong, have all made a central feature of syncretism. They happily morph other religions into their faith.

In contrast to these religions, Christianity, along with Islam, does not accommodate itself to any other religion, other than to build upon a common Jewish heritage.

So, does this mean that Christianity is particularly wrong?

Not necessarily.

It would be totally outrageous for Christianity to claim it was the only way to reach God...if it were not for one tiny, eensy-weensy, fact. And that fact is – unless it was true.

Are there many ways to God?

How can we respect other faiths for their good qualities, yet be convinced of Christ's unique authority as God's Son? What are we to make of the many excellent qualities of Mohandas Gandhi? What are we to make of the compassion and gentleness of Buddha, or the sensitivity and wisdom of Confucius? What does God want us to believe about other faiths?

Christianity is uncompromising. The Christian gospel makes it plain that people are not made acceptable to God by their moral leadership (Gandhi), or their wisdom (Confucius), or their piety (Hinduism). No one is good enough to earn the right to God's acceptance. The Bible says that the wisdom of humankind is foolishness compared to God's standards (1 Corinthians 3:19). The sad reality is: the piety of humankind is never enough to reach God, and often amounts to humankind trying to make God controllable and accessible by their own efforts.

It's probably wise, at this point, to let God have a say. Why? Because if God exists, we must all come to God on his terms, not our own.

Whilst some faiths believe that God requires moral, wise or pious acts to reach God, Christianity does not. It declares that it would be cruel to require the standards of morality and piety necessary to reach God, because they are impossible to attain. The reasoning behind this is simple: God is morally perfect. He cannot accommodate anyone who is less than perfect, and still retain his perfection. Humankind is therefore in an impossible dilemma, for we can never reach God by our own efforts.

In the end, only God could solve the dilemma. His love found a way through the impasse. As he knew we could never reach him through our own merit, he came to us. He came as the person, Jesus Christ. Jesus came to die on a cross to pay the penalty for our sins. It only remains for us to put our faith in him...and to ask him to be the one in charge of our lives.

And that, in a nutshell, is the Christian gospel.

Is Christianity just another way to God?

The dilemma we have by saying that Christ's death on the cross is indispensable for salvation, is that we appear to condemn other faiths as inadequate. But if we say that other ways to God are equally valid; the cost is giving up Christ as the only person able to rescue humankind to God.

So, what's the solution?

Logically, there are only three possible answers.

Position 1) Pluralism

Pluralism says that all religions lead to God. (Some pluralists would like to add that all morally 'good' religions lead to God, which raises the interesting question of who decides what ultimate 'good' is.)

There are two main types of pluralism:

The first is 'ethical pluralism'.

This says that only those religions that are effective at caring for the poor, and which insist on justice, are valid. Some feminists support this position. For them, saying that only one religion is right has clear parallels to sexism. (It is like saying one gender is superior.) They say that 'justice' is to be the fundamental value of faith, and this should be the focus of all talk between religions. There should be a shift of focus from right religious belief to right ethical behavior.

The other type of pluralism is what I call 'existential pluralism'. It's a frightening name for something that is essentially very simple. Existential pluralism suggests that all religious experiences are just various experiences of the same God. Different religions are simply culturally and historically conditioned human responses to the one God.

Unfortunately, in order to hold this opinion, Jesus is not allowed to be God, for that would make Christianity unique. The religious philosopher, John Hick, for example, simply regards Jesus as a human being who was open to the presence and reality of God in such a way that he made an impact on everyone he met. Pluralists like Hick, don't believe that very much in the biographies of Jesus (written by Matthew, Mark, Luke and John) is historically true. They say that the stories about the divinity of Christ are 'myths'. Hick defines myth as: "a story which is told but which is not literally true, but which invites a particular attitude in its hearers."[1]

One can quickly see that central to debate about other faiths is the identity of Jesus. Jesus' question to his disciples "Who do people say I am?" (Mark 8:27) has never been so relevant!

In order for pluralists to make Christianity palatable and fit in with their thinking, they have to remove everything that is diagnostic about Christianity (e.g. Christ's saving action on the cross, Christ's resurrection, and the authority of Scripture). When this is done, nothing is left other than a bland form of moralism – which has its equal in most other religions.

Quite a lot of pluralists have an overarching ideological cause (e.g. eco-justice, feminism or social justice), which they tailor their faith to serve. In other words, they build their own god. To help in this, they borrow selectively from those sections of Scripture that support their cause.

The necessary consequence of pluralism is that the god it defines lacks identity, is impersonal, and is unknowable. The pluralist god is simply a vague abstract form that hides behind the face of many religions – able to be revealed as any or all of them.

Pluralists can be passionate about their cause, and this can result in those who don't subscribe to their faith being accused of being imperialist bigots. In reality, pluralism tries to silence a lot of people. Pluralism is equated with social tolerance, so if you don't embrace pluralism, you are considered to be intolerant.

What can we say in response to this?

The first and rather obvious point is that any god created to meet the need of humankind is not much of a god. Sadly, inventing such a god stands in a long tradition of humankind wanting to control their own destiny and salvation.

Secondly, pluralism fails to address the reality of the sinful nature of humankind. Neither does it explain the suffering that occurs naturally in nature. It has no answers to these issues, and offers no hope to overcome them.

Thirdly, the pluralist god is one that allows religious confusion because he (or she) refuses to reveal himself in any definitive way.

In sharp contrast to this, conventional Christianity teaches that God has chosen to reveal himself to us as Father, Son, and Holy Spirit. Christianity makes it clear that whilst the themes of justice and environmental care are important, our main purpose in existence is to accept the loving friendship of a self-revealing God.

Christianity therefore cannot be reduced to being simply a moral philosophy to live by. Its claims are too exclusive. Jesus' words: "I am the way and the truth and the life. No one comes to the Father except through me," (John 14:6) leave little leeway for debate.

The reality is: Jesus' life, death, and resurrection are not an optional garnish to Christian faith, they *are* the faith. Jesus did not come primarily to show the right, ethical way to live. Jesus came primarily to restore our relationship with God, a God who insists that we live in a way that is ethical and compassionate.

Jesus made it plain that life with God is only possible because he died to pay the penalty for our sins. These sins would otherwise make us ineligible for life with God. As such, Jesus opens the way to God.

Christianity is therefore not just another way to God alongside many other religions.

Position 2) Exclusivism

If pluralism is wrong, do we need to hold an 'exclusivist' position, which believes that those who have not heard the gospel, or who belong to other faiths, cannot be saved?

If we did believe this, it would seem to contradict God's expressed will that everyone should be saved (1 Thessalonians 5:9; 2 Peter 3:9). It also contradicts the three things we know about God's character:

1. God is righteous (Psalm 19:9; 145:17)
2. God is loving (1 John 4:7-10,16)
3. God is just (Psalm 89:14; Revelation 16:7)

The Bible makes it clear that God is 'just' in that he takes into account what we know when dealing with us (Luke 12:47-48; 1 Timothy 1:13). It goes on to teach that God will judge us according to two things. The first is how we have responded to Jesus (John 3:36; Hebrews 10:29). The second is how we have responded to our conscience and the ethical laws we instinctively know to be right, i.e. what we have done (Romans 2:14-16; Revelation 20:12).

This is significant, for whilst not everyone has the opportunity to respond to Jesus, everyone has the opportunity to faithfully live the values they instinctively know to be right.

The Bible teaches us that the incredible wonder and complexity of the universe should point people to the possibility that God exists (Psalm 8:3-4; 19:1-4; Romans 1:19-20). As such, it is reasonable to expect people to seek God, and to live life as morally as they know how in response to his existence.

We are surrounded by evidence for God. Nature shouts it out. When people acknowledge the truth of that in their heart, from whatever culture, they have the beginnings of faith. I heard that a Confucian monk once said (on hearing the gospel of Jesus Christ), "I've always known him, but now I know his name."

It is reasonable to agree with the Bible's judgment that where people allow rebellion against what they know to be 'good' to obliterate the possibility of a relationship with God, then that is a bad thing. The reality is: it requires a certain selflessness and humility of heart to acknowledge God – and not everyone has it.

As we've seen, the Bible says that God will judge justly, taking into account what people know. However, for many people, the thought of God dealing with them with perfect justice is terrible, for most of them know that they haven't measured up to their own standards, let alone God's. This is why the Christian gospel is such good news. By putting our faith in Jesus, we are rescued from such judgment (John 3:16; 5:24).

So, all of this leaves us with mixed messages regarding exclusivism. In its raw form, it doesn't sit well with us. However, if pluralism is to be rejected, and exclusivism is not right, what can we believe?

Position 3) Inclusivism

Inclusivism maintains that the central claims of Christianity are true, but it adopts a more positive view of other religions than exclusivism. Jesus is still held to be unique and essential but God is said to be revealing himself and providing salvation through other religious traditions as well.

This position seems reasonable, but it is dangerous. Its danger comes from the very flexibility of what is meant by salvation of people 'through' other faith positions, for the Bible makes it clear that there is no other name than Jesus through whom we can be saved. The apostle Peter was fairly blunt when he said: "Salvation is found in no one else, for there is no other name under heaven given to men by which we must be saved" (Acts 4:12).

So, where does that leave us? If pluralism, exclusivism and inclusivism are not satisfactory, is there a better understanding?

I think there is.

The inclusivist position can be modified slightly so that it takes better account of the essential work of Christ.

Modified inclusivism

Modified inclusivism allows that there is some undeniable truth and beauty in other religions. However, these truths do not add anything new to the essentials of salvation spoken of in the Bible.

Modified inclusivism suggests that it is not true that people can be saved *through* other religions, but it may be true that they have access to Christ's saving action *from* their own sincerely held faith position – a faith position that they live out through godly behavior (Romans 2:13-16; Matthew 25:31-36). This was the position held by Karl Rahner, a German Jesuit priest who was one of the most influential Roman Catholic theologians of the 20th century. He called those who lived faithfully according to the moral and spiritual code they instinctively knew to be right, 'anonymous Christians'.

This, however, raises the question of what happens to people who have been faithful to the religious truth they know, but their faithfulness includes sanctioning things that most of us would consider terrible, such as female genital mutilation, or the killing of 'infidels'.

At this point, I think we need to back away from dogma and leave the judging to God—to the one who *really* knows what is going on in a person's heart.

One of the things that modified inclusivism allows, is that some teaching from other faiths can be helpful in emphasizing aspects of biblical truth. Their perspective can highlight forgotten or undiscovered applications of Christian truth, and challenge us to live out aspects of the Christian gospel more faithfully, e.g. to recover the gospel mandate for environmental care.

Crucially, modified inclusivism preserves the need for the essential work of Christ, and maintains the urgency of mission and evangelism. After all: why should anyone risk judgment on how well they have lived up to their own standards? And why allow people to 'hope' for a future with God, when they can have a loving friendship with God right now?

Christians have been given something very special to share with the rest of the world. It is the good news of God's revelation of himself to us. It is the good news of God's love. It is the good news of God's provision for our forgiveness through Jesus. Christians have a Godly mandate to share this good news (Matthew 28:18-20; John 20:21).

It is significant that the Bible makes reference to people who knew about the existence of God, but who didn't really know and love him personally (John 4:22; Acts 17: 16-17, 22-23). This teaches Christians not to be content for anyone to live in the shadow of truth – when they can know the reality of truth.

God came on a mission to win us to himself, and we, who are his people, are similarly called to mission. The option of lazily falling back into a theology of modified inclusivism, and not telling other people about Jesus is not open to us.

Let's pause at this point, and do a quick review of what the other main religions in the world teach.

Hinduism

Hinduism is the main Indian religion. It has no founder and no distinct creed. Hinduism is an ancient religion that is an amalgam of many religious influences. The central core of the Hindu scriptures is called *Sruti* (literally, 'that which is heard'). This collection includes the four Vedas that contain teaching, poetry and hymns. The Hindu book *Rig Veda* is a collection of ancient hymns compiled in 900BC – which makes it the oldest religious book in the world.

Hindus believe in one 'High' God, Brahma (the ultimate reality), who is aided by lesser beings which the peasant classes of India regard as Gods, but which many of the higher classes regard as saints or angels.

There are three sects of Hinduism. Each has a different name for the one high God, and each attributes a different type of character to him. The three different names are: Vishnu, Shiva, and Shakti.

Vishnu is a god of goodwill who visits earth occasionally in the form of an incarnation. He is usually worshiped in the form of one of his ten incarnations, some animal, others human.

Shiva is seen by some as being a grim destroyer and by others as a grim ascetic. He is worshiped as an image, and also as his emblem: a rounded phallic pillar, representing the creative power of God.

Shakti is the great mother goddess who is worshipped in her fierce, ugly form (of Durga or Kali) or in her mild form (of Parvati or Uma).

Historically, there have been some nasty practices, including human sacrifices and the burning of widows (*sati*) associated with the Hindu religion. Happily, these practices no longer take place.

Traditional Hindus worship as individuals or families rather than as congregations.

The many idols that exist in Hinduism are not necessarily seen as Gods (except perhaps by the peasant class) but as icons that help in the worship of God.

Hindus believe in reincarnation, i.e. that the soul passes into another animal or human, depending on the merit of their actions (karma) whilst they were alive. The eventual goal, after rebirth into the higher orders, is to earn enough merit to escape from this continual cycle of rebirth, and reach God.

This end point of Hinduism is a bit vague. Hinduism tries to balance the belief in many gods, with pantheism – the belief that God *is* everything that is created. It is not an easy balance to find. Pantheism requires you to believe that you (as part of everything that is created) are God. As such, it has much in common with New Age thinking.

The Hindu religion offers three ways to God. The way of philosophy (salvation reserved for the wise), the way of devotion (salvation earned by acts of piety), and salvation by faithfully living out your fate and station in life.

Unfortunately, this belief discourages people from trying to better themselves, or to question the justice of factors that keep them in their place. People are expected to know their place and to live out their path of duty as one of four classes of people. These are: 1) the priestly cast (the Brahmins); 2) the warrior class; 3) the merchant class; and 4) the laborer class.

As well as these, there is a lower group of people who are considered to be outside of society, known as 'untouchables'. Untouchables (more properly called 'Dalits') account for approximately 25% of the population of India.

This passive aspect of Hinduism teaches people that they should cope with evil and injustice not by addressing the issues that cause them, but by changing their perception of what constitutes evil and injustice.

Buddhism

The founder of Buddhism was Gautama who lived from 563 to 483BC in Nepal. He led a sheltered and privileged existence, but was eventually disturbed by the suffering he observed. As he viewed the harshness of life, a wandering beggar clad in a yellow robe impressed him with his serenity.

Trying to make sense of it all, Gautama left his wife and son to embrace a life of severe asceticism. However, he found that wasn't the answer. Whilst meditating under a Bo tree by the river Gaya, Gautama had an 'enlightenment', which convinced him that the root of all evil and suffering was 'desire'. He was also convinced that desire could be stopped by living a pious life that was neither too ascetic nor too sensuous.

Buddhists therefore seek to follow the 'noble eightfold path' of eight disciplines that teach aspects of wisdom, morality, gentleness and meditation.

Worship in the Buddhist tradition is an individual rather than a corporate activity.

The goal of all Buddhists is to escape the wretchedness of life (karma) with its incessant cycle of cause and effect, and achieve a state of spiritual bliss (nirvana).

The basic teachings of Buddhism were not written down until 400 years after Gautama's death (which is a very long time!) In fact, a full biography of Gautama's life (considered to be less important than his teaching) was not written down until the second century AD.

There are two main types of Buddhism. The first is 'Theravada'. This teaches that salvation is earned by doing enough good works. However, it is for monks only. The second is 'Mahayana'. This teaches that salvation is for everyone – provided they have enough faith and devotion. This form of Buddhism is particularly popular in China and Japan.

Buddhism believes the main problem in life is not sin but suffering, and that the root of this suffering is, as I've said, 'desire'. The aim of life is therefore to rid yourself of all desire through meditation and self-control.

The second last words of Buddha to his disciples were, "strive without ceasing." His last recorded words were: "always exert the mind, seeking the way out."[2]

These words are very different from the last words of Jesus before he died, "It is finished." Christians understand that Jesus has provided the "way out." He won the right for us to be with God by dying in our place on the cross.

Islam

Islam has much in common with Christianity. It arose at the start of the 7th century, largely from Jewish and Christian influence. As such, Muslims revere the Old Testament prophets, but believe that Jesus was only a prophet and not God. Like Christianity and Judaism, Muslims believe in the one God, whom they call Allah.

Islam was founded by Muhammad (whom Muslims regard as

the greatest prophet of God). Muhammad was born in Mecca in about 571AD. When he was 25, a wealthy forty-year-old widow put a proposition of marriage to him. They were married and she bore him three daughters. From time to time, Muhammad would withdraw to lonely places to contemplate. Whilst doing this, he had divine revelations calling him to preach the existence of the one true God, Allah.

Unlike Jesus (who chose the path of love), Mohammad was not above attacking trade caravans from Mecca in order to further his cause. In fact, the initial spread of Islam was through conquest.

Islam's scripture, the *Qur'an*, teaches that it is perfectly legitimate to fight against other nations or people-groups in a 'holy war' (*jihad*), but that Muslims should not be the initial aggressor. It also says that those who worship other Gods should be killed or expelled from the land unless they pay tax (*dhimmi* or *jizya*). This concession was originally only offered to Christians and Jews, ('people of the book'), but was sometimes extended to those of other faiths.

Muslims believe in angels, demons, and prophets. They believe that each person will eventually face God's judgment, which will determine whether they spend eternity in paradise (heaven) or in hell. As such, they need to be careful how they live their life.

Islam also talks of the divine scales of justice in which bad deeds are wiped out by good deeds. In other words, you can be as bad as you like – provided you do enough good later on to counter it. This must cause many to despair of ever being good enough to earn the right to go to heaven. It also means that heaven (which Muslims call 'Paradise') may have to accommodate up to 49% evil – which does not sound very attractive.

Christianity, by contrast, teaches that God has a zero tolerance to sin, and his one answer to it is to kill it off. Christianity teaches that Jesus took the sins of all humanity on himself, and died on a cross to pay the price for them. What we couldn't do for ourselves, God did for us.

Good Muslims pray five times a day; fast during the month of Ramadan; give to charity; and make a pilgrimage to Mecca at least once in their lifetime.

Their scriptures not only consist of the *Qur'an* (a collection of Muhammad's revelations, together with regulations concerning religious and social behavior), they also have the *Shari'a*. This is a book that defines in great detail the code of behavior Muslims must live by in everyday life.

Some of the writings of the *Qur'an* are beautiful. Some of it is ambiguous and contradictory. This is because Muhammad's thinking changed during his lifetime so that his later writings (after he moved from Mecca to Medina) were less conciliatory toward those of other faiths. This lays the *Qur'an* open to a number of different interpretations, and places great responsibility on spiritual leaders to interpret the *Qur'an* appropriately for their local community. The *Qur'an* was written in Arabic, and Islamic leaders insist that it always be read in Arabic so that nothing of its original inspiration is lost.

There are two main groups of Muslims. One group is the *Sunni*. Most Muslims are *Sunni* Muslims. They seek to determine what God's direction is for them by community consensus.

The other main group of Muslims is the *Shi'ite*. *Shi'ite* Muslims appeal to their 'inspired leaders' (Imams) for God's direction. This can increase the potential for a community to adopt more extreme (and sometimes violent) courses of action.

A key culture of Islam is one of 'dominance'. The *Qur'an* does not countenance anything else. No other faith is seen as valid. Dialogue with those of other faiths will only be pursued if it is seen to be of benefit to Islam. Faithful Muslims honor Allah, Muhammad and the *Qur'an*, and will not tolerate anyone who demeans any of them.

Muslim culture differs from that of the West. Whilst secular Western culture compartmentalizes society, (seeking to marginalize Christianity to a private belief), Islam does not. Islam is a total package of religious practices, legal system (*Sharia* law), education, and politics. Any country where Islam is taking hold soon discovers that demands for Islamic schools, *halal* meat, *Sharia* law and a parallel Islamic government within their host nation soon follow.

Muslims greatly esteem Jesus (whom they call *Isa*) as an honored prophet, but do not believe he was God in human form. Muslims don't believe Jesus was crucified, despite overwhelming historical evidence to the contrary.

People unfamiliar with religion can mistakenly believe that Jesus and Muhammad are much the same. They are not.

Muhammad led a warrior force that killed, executed, and enslaved, justifying it by declaring it *jihad* (a holy war). Those still doing that today quote a verse from the Qur'an (Surah 9.5) which has come to be called, 'the verse of the sword', which says: "…fight and slay the pagans wherever ye find them, and seize them, beleaguer them, and lie in wait for them in every stratagem (of war)."

Muhammad also taught that non-Muslims living in a Muslim country should be made to feel inferior. Part of this involved the exaction of the tax we talked of earlier, *jizya*.

Mohammad became increasingly hostile toward non-Muslims, particularly the Jews, during his lifetime. He allowed 600 of them to be beheaded after the Battle of the Trench in 627AD.

Umar ibn Abd al-Aziz, commonly known as Umar II, was the eighth Umayyad caliph, who ruled the Islamic kingdom from 717 until his death in 720. He reported that the last words of Muhammad were: "O Lord, perish the Jews and the Christians …Beware, there should be no two faiths in Arabia."[3]

This attitude is in stark contrast with Jesus, who taught that we are to love our enemies (Luke 6:27; Romans 12:20). This teaching is one of the most diagnostic teachings of Christianity – and sadly, is not one that those calling themselves Christians have always followed!

Despite this, it is highly significant that nations with a Judeo-Christian heritage have become a sanctuary for refugees who seek out that nation's peace, civility, schools and hospitals. It should be of some concern that opinion leaders in these Western nations are now trying to trash their heritage, for nowhere in history has it ever been shown that morality and civility can thrive without God.

Muhammad married a number of times. He married Ayishah when she was just nine, although he didn't live with her until some years later. And his attraction to Zainab led to her being divorced so

Muhammad could marry her. Muhammad justified his actions by claiming he had a revelation from God.

Jesus, however, never married. Significantly, he taught that God hated divorce (Matthew 19:1-9). The New Testament also makes it clear that a man should only have one wife (1 Timothy 3:2;12; Titus 1:6).

Islam teaches that salvation has to be earned by doing enough good works.

Christianity teaches that we can never reach God by doing enough 'good works' (Ephesians 2:8-9). It required Jesus (who was perfectly holy) to die on a cross to pay the price for our sins, for us to have the right to be with God.

Islam teaches that women are required to be subservient to men. Women who are faithful will make it to *Jannah* (paradise). But whilst faithful Islamic men are promised eternal sensual (sexual) rewards, the Qur'an is silent about any rewards for women. (This doesn't necessarily mean there aren't rewards for women in paradise, it is just that nothing is mentioned.)

The Bible has no ambiguity. It makes it very clear that men and women are equal in the sight of God (Galatians 3:28).

One of the worrying features of Islam is its inability to self-evaluate. The reason for this is that self-evaluation of Islam is seen as impiety, something which is liable to bring about harsh consequences from other Islamists. Reform is therefore difficult to achieve, and moral questions such as those raised by 9/11 have not been addressed.

This is a concern. The percentage of Christians in the Middle East has declined from 25% to 5% in the last few decades. This has been almost entirely due to rape, crucifixions, shootings, and beheadings carried out in the name of Islam. Despite this appalling statistic, the Islamic community, as a whole, has remained disturbingly quiet. Sadly, if you have a cultural and theological heritage that sanctions the use of violence as a missional tool, silence is understandable...but, "oh dear, oh dear, oh dear." I weep.

. . .

New Age

The New Age movement has sprung up in the spiritual vacuum caused by people having an inherent spirituality, but not knowing what to do about it. Many people have despaired of finding any ultimate truth, and feel that all the major faiths have been discredited. As such, they are looking for something that is new and non-institutional. They are looking for something that: 1) is spiritually satisfying; 2) will help them realize their potential; 3) won't require too much personal sacrifice; 4) dispenses with the notion of 'sin'; and 5) is infinitely flexible and allows them to design their own belief.

The Australian Anglican theologian, Peter Corney writes:

The dissatisfaction with rationalism and materialism has led to a new search for the transcendent, the mystical, the mysterious and the magical. You see it everywhere from New Age crystals to the revival of Celtic myths and Gothic images. Add extreme feminism and environmentalism ...and the distinction between God and nature has blurred to create a new paganism.[4]

New Age is a spiritual quest for transformation. It believes in a universal life force. Another fundamental tenet of New Age thinking is the belief that spiritual energy can be manipulated for the benefit of self and others. The American author, Russell Chandler writes:

The New Age world view holds that God is an impersonal force, or a field of energy that holds everything together ...In essence, God is everything; everything is God; and humans are part of that process – so we are God. We create our own truth, our own reality ...The New Age movement promises a 'quick fix' spirituality, global harmony, and self-empowerment from the 'divine within', without the troublesome demands of personal accountability.[5]

New Age has no firm doctrine, but is a loose collection of beliefs and philosophies, from which you are able to choose a selection that suits your thinking and lifestyle. Typically, the beliefs you can select from (to design your own new age philosophy) include: eastern mysticism; the ecology movement; the human potential movement;

some aspects of feminism, psychic phenomena, and pantheism (the belief that God *is* the universe).

Because New Age has so many component parts, some facets of it (such as identifying the worth of nature, justice for women, and developing your potential) are good. However, others parts of it that deny the person and work of Christ are not.

One of the features commonly associated with New Age is the belief in the special power of crystals (which are sometimes worn around the neck). The belief is that crystals can harness and focus 'energies' that can improve your well-being. This is often described in pseudo-scientific language. It is, of course, nonsense and is something that has no integrity in the field of real science.

The fact that people can believe in it at all is testimony to the fact that many people have become disillusioned with science. It was once thought that science would give us all the answers to life – and even explain away God. Many people no longer have this optimism. They have therefore turned their quest for truth inward to the world of subjective experience; to the world of the mystical and mysterious.

Cults

A cult is simply a small religious group of people (relative to the main religions) who hold to an unconventional doctrine. The term is sometimes a disparaging one used to suggest that its members hold to a belief that would not withstand general scrutiny and analysis. (It is perhaps sobering to remember, however, that Christianity once looked like a cult – a strange offshoot of Judaism.)

Sadly, there is no shortage of cults. New ones seem to appear every decade. Children of God; Christian Science; Moonies; and Scientology can all be called cults.

A number of factors commonly (although not invariably) typify a cult.

Cults often develop around a strong, charismatic leader. The public face of a cult may appear very reasonable at first glance. (It has to be if it is to recruit people.) Cults often set out to meet people's immediate needs. This can be: 1) the need to belong and have identity; 2) the need for love; 3) the need for self-improvement; and 4) the need to know truth and have purpose.

Cults often enroll people into an initial period of intense training. A significant part of this involves getting people to define themselves against 'normal' people. Typically, they do this by teaching that normal people are deficient in some way. Cult members, however, are 'chosen' and 'special'. (Islamic terror groups use this technique to recruit young adults who are still in search of their identity.)

Cults claim an exclusive handle on truth. They often find room for Jesus or borrow selectively from the Bible to lend themselves credibility. However, they feel free to augment or re-interpret it, or to place the Bible alongside their 'more adequate' literature.

It is by no means unusual for cults to remove their members from society and become reclusive. They do this to keep themselves free from wider society's polluting ideas. Some even develop a persecution complex, believing that society is evil and antagonistic. This has the effect of removing its people from public scrutiny and reasoned criticism.

The moral behavior of some cults has sometimes been bizarre. They are very prone to scandal. Some, however, live by a very strict moral code.

Most cults are short-lived, many not lasting 100 years.

Be careful

Please don't join a cult. The Bible says that false prophets will appear and will deceive many (Matthew 24:11-12; 2 Peter 2:1-3). It says that false teachers are identified by the 'fruit' of their actions (Matthew 7:15-20). They can also be identified because what they advocate does not line up with the consistent principles God has made clear in the Bible (1 John 4:1-3). It is vitally important to know your Bible well, and to be on your guard.

. . .

Be gracious

There is never any excuse for anyone, particularly Christians, to be anything other than gracious toward those of other faiths. The central feature of Jesus' ministry was love, and we his Church need to show it.

I was a pastor of a church when Islamic terrorists flew planes into the twin towers of the World Trade Center in 2001. The Sunday after that terrible event was an extraordinary time. Our church was full. One of the people who came to our night service was a Muslim refugee. He had come to the service to thank the church for providing him and his family with furniture and provisions. However, he came in some fear and sat in the back row, unsure of how his presence might be taken in the light of what had happened. After I finished preaching, I walked down the length of the aisle and embraced him with a hug. Everybody watched. It is probably the only thing people remember from that service.

What is special about Christianity compared with the other major religions?

Let's do a review of what it is that makes Christianity special.

Quite apart from the historical reality of Jesus and the ethical integrity of his life, there are three aspects of Christianity that indicate that we should take it seriously.

The first is that Jesus is the only historical person who has been raised from the dead. It's important to note that Jesus was not merely resuscitated from death; he was *raised* from death, never to die again. This extraordinary feature formed the heart of the message of the early church. It was what energized and compelled them into mission.

If you want to make sense of life after death, may I recommend you ask the one person who has beaten the power of death – Jesus. As a Finnish missionary to Russia once said, "If you come to a cross roads and do not know which way to go, and you see a dead person and a live person: which one are you going to ask the way?"

The second factor that makes Christianity special is that most religions require you to pray, meditate, or perform acts of piety in order to reach God (or attain eternal bliss). Christianity is unique in that God recognizes that we can never do enough to earn salvation in our own strength. God therefore does it for us in sending Jesus to die for our sins. We only need to accept it, and respond to God's love by loving God in return.

Thirdly: Christianity makes the claim that God indwells Christians with the empowering presence of his Holy Spirit. Christians testify to the power of God to change them when they allow the Spirit of God do so. In other words, there is *power* in authentic Christianity. It is not just a belief or philosophy.

Jesus teaches that fundamentally, the purpose of God creating the universe was to establish a relationship with us – a relationship based on love. Whilst other faiths show aspects of truth, Jesus claimed that it was only through him that people could have the sort of intimate relationship with God that he had. He taught us to call God 'Father'. This level of intimacy with God is not found in other religions. Rajiv Gandhi, who served as the sixth Prime Minister of India from 1984 to 1989, wrote in his autobiography that he had searched for most of his life for intimacy with God. However, he felt that he never attained it because he was acutely aware of his own lack of holiness.

So, what can we say in conclusion?

Simply this: There are many ways that people have tried to reach out to God. Christianity is unique. Christianity is all about God reaching out to us.

And that's good news.

Isn't Christianity just a Western religion?

I've heard people claim that Christianity is just a cultural religion of the West. This assertion ignores the rather obvious fact that most of the world's Christians are now not from the West, and that the West is rapidly trying to shrug off its Christian heritage. So, can it still be reasonably said that Christianity is a Western religion?

It's fair to say that everything has to start somewhere. In the case of Christianity, it was born in the Middle East. Jesus was a Jew. However, Christianity was nurtured for many centuries in Europe. This means that Europe's culture has influenced how Christianity has been expressed and is perceived by many today. (It has been said that England turned Christianity into a national establishment, and America turned it into a commercial opportunity!)

The truth is, God speaks to all nations through their own culture. As such, the Western church should be careful not to saddle other nations with its cultural baggage when teaching the good news of Jesus. The apostle Paul didn't insist that all non-Jewish Christians should be circumcised to be like Jewish Christians (Galatians 2:14-16). He celebrated diversity of culture and worked within it when presenting the 'good news' of Christ (Acts 17:22-23,28; 1 Corinthians 9:19-20; 12:12-27).

We should do the same.

Aren't all Religions fundamentally the same?

We've already addressed this issue, but it's worth tidying up some loose ends.

There is a sentimental attraction to the idea, isn't there, that all religions are fundamentally the same. It is tidy and diplomatic, and overlooks all the messy divisions that have caused so much strife in history. It would also suggest that all of humankind has a handle on truth. So, what can we say?

There is no doubt that there are similarities between some religions. For example, the Zoroastrian religion has much in common with Christianity.

There are probably five things that most religions have in common.

1. Most religions have a sense of 'the other'. They believe
2. in a god (or gods) that is/are responsible for the existence of life.
3. Most religions believe this god (or gods) require our worship and devotion.

4. Most religions require a level of self-discipline.
5. Most believe in an existence beyond death.
6. Most religions have a similar sort of moral code.

Unfortunately, however inconvenient it is, we also have to acknowledge that there are fundamental differences between religions that simply can't be reconciled. Here a just a few of them.

Pantheists e.g. many Hindus, believe that God is all of creation. But Christians, Jews and Muslims believe that God exists independently outside of creation.

Hinduism has many gods. But some branches of Buddhism say that there are no gods.

Islam teaches its followers that they can earn their way to heaven (paradise). But Christianity says you can't earn your way to heaven, Christ had to do that for us.

These issues are not reconcilable. They can't all be right.

Neither can we say that 'truth' is something that can vary from one person to another. Either something is true, and is true for everyone, or it is not real truth. Truth is not a subjective and variable idea. The truth about gravity always requires a brick to fall to the ground. This will be true for all bricks anywhere on planet Earth.

If you believe that all religions are fundamentally the same, Christ's teachings, as recorded in the Bible, also present a difficulty. Jesus said: "I am the way and the truth and the life. No one comes to the Father except through me" (John 14:6). Similarly, the apostle Peter spoke about Jesus saying: "Salvation is found in no one else, for there is no other name under heaven given to men by which we must be saved" (Acts 4:12).

...and that is a wonderful note on which to end.

9

Church, Its Moral Failure, and Me

Atheists have pointed to the moral failure of Christianity in history as a reason for it to be scorned and avoided.

Leaving aside the rather obvious fact that atheists do not put the humanist ideologies of Stalin, Hitler, Mao, and Pol Pot under the same scrutiny, what can we say?

I believe that Christians need to take this particular criticism very seriously, and to use it to motivate reform. Why? Because the institutional church needs it.

In this chapter, we'll look at two issues. In part 1) we will ask the question: "Is Christianity bad?" In part 2) we will ask the question: "Is God bad?"

Part 1) Is Christianity bad?

One of the main planks in the argument of militant atheists such as Richard Dawkins, Sam Harris, Christopher Hitchens, and Daniel Dennett, for why Christianity should be spurned, is its moral failure in history. Certainly, the dreadful abuses of the Crusades, the Spanish Inquisition, and more recently the sectarian violence of Northern Ireland and Bosnia have reflected poorly on Christianity.

Particularly recently, of course, the church has had to deal with the obscenity of child abuse within its institutions.

It has to be said that the institutional expression of church has often been imperfect, and un-Christ-like. People with a hunger for power have sought to use Christianity as a means to further their ambitions or satiate their lusts. But alongside and within the fallible institutional church, there has been the 'true church', the church that embodies the grace and truth of Jesus. We see its beautiful influence on individuals, families, cities and nations. We see it in Mother Teresa working amongst the beggars of Calcutta. We see it in the wonderful priests working amongst the beggars living on the rubbish dumps in Juarez, Mexico.

None of us should dare say who belongs to which church – only God can do that. In reality, most Christians know themselves to be living in *both* the fallible church and the faithful church. We know this because the church is a reflection of us. We are both. That is why every single one of us needs God's grace and forgiveness.

The story is told (probably apocryphal) that *The Times* once sent out an inquiry to famous authors, asking the question, "What's wrong with the world today?" to which the Christian writer and philosopher, G.K. Chesterton, responded: "Dear Sir. I am. Yours, G.K. Chesterton."

The problem of being good

Christians understand themselves to be imperfect, broken, and a 'work in progress'. They see themselves as 100% flawed because of their human nature, and 100% righteous in the eyes of God because Jesus has paid the price for their sins. In other words, Christians see themselves as both saint and sinner.

My wife and I once had the privilege of starting a youth group in Adelaide. Rather bewilderingly, it grew – largely due to the influx of young adults who had no previous experience of Christianity. To teach the team that they were both saint and sinner, we had T-shirts made with the emblem of a princess kissing a frog, underneath which was written: DGMAMGH-

FWMY, which stood for: "Don't get mad at me, God hasn't finished with me yet."

Now, don't get me wrong, I am not suggesting that becoming a Christian makes no difference to people's moral behavior. Quite the reverse: In my experience, (and I would argue, the experience of history), nothing is as transformative of individuals, families, towns or nations as authentic Christianity. The teaching of the apostle Paul in the New Testament made it clear that if he didn't see evidence of the Holy Spirit's work in a person or a community, he would challenge that person or community. When someone becomes a Christian, God's Holy Spirit indwells them (Romans 8:9). Paul expected two consequences to follow from this. The first was a transformed character. The second was an empowered ministry. If he didn't see evidence of either of these things, he would ask why. However, whilst these changes begin at the point someone becomes a Christian, change does not fully occur instantaneously. In other words: at conversion, divine 'perfection' is not conferred, but divine 'infection' begins.

One must also point out that the behavior of the church is irrelevant to the question of whether or not God exists. The philosopher, Anthony Flew, put it well when he said, "The excesses and atrocities of organized religion have no bearing whatsoever on the existence of God, just as the threat of nuclear proliferation has no bearing on the question of whether $E = mc^2$."[1]

Two guiding principles

Two principles should guide us as we explore the question of whether or not Christianity is morally deficient.

The first principle is this: Living in a biscuit tin doesn't turn a mouse into a biscuit. In other words, not everyone who goes to church is necessarily a Christian.

Here's the second principle: If people behave badly because they are obeying their leader – blame the leader. But if people behave badly because they are disobeying their leader – blame disobedient people.

It's common sense really, but many seem to forget it.

The danger of institutions

Christian institutions are necessary because they enable the church to organize itself and work efficiently. When functioning well, they also help keep people accountable. However, they are also dangerous. Institutions can too easily develop their own *raison d'être* and become self-serving monsters. People within them can take their eyes off Jesus and become swayed by the rather more grubby things of power, prestige and wealth. The three Borgia popes, who became prominent during the Renaissance, turned murder and unbridled hedonism into an art form.

Christian institutions have always been deeply flawed, and have sometimes lived in contradiction to the teachings of Jesus Christ. It is significant that Jesus' most implacable enemies were religious leaders.

The failings of religious institutions are not a new phenomenon. The Bible has consistently addressed inauthentic religion, sterile formalism, greed, and ego. Why? Because it has been necessary. It has particularly targeted idolatry, hypocrisy, and religion that had no regard for social justice (Isaiah 1:10-17; 58:5-12; James 1:27). In other words, the church doesn't need militant atheists to point out its shortcomings because God already does.

Religion is bad, therefore Christianity is bad

Some atheistic opinion leaders trumpet the idea that religion is bad for society. They echo the sentiment in John Lennon's song *Imagine*, in which he asks us to imagine a utopian world without religion. It is also the sentiment echoed in Christopher Hitchens' book: *God is Not Great: How Religion Poisons Everything*.

Their reasoning goes something like this:

- Most terrorism in recent years has been carried out by Islamic extremists in the name of religion.
- Christianity is a religion.
- Therefore, Christians are terrorists.

Yes, it can really be that crass.

Richard Dawkins is particularly guilty of this sort of folly. He lumps the morally repugnant practices of some religions with Christianity, and by so doing, makes a totally inadequate distinction between a hate-crazed suicide bomber and Mother Teresa. This brings to mind a comment by the American psychologist, David Myers, who said: "To judge religious faith by vulgar caricatures that would make a first-year theology student wince, is like judging science by eugenics, nuclear warheads, and chemical pollutants."[2]

The Christian apologist, Ravi Zacharias, says this sort of logic ruptures the law of logic called the 'Undistributed Middle,' and makes the point by giving this delightful analogy:

> *Elephants have ears*
> *I have ears*
> *Therefore, I am an elephant.*[3]

My challenge to atheists who want to denigrate Christianity in this way is this: Show me a single piece of teaching from Jesus that is morally repellent. Tell me if you find a morally repugnant action committed by him. And as you ponder this challenge, consider this: The most diagnostic feature of Jesus' morality was "love your enemy." Tell me if you see that sentiment in any other religion, philosophy, or world-view.

Religion causes war

This accusation is thrown carelessly at Christianity by the likes of Richard Dawkins. He rarely lets facts get in the way of his bigotry, and what he says wins plaudits from his adoring acolytes. But let's dare to look at some facts.

What has been responsible for the most deaths in war?

Let me list only those wars where over 1 million people died. (My list is taken from a larger list compiled by the American author, Piero Scaruffi.[4]) With the proviso that it is difficult sometimes to get exact figures, here are the number of people who have died in wars between 1900 and 2018.

- World War 2 (1939 - 1945) – including the holocaust and the Chinese revolution = 55 million
- World War 1 (1914 - 1918) = 20 million
- Mao's cultural revolution (1966 - 1969) = 11 million plus (Other reputable sources put this figure at 42 million)[5]
- Stalin's purges (1936 - 1937) = 7-13 million
- Soviet war with Ukraine (1932-1933) = 10 million
- Soviet revolution (1917-1921) = 5 million
- Korean war (1950 - 1953) = 3 million
- Vietnam war (1964 - 1973) = 3 million
- Chinese revolution (1911) = 2.4 million
- Chinese civil war (1928-1937) = 2 million
- Khmer Rouge, Cambodia (1975 - 1979) = 1.7 million
- Menghitsu, Ethiopia (1975 - 1978) = 1.5 million
- Japanese Manchurian war (1931) = 1.1 million

You will immediately see that not one of these wars was caused by religion. You might also note the horrendous number of deaths caused by the atheistic ideologies of Pol Pot (Khmer Rouge), Mao, and Stalin.

I fully understand that Islamic terrorists have carried out most terrorist acts conducted in the last sixty years, but to say that Christianity (or religion in general) has caused most of our wars is manifestly false.

The three things that non-Christians should see in the church

The Bible lists three things that a church should display, that will win the approbation of those not yet in the church. It's worth noting that none of these factors include the architectural merit of its buildings, the professionalism of its music, or the pageantry and performance of its services. No. The Bible mentions just three things.

The first is the good deeds we do in society (Matthew 5:13-16). The second is the quality of our love (John 13:34). The third is the quality of our unity (John 17:20-21). So, if we are looking to attract the favor of wider society, these are the three qualities the church needs to show.

A plea to the church

Let me dare to make a plea to the church. I do so because the consequences of its imperfections are washing up on my shore. It is wounding me and wounding society.

I also dare because I care.

At the risk of causing huge reaction and umbrage, let me express my heart's cry to the three main sections of the institutional church in the West: the Roman Catholic Church, the Protestant Church, and the Pentecostal Church.

My heart's cry to the Roman Catholic Church

When Cardinal George Pell debated Richard Dawkins on television in Australia (April 9, 2012), it wasn't a very edifying affair. Dawkins complained about Pell's lack of understanding of the finer details of evolution, and Pell scored a hit by telling Dawkins that Darwin was a theist, not an atheist. Dawkins protested that this wasn't true, but Pell was right. It was something Dawkins should have known, and it again showed up Dawkins' extraordinary ignorance of things outside his field of biology.

Where Pell came unstuck was in seeking to defend some of the idiosyncratic beliefs peculiar to the Roman Catholic Church. The cardinal, caged within his denominational institution, gave an expression of the Christian faith that made my toes curl with embarrassment. I was acutely aware that some of my non-Christian friends would be watching, and whenever Pell strayed from consistent, biblical principles, what he said was not credible. It is these non-credible accretions on the gospel that have been pursued by an increasingly scornful media.

The other thing the media have hounded the Catholic Church about, is its handling of cases involving the sexual abuse of children within Catholic institutions. The appalling things that have occurred defy belief. It has been vile, shocking and ruinously destructive of so many lives. It is therefore vitally important that this evil is brought to light. God gave warning that bad behavior in the church will always be judged. The Bible says in 1 Peter 4:17, "the time is come that judgment must begin at the house of God."

In recent years, judgment has come.

My plea to the Catholic Church is this: Please don't be defensive about this sin. Don't minimize it. Don't fail to examine the culture that has allowed such abuse to develop and fester for so long. Take seriously Jesus warning: "If anyone causes one of these little ones – those who believe in me to stumble – it would be better for them to have a large millstone hung around their neck and to be drowned in the depths of the sea" (Matthew 18:6).

If you have detected a plea for the Roman Catholic Church to return to the consistent principles of Scripture when determining their belief and culture, you are right. I believe the Roman Catholic Church has been ill served by the additions of institutional history, which have sought an authority equal to that of Scripture. Whilst its leaders may, on reading this, sigh and reach for well-worn rebuttals formed over the centuries by theologians squirreled away in the Vatican, these theological accretions are wreaking havoc in the real world. Superstition is replacing faith, tradition is replacing biblical principles, and immorality is flourishing. These theological additions have given rise to barely credible theologies and practices within the Catholic institution that have caused the rest of Christendom to cringe with embarrassment.[6] They have given poor witness to the apostolic, biblical witness of Christ and his church.

Some of my finest friends are Catholic. I have worked alongside many of them in a professional capacity and have been proud to do so. I've attended Bible studies in their sitting rooms, shared hilarious lunches with Capuchin monks, participated in weddings with wonderful priests, and rejoiced in the brilliance of my Jesuit friends, savoring their wisdom, compassion – and the occasional whiskey.

I am in awe of the beautiful side of the Roman Catholic heritage. Thank you for your heart for mission. Thank you for providing schools and hospitals when no one else was doing so. Thank you for caring for the poor when most of the rest of the world did not care. The work of Mother Teresa and those like her has been, and is, beautiful.

It is all too beautiful for me not to care.

My heart's cry to the Protestant Church[7]

The lingering death of the church in the West (and in particular, Australia) has largely come about because two inauthentic things have posed as Christianity. The first is the belief that it is religious denominations that define Christianity. This is not so. It is Christ who defines it. Whilst most denominations began because of a sincere attempt to recover authentic Christianity, too many have morphed into bureaucratic organizations riddled with politics and power.

Now, don't get me wrong; there are many lovely Christians in denominational churches, but religious institutions are not the measure of Christianity. At times, they have been severely dysfunctional.

The other thing that has masqueraded as Christianity, is 'liberalism'. Religious liberals have sought to radically revise Christianity, removing its defining features so that it bears little resemblance to the gospel teaching contained in the Bible. In order to do this, they have needed to cut Christianity free from scriptural authority.

Liberal revisionists don't believe Jesus Christ to be the Son of God in anything like the biblical sense. Essentially, they believe in little more than moralism, and the acknowledgment of a vague sense of internal spirituality. This thinking, which has infiltrated the church under the banner of Christianity, is actually a completely new religion.

Its effect on the Protestant Church has been devastating. It has enfeebled the church and caused people to leave. A church which can't decide whether Jesus did, or did not die, for our sins; which can't decide whether Jesus did, or did not, overcome death; which can't decide whether prayer is efficacious, or not; a church which lamely follows the moral lead of secular society – has manifestly lost its prophetic voice to the world, and I might add, any right to respect.

The irony of this is extraordinary. The Protestant church was a movement that came into being as a protest against the spiritual laxity of the Catholic Church. But now it too has become spiritually dead and offers little more than theological confusion and politically correct moralism. John Wesley was terrified that this would happen. In 1786, he wrote:

> *I do not fear that the people called Methodist shall ever cease to exist either in Europe or America. I only fear that they shall exist as a dead sect having the form of religion but not the power thereof, and that undoubtedly will be the case unless they hold fast to the doctrine, discipline and spirit with which they first set out.*[8]

The movement that John Wesley was instrumental in leading began as a renewal movement. It exhibited many of the factors associated with the work of the Holy Spirit, which were to re-emerge with the Charismatic renewal 200 years later. The Methodist revival resulted in a renewed love of Scripture, a renewed zeal for mission to the poor, and a renewed passion for evangelism.[9]

And then in recent decades, the Protestant church took its eyes off the Bible, and off Jesus. As a result, it has now largely lost its passion, and its distinctive Christian flavor. The main reason for this has been the influence of liberal revisionist thinking.

Liberal thinking offers spirituality without the troublesome demands of living according to God-given standards of holiness. It also divests Christianity of all its distinguishing features, so that all that is left is moralism, and tolerance of things hitherto forbidden. Anything supernatural or hope engendering is denied.

Let's explore the issue of miracles a little.

Most Christians understand full well that God usually chooses to work within the laws of nature he has put in place. We don't live with miracles every day. God's presence is often subtle. He chooses to stand behind a veil of mystery so that he can only be approached by faith. In this way, God does not compel our faith by dramatic shows of strength, but invites faith that is voluntarily given. Everyone, whether they are a child, or a brilliant academic, must stoop through the humbling door of faith to reach God.

Sometimes, however, God declares his sovereign authority over the laws of nature he instituted by performing a miracle. These miracles prefigure the reality of God's coming kingdom – which was one of the reasons Jesus performed them.

Miracles, therefore, encourage faith, but are by definition, rare. This does not stop us from asking for God's sovereign power to be manifest in a situation, particularly in a situation where healing is required. Jesus instructed his followers to pray prayers for healing, therefore we should do so (Luke 9:1-2).

God's involvement with humankind in history, particularly when he came to us as Jesus, were occasions when miracles occurred. In a sense, they heralded God's authority and holiness. The miracle of Jesus' resurrection is, of course, particularly significant, as we discussed earlier.

Having a Christian faith that makes no room for miracles is like throwing a wedding banquet and not inviting the bridegroom.

One of the main exponents of liberal theology has been the American Episcopalian John Spong. He scorns the idea of prayer, saying "Prayer cannot be a request made to a theistic deity to act in human history in a particular way."[10] He goes on to say that God has no identity and does not exist in any form in which a relationship can be established. God is merely the source of life, love and meaning, but other than that, he does not engage with us. We must "turn inward to meet God" so that we can have "an expanded transcendent consciousness."[11] Spong says that God has not entered history or the realm of human experience, and so any notion of God entering our world as Jesus Christ must be dismissed. "The Christology of the ages is bankrupt."[12]

Oh dear! There goes 2,000 years of Christian theology.

In my own country, Australia, a progressive stream within the Uniting Church has helped sponsor a number of trips to Australia by John Spong. The schizophrenia this helped to develop in that denomination was extreme. The national president of the Uniting Church at the time tried to hold things together using the mantra: "Unity in diversity." He'd forgotten that the Bible makes it clear that unity is not found in diversity, it is only found 'in' Jesus Christ.

The fact is: it is impossible to put light and darkness in the same place. It is impossible to put two mutually exclusive philosophies together and claim any sort of credibility from a watching world. Light and darkness cannot co-exist.

One of the factors that helped accelerate the decline of the Protestant church in the West has been the tendency for liberal clerics (who have little interest in leading people to faith) to migrate either toward academia or church governance. This has resulted in liberalism being over-represented in theological education and church politics – to the denomination's great misfortune.

Richard Niebuhr, one of the most significant American theologians in the twentieth century, summarized how liberal Christianity both weakens and cheapens the Gospel. He wrote, "It proclaims a God without wrath, who has brought people without sin into a kingdom without judgment, through the ministrations of a Christ without a cross!"[13]

Spong reduces the gospel to a therapeutic invitation to come as you are and stay as you are. There is no need for repentance, no need for obedience to Christ. It proclaims what Dietrich Bonhoeffer called 'cheap grace'. "Cheap grace is the preaching of forgiveness without requiring repentance, baptism without church discipline, communion without confession. Cheap grace is grace without discipleship, grace without the cross, and grace without Jesus Christ, living and incarnate."[14]

David Gushee and Glen Stassen, professors of ethics at Fuller

Seminary, write, "When Jesus' way of discipleship is thinned down, marginalized, or avoided, churches and Christians lose their antibodies against infection by secular ideologies."[15] Sadly, this has proved true. We are seeing the fruits of Proverbs 29:18 come into play. That proverb warns that when godly leaders don't give a clear lead, society casts off restraint and goes into moral free-fall.

This is what happened in the time of the Old Testament prophet, Jeremiah. The Hebrew people had become stubborn and rebellious and had taught themselves to no longer "fear the Lord" (Jeremiah 5:24). Later, in verses 27-28 we learn that economic rationalism, designed to make the rich richer at the expense of the poor, had become rife. All of society, from top to bottom, had become corrupt – even the religious leaders. The prophets, who should have spoken God's word, spoke lies instead – something which God condemned as being "a horrible and shocking thing" (v.30). Similarly, the priests, who were meant to present the authority of God, were presenting their own authority as if it were God's. They had also become greedy for prestige and money, and were deceiving people by telling them that their moral failures were "not serious" (Jeremiah 6:13-14).

God's answer to this was to tell them that they were standing at a crossroads, a place of choice. They needed to make a decision about which way they would go. God urged them to "ask for the ancient paths" (Jeremiah 6:16). In other words, God wanted them to choose the time-honored, traditional values he revealed to their ancestors.

I weep for the once beautiful Protestant church. You used to be so fresh, powerful and committed to Christ. You had reformed yourself on scriptural principles and were on fire. Now you are dying. Whilst there are a few among you who are still faithful, your light has almost gone out, and there is now little left to give anyone direction.

The question is: Are you content to let this be so? Are you content to let this happen on your watch, during your particular period of history? Or will you pray, fast, and network with other faithful Christians to bring about reform?

My heart's cry to the Pentecostal Church

Wow! What a whirlwind. See how much you have grown since the revival in Azusa Street, Los Angeles, in 1906. You started out small and were dismissed, for the most part, by the mainstream denominations as being little more than a cult. Then the worldwide Charismatic renewal swept through every main denomination in the world.

Just as the Reformation returned the church to the Bible, the Charismatic renewal returned the church to an authentic engagement with God. It reignited a love for God and allowed the possibility of God's supernatural action within his church.

The Pentecostal church played a pivotal role in this. Whenever a mainline denominational church did not condone spiritual renewal, you opened your arms and accepted the people it displaced into your churches. The Protestant churches in particular emptied into you. People who were tired of liberalism, spiritual dryness, formalism and irrelevance; people who were hungry for an experience of God, came to you in huge numbers.

Thanks for providing a home for them.

Paradoxically, the monster that now seeks to pollute the Pentecostal Church comes from its very success. What is threatening it now is a distorted theology of prosperity. Like the most dangerous of lies, this idea is nearly correct. But corruption always comes from pushing something too far, so that a good principle is turned into something bad.

In essence, the Pentecostal theological argument for success goes like this: God is active in our midst today and chooses to act in response to the prayers of his people. He does so because he loves us and wants us to thrive. As we center ourselves on God and honor him with worship, our faith rises to a point where we can take hold of God's promises. Then we can pray God's healing on our sicknesses and blessings on our finances, family and ministry.

The theology is so nearly right, but it is nonetheless a distortion of the gospel of Jesus Christ – a distortion that has resulted in a number of unfortunate symptoms.

The first is that success is seen as the result of God's blessing, which has come about as a result being faithful. 'Big' is therefore seen as a symptom of faithfulness. This has resulted in what some of my Pentecostal pastor friends call: 'dog sniffing'. When two dogs meet, they circle around each other, trying to sniff each other's bottoms in order to determine their identity and importance. The same happens in a Pentecostal setting. When two Pentecostal pastors meet, they will ask: "How big is your church?" In other words, they want to know whether the other person is someone worth meeting and has more spiritual stature than them.

This culture is encouraged by the practice of ushering senior pastors to front row seats, inviting them to special lounges reserved for the elite, and putting them up in luxury hotels. To be spiritual is to be successful and big. To be big is to be guaranteed respect and the right to speak at conferences.

Now, please don't get me wrong. I love effective, faithful leaders, many of whom are worth listening to. They are usually inspirational and charismatic – after all, that's what makes them successful. But 'big' isn't the only definition of Christian success.

Success is being able to sit on an ash-heap while dressed in sackcloth, refusing to curse God, even though you are covered in sores and have lost everything (Job). Success can look like a man dying on a cross – Jesus (John 19:30). Success can include being shipwrecked, beaten, abused, maligned, deserted, and executed, e.g. the apostle Paul (2 Corinthians 11:23-30; 2 Timothy 1:15). Success can look like being fed to the lions, or staying faithful even when you are raped, crucified, or in any other way persecuted for your faith (Hebrews 11:32-40).

Without losing its emphasis on the importance of faith, the Pentecostal church needs to find a more adequate doctrine of suffering, a more adequate doctrine of healing, and a more adequate doctrine of success. The insidious nature of the prosperity doctrine, which has taken root amongst the Pentecostal church, is exacting a terrible toll.

It has given rise to a celebrity cult. This has forced leaders of big churches to run ever faster on the treadmill of excellence and busyness, fueled by an addiction to expansion. Some of this expansion can be more parasitic than godly. One megachurch in Queensland, Australia, sought to plant satellite campuses in other areas by taking over some small churches around it. When one of these churches did not want to be taken over, the megachurch stole its name and planted another church right beside it. The megachurch then poured its considerable resources into the new church, so that the original church was killed off.

I hope you find this as troubling as I do. I don't see Jesus' passion for love and unity in that sort of behavior. I see an addiction to bigness masquerading as a desire to further the gospel. It looks dangerously like building one's own kingdom rather than God's kingdom.

Another symptom of an addiction to bigness is the faking of a spiritual 'wow' factor.

The fact is, people will turn up to church if God is seen to show up. This is usually evidenced by miracles of healing. This exerts huge pressure on churches to be seen to 'perform' spiritually. At its worst, this results in sensationalist healing meetings, some of which are aired on TV. An investigation into all the healings conducted by one TV evangelist revealed that not one of the healings claimed on the show could actually be substantiated. Not one!

This sort of phenomenon has given rise to the term 'evangelastics'. Evangelastics is when someone stretches the truth for the sake of the gospel.

Please don't do this. If you do, Christianity will be scorned and lose credibility – and so will you.

Curiously, a doctrine of prosperity can also result in a lack of spiritual engagement with God. It works like this: When a church gets big, it quite properly becomes committed to excellence and expands its ministries and mission. Competent leaders are appointed, and a huge army of volunteers is mobilized. However, this means it can be very easy for reliance on God's supernatural provision to fall away. After all, you already have the finances and leaders necessary to do everything you want. Who needs the Holy Spirit when you have everything under your own control?

An addiction to bigness often starts a busyness treadmill that burns people out. The casualty list can be huge. Church leaders are required to motivate people to do more and more, and give more and more, so that the church can get bigger. Eventually, the church can become a monster, not a blessing.

I love worshiping with Pentecostals. I love it when someone provides an environment within which I can be real and express my love for God. However, I am troubled when people speak about needing to worship in order to cause "faith to rise," an essential prerequisite if God is to operate supernaturally amongst them.

Whilst God usually chooses to work amongst people who have faith, working to cause faith to rise through music, singing and emotion can easily morph into manipulation. It can too easily become a necessary act we are required to do to 'switch God on'. In other words, it can become a means by which we seek to control God.

People have been trying to control God since the dawn of time. It's our oldest heresy.

The idea of 'calling God down from heaven' through praise and worship also presents a theological problem. The Bible teaches that God is everywhere fully present. As such, he doesn't need to be called down from heaven – ever. Rather, encountering God is a matter of focusing on him so that we become aligned with him who is always fully present. Singing in order to manipulate God is invalid. However, worship that helps us center on God and celebrate God is perfectly legitimate.

A CEO (Chief Executive Officer) is <u>not</u> one of the five-fold ministries listed in the Bible as being essential for training people to be fully functioning disciples of Christ (Ephesians 4:11-13). I say this because the actions of some senior pastors can suggest that it is. Certainly, Senior Pastors can look very much like CEOs. Any pastor organizing a team to help grow the church can't help but do so. However, a pastor is so much more. Pastors pray, love, shepherd, preach and model Christ's lifestyle.

Pentecostal churches sometimes label those responsible for large organizations 'apostles'. This can have the effect of spiritualizing CEO behavior. I've seen the title 'Apostle' written on business cards. So, for the sake of biblical integrity, it may be helpful to remind us what an apostle actually is.

The word 'apostle' comes from the Greek word, *apostolos*, which means 'sent one.' Apostles are those sent to speak about Jesus, who has made God's kingdom available to everyone. Essentially, they are missionaries. They are those who plant churches (either overseas or in their own nation).

According to the Bible, there are only two qualifications required for being an apostle. The first is that an apostle must be called by God (Romans 1:1; 1 Corinthians 1:1). The second is that an apostle must to be so familiar with Jesus' life and teaching, that he or she imitates it, embodies it, and reflects it in his or her words and deeds (Acts 1:21-25).

That's it. Being an apostle has nothing to do with having political influence with governments, building a megachurch, or being a CEO with a large salary. Leaders of the church are called to model the servant-heart of Jesus.

> *Jesus called them together and said, "You know that those who are regarded as rulers of the Gentiles lord it over them, and their high officials exercise authority over them. Not so with you. Instead, whoever wants to become great among you must be your servant, and whoever wants to be first must be slave of all. For even the Son of Man did not come to be served, but to serve, and to give his life as a ransom for many."* (Mark 10:42-45)

I can't help but contrast Jesus' attitude to the following experiences:

I was once sent a free gift of a book and DVD from a pastor of a Pentecostal megachurch in the United States. Evidently, he'd sent the same gift to hundreds of pastors in Australia. The DVD was a long advert explaining why I should donate money to him so that he could buy a one-third share in a luxury private jet.

I threw the book and DVD in the bin.

A friend who is a pastor of a vibrant church once told me how he'd had to write to a well known overseas pastor who had volunteered his services, and explain why he wouldn't be needing them. He would not be supplying the prescribed make of luxury car for him to drive during his visit. Nor would he pay the umpteen thousand dollars required for his mission costs, or guarantee the visiting pastor a certain grade of luxury in a hotel.

On another occasion, I listened uneasily as a senior pastor of a Pentecostal megachurch boasted that neither he nor any of his family had ever flown economy class in their life.

Whilst I fully appreciate the need for exhausted pastors on international mission to be comfortable and cared for, I can't help but think that a boundary has been crossed here. I'm forced to ask whether this culture of excess is what the widow's mite, given so faithfully and sacrificially, is meant to support? Does this sort of behavior faithfully represent the humble, servant heart of Jesus? Is it good for the gospel?

Personally, I think it is exactly this sort of abusive behavior that the Apostle Paul railed against in his letters to the church in Corinth. Paul needed to expose the exploitative behavior of supposed "super-apostles" who were demanding extravagant payments and provisions (2 Corinthians 11:5-15). In contrast to them, Paul simply showed the compassion of a father's heart (1 Corinthians 4:11-16). And so must we.

I've noticed that when the media ridicule Pentecostalism, they attack two things in particular. The first is their prosperity doctrine – which we've already talked about. The second is its barely credible belief about science.

Pentecostalism's antagonistic stance against conventional science can be hugely damaging to Christianity.

Christians have no right to put obstacles in front of those coming to faith by requiring them to believe ridiculous things. Exaggerated claims have been publicized by some Christian organizations aimed at discrediting the evolutionary theory. Sadly, these are almost always distortions of scientific truth as we currently know it. Such writings have helped generate a self-fueling sub-culture amongst Christians that promote views not held to be credible by most scientists.

In reality, the theory of evolution is remarkably well supported by scientific fact. It has earned so much credibility that almost all scientists operate on the basis of it. This means that if you allow scientific truth to be ridiculed in your church (in the mistaken belief that you are protecting biblical authority) you will be scorned by society. Worse, you may earn God's displeasure for putting obstacles in front of thinking people who want to believe in Jesus.

I have some sympathy for pastors, because, for many of them, science is outside their field of expertise. This makes them wide open to the influence of noisy minority groups holding views on science which are not credible – which they promote in the name of protecting biblical authority.

Here's an elemental truth: All truth, whether scientific or theological, has its origin in God. So, don't set scientific truth against theological truth. Just don't. It is wrong, and it is damaging. Have the courage to go for truth – all truth.

Here's a question I want to put to the Pentecostal church: How do you want the Pentecostal movement to die?

Let me explain:

Every organization carries within it the seeds of its own destruction. Every organization normally completes a cycle of birth, maturity, corruption and death.

My question to the Pentecostal church is: How much do you want to control and manage this cycle?

I would urge caution before you protest that Pentecostalism will never die. Whilst Jesus promised that his church would never cease to exist, no such assurance is given to denominational institutions. The Pentecostal church in the third century AD had its equivalent in the Montanists. Although Montanism began as a Christian sect, it eventually spiraled away from apostolic and biblical truth until it was declared heretical. The movement petered out early in the sixth century.

All Christian movements have a lifecycle.

The church of Jesus Christ was born at Pentecost when God

caused his Holy Spirit to indwell people to empower their ministry. As a result, a vibrant church was born that was soon engaging in mission and in preserving the words of Christ in Scripture. Then, sadly, the church became institutionalized. It took its eyes off Jesus and wandered off from biblical principles.[16]

The church was protested against when Holy Spirit renewal broke out during the Reformation, and the Protestant church was born.[17] This returned the church to a love of Scripture, a love of Jesus, and a love of mission. But then it too became institutionalized and lost its edge. New revivals and renewal movements (including the Methodist movement led by John Wesley) protested against the institutional church, and reignited a love of Jesus, a love of Scripture, and a love of mission.

But the Methodist church has since had its edge blunted by liberalism, formalism and institutional folly. It too was subject to a protest movement when the Holy Spirit gave birth to the Pentecostal church and brought about the charismatic renewal.

So, now it's your time. What will be your story?

The date of your death and the manner of your death are entirely in your hands. May I encourage you to write large on history's page. But this will only be possible if you stay faithful to Scripture, and foster a love of Jesus – because that's where the Holy Spirit never fails to return the church every time he brings renewal.

Part 2) Is God bad?

Part 2 is a consideration of a conviction that is deeply shocking to all Christians: the conviction that God is bad.

Richard Dawkins describes the God of the Old Testament in this way:

> *The God of the Old Testament is arguably the most unpleasant character in all fiction: jealous and proud of it; a petty, unjust, unforgiving control-freak; a vindictive, bloodthirsty ethnic cleanser; a misogynistic, homophobic, racist, infanticidal, genocidal, filicidal, pestilential, megalomaniacal, sadomasochist.*"[18]

Those making this sort of accusation usually point to two particular events in the Old Testament to support their accusation. The first is God's instruction to Abraham to sacrifice his son Isaac (Genesis 22:1-18). The second is God's instruction to his people to kill off all the Amalekites – to "spare them no mercy" (1 Samuel 15:3).

So let's have a look at both stories, for they have proved to be very much at odds with the rest of Scripture that makes a big feature of God's love.

The destruction of the Amalekites

In January 2004, *The Advertiser* reported that a Hindu priest from the state of Orissa in India had gone to prison for chopping the head off an eight year old boy as a placatory offering to a god.[19] Sadly, killing children in order to win the favor of a god has been a nasty habit of humankind for a long time.

The famous Paris museum, the Louvre, contains a dark Moabite Stone from the ninth century BC. On it is inscribed the record of how King Mesha of Moab rebelled against his nation's Israelite overlords and drove them out of Moab. However, what the inscription does not say is that the king of the Moabites sacrificed his oldest son to the Moabite god, Chemoth, in order to recruit the god's help in securing victory over the Israelites. The account of him doing so is told in 2 Kings 3:26-27.

Another very nasty god was Moloch. Moloch was the Assyrian and Canaanite god of fire. Jewish accounts say that the statue of Moloch was made of brass, and that children were placed in his arms, or in compartments within the idol, and burned alive as an offering.

Moloch was worshiped as early as the third millennium BC, so the practice of burning children was occurring at the time of Moses. However, most references to Moloch come from a later period of Jewish history.

The Bible reports that Solomon reintroduced the worship of Moloch at Topheth in the valley of Hinnom that bordered the southern edge of the city of Jerusalem (Jeremiah 7:7-31; 1 Kings

11:7; 2 Kings 23:10). He did so in order to accommodate the wishes of his many foreign wives. It was an abhorrence that God could not ignore, and God's judgment on Topheth is spelled out in Jeremiah 19:6-7.

Tragically, he was not the only king to allow this terrible practice. Two kings of Judah, Ahaz and Manasseh, also sacrificed their sons to Moloch (2 Kings 16:3; 2 Kings 21:6). Their "detestable" actions were never going to be unchallenged by God, as we will see later.

However, one nation particularly made a practice of sacrificing children to their gods, and that was the nation of the Amalekites. God found their actions particularly offensive. The events recorded in the Bible show that whenever a nation allowed the obscenity of sacrificing children to false gods, God *always* ensured there was a consequence. This usually came in the form of invasion by a foreign nation.

It is significant that the Amalekites were descended from Amalek, the grandson of Esau – a man who broke covenant with God by spurning his birthright. It is also significant that the murderous Haman who tried to exterminate all Jews (as recorded in the Book of Esther) was an Amalekite. He is described as "the Agagite," i.e. descended from the agags – the Amalekite kings (1 Samuel 15:7-8). The Amalekites were the Jews' implacable enemy. They consistently sought the annihilation of the Jews (Exodus 17:8-14; Numbers 14:41-45; Judges 3:12-14; Judges 6:3,33-35).

It was the Amalekites' implacable stance against the Jews, coupled with their practice of sacrificing children to false gods (Deuteronomy 12:31) that resulted in God condemning them to total annihilation. He warned the Kenites who lived amongst the Amalekites to come out from them lest they also be destroyed (1 Samuel 15:6).

Although Solomon was, at one time, the wisest person of his generation, he lost his wisdom when he married foreign wives who turned his heart away from God. As we said earlier, Solomon began to set up altars to false gods, including Chemoth and Moloch – both of whom required child sacrifices (1 Kings 11:4-7). Solomon's act of rebellion resulted in the Jewish nation being divided into two nations that often fought each other (1 Kings 11:29-33). God could never be indifferent about such a terrible thing. He never failed to bring consequences to the foreign nations around Israel and Judah for worshiping these gods, e.g. that nation of Moab (Jeremiah 48:46), so he was certainly not going to allow his own people to get away with it.

The Old Testament records how King Josiah of Judah rediscovered the scriptures, and used them to return his people back to the worship of the one true God. One of the first things he did was to destroy the idols of false gods (2 Kings 23:13).

Sadly, God's people did not remain faithful, and as a consequence, suffered God's judgment – deportation and captivity. When God's people eventually returned from captivity, Ezra the priest and Nehemiah the governor, insisted that the Jewish people separate themselves from their foreign wives (as foreign wives had led Solomon and the Jewish nation astray: see Nehemiah 13:23-26).

The Old Testament makes it clear that God has an implacable hatred of people sacrificing children to false gods. It was this practice that caused God to show them "no mercy."

Abraham and Isaac

Many people find the story of Abraham and Isaac deeply disturbing. It is a story in which God asks Abraham to sacrifice his own son in an act of worship. This prompts the question: Does God require the sacrifice of children? So, what can we say?

God loves people who totally commit to him, who withhold nothing, and honor him with everything. And yet, as we have seen, God hates the killing of innocent people – particularly children. So when God tells Abraham to sacrifice his son Isaac, God is making it clear that God loves devotion to him that is *total*. However, by preventing Abraham from sacrificing his son, God made it clear that he was not the sort of God who required the sacrifice of children.

In fact, The Old Testament makes it clear that God considers the sacrifice of children a "detestable" practice – a practice which he did not "command or mention, nor did it enter my mind" (Jeremiah 19:5; 7:31). God says specifically to his people, "Let no one be found among you who sacrifices his son or daughter in the fire" (Deuteronomy 18:10).

The term "detestable things" is used in the Old Testament in relation to the worship of false gods (Deuteronomy 20:16-18; Jeremiah 16:17-18). But it was particularly used to describe the practice of sacrificing children to false gods (2 Chronicles 28:1-4; 33:1-6). This behavior was practiced by the nations the Jews dispossessed and slaughtered when they invaded Canaan (Deuteronomy 12:29-31; Psalm 106:34-43). God couldn't allow their actions to remain unchallenged.

We have learned when faced with a difficult theological question, to define the issues relating to that will help us understand the answer. So, let's do another octagon.

The question we want the answer to is: How do we makes sense of God's violence in the Old Testament?

The following eight truths are the boundaries within which the answer will be found:

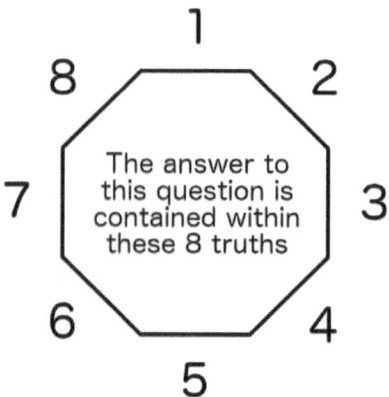

1. God is loving (1 John 4:8). He is the final definition of love
2. God is just (2 Thessalonians 1:6). He is the final definition of what is just (Job 40:2,8).

3. God is holy. He has a zero tolerance for evil. God will kill it off. The sobering reality is that there is a sense in which we all deserve death (Romans 6:23).
4. The nations displaced by the Jews when they invaded Canaan had engaged in "detestable things" when worshipping their false gods (Deuteronomy 20:16-18). This particularly included the sacrifice of children (2 Chronicles 28:3).
5. God commanded the Jews to offer the option of peace to any people-group living in Canaan if they were not a threat to God's people, and if they were willing to serve the Jews (Deuteronomy 20:10-11).
6. Jesus is the perfect picture of God. He completes and perfects our understanding of him and is therefore the true and authoritative representation of God's character.
7. This present life is not all there is. Nor is it of central importance when viewed from the perspective of God's eternity (Matthew 6:19-21). No 'good' person, of any nationality, will fail to receive his or her reward in eternity (Matthew 25:31-46).
8. God allows us to represent a little of his authority in commissioning us to bring order to what is unruly in his creation (Genesis 1:28; 2:15).

The answer to our question lies within these truths.
Let's now turn to the New Testament.

Is God guilty of infanticide?
The militant atheist, Richard Dawkins, has said on a number of occasions that any God who could cause his son to die a horrible death to pay the price for the sins of humankind, is nasty and vindictive!

What do you think about that?

In order for Dawkins to say such a thing, he needs to have a theological understanding that is both paper-thin and willfully distorted.

The reality is: God was not driven by vindictiveness to force someone else to die in order to appease his anger at sin. No; quite the reverse. God *himself* chose to die. He *himself* took the blame. He took on himself the penalty for our evil, which was death, and died on a cross. Quite simply, his was the greatest act of selfless love in history.

Now here's the important bit (and one that I have mentioned in an earlier chapter): *All* of God paid the price for our sins. Jesus made it plain that he and the Father were one (John 10:30). This point was made in William Young's book, *The Shack*, in which the book's hero accuses God the Father of callousness in asking Jesus to die for our sins. God the Father's reply was simply to show his accuser his hands...that had the same crucifixion scars as his Son.

My speech to Richard Dawkins:

Let me finish with a rave:

Richard Dawkins; don't you dare, in your arrogance and ignorance, call the greatest act of sacrificial love in history "vile" or "vindictive." The very violence you accuse God of is the very violence that he is protecting you from.

I want to ask you, Professor Dawkins: What was the alternative to God not killing off the sins of humanity in himself? Do you seriously want rape, abuse, injustice, untruth, cruelty and selfishness to continue forever – unresolved and unchallenged?

Let me help you with the answer: If a good God exists, that cannot be allowed. And because a good God does exist, it is not allowed.

Please don't trivialize God's love. God's love is powerful, perfect and persistent. A fair description of it is given in the Old Testament book, The Song of Songs. This is what it says:

> *Place me like a seal over your heart,*
> *like a seal on your arm;*
> *for love is as strong as death,*

> *its jealousy unyielding as the grave.*
> *It burns like blazing fire,*
> *like a mighty flame.* (Songs of Songs 8:6)

That's what God's love for you is like. He wants you to place him over your heart, because his love for you is strong as death. It is unflinching, and it burns like a blazing fire. That's the nature of God's love for you. And that's the love you are impugning.

God's love for you and me was such that he could not allow our evil to keep us from him. But neither could he turn a blind eye to it. Why? Because God is holy. As such, he can't ignore sin. God therefore chose to die in our place to kill off our sin that would otherwise keep us from him. Why? Because that's what perfect love does.

God died. He didn't force anyone else to die because of our sins. He was motivated by love to die in our place.

So, Richard Dawkins: don't turn the greatest act of love in history into an evil thing, and throw God's grace back into his face. To do that would be a terrible injustice and a terrible evil. In saying what you have, I fear you are standing in a very dangerous place.

My prayer for you, dear reader, is that you are standing in a better place.

10

Sex, the Bible, and Me

Many young adults find the church's teaching on sexuality negative, judgmental, or irrelevant. I'm sorry about that. Let's see if we can say something more useful.

As I look round the university scene, I see a lot of people who are conflicted because they feel let down by the realities of the 'hook-up' culture. The fun, fun, fun loving thing hasn't delivered. Woman particularly can end up with a loss of self-esteem, anxiety, depression, and sometimes post-traumatic stress if they have been victimized. They can feel that something of their essence has been violated or trivialized – but they may not always be able to put this into words.

So, what do you do when you're at a party at which people are hooking up? (Big hint here: Don't put yourself in situations where things are likely to head that way.) Here's a radical answer: Imagine what Jesus would be doing and saying if he were with you. Remember, he was the one who said: "I have come that you might have life, and have it abundantly" (John 10:10). So he is all about fullness of life, not denying life. So: whatever you picture Jesus doing, do the same.

Jesus knew who he was, and why he was. In the same way, he

invites you to know yourself, your sacredness, your destiny, and to know the person God calls you to be, i.e. the best and most fulfilled 'you' possible.

Godly sex is not about 'using' people, or allowing yourself to be used. A word of caution here: Men's brains are hard-wired to go after sex as often as possible. That is the reality women have to navigate, and men have to manage.

Women generally look for emotional commitment or security before they have sex – although this is becoming less true these days. Men, however, are visually driven. This makes them sitting ducks when it comes to pornography – and that's a tough fight most men have to win. Women know this, at least instinctively, so it's something worth bearing in mind when you go shopping. In a very real sense, when you shop, you are buying the identity you want to advertise. If you advertise a particular identity, please don't be surprised if people interpret it correctly and behave accordingly toward you. By all means, look fabulous, but go steady on the sexually provocative stuff. Keep that for your spouse.

God has a great plan for sex, and he should know, because he invented it. "Tonight we will fake love…" is a paltry, pathetic shadow of a beautiful reality that God wants to reserve for you.

The excuse, 'everybody's doing it' didn't work out so well for lemmings – so take the hint. Your self-esteem is never going to be improved by someone who just wants to use you for sex. So, embody Jesus' way of living – in particular, the way he was so comfortable living within his own skin.

Peer pressure

It's worth dwelling for a moment on the subject of peer pressure. It is a significant factor that determines the thinking and behavior of people today. This pressure to conform has been exacerbated in recent decades by social media. The pressure to 'toe the party line', is now both relentless and intense. And the consequences of not conforming (of being anything other than 'average') can result in you being attacked in a feeding frenzy of ridicule by those who hide behind the anonymity of a silicon chip as they tap away on a keyboard. It can be deeply wounding. This is because we are herd animals. We derive our identity and significance in relation to others.

So, do choose carefully whom you socialize with, and whom you choose to be influenced by. Choose those who model the character you want to have.

Some profound questions lie at the heart of issues concerning sexuality. They are: Who are you? What does it mean to be made in the image of God? Whose are you, and what is the destiny you hope for?

Let me give a word of caution about herd (or tribal) thinking.

Every vile abuse committed by humankind – all the concentration camps, all the moral decadence, all the gulags and killing fields – were technically legal according to the laws of the land that existed at the time. Conformity to herd thinking allowed it to happen. So be careful with conforming to society's norms.

Feeling good about yourself

How are you going so far, reading this? I hope you are feeling okay and are not beating up on yourself. Let me give you a gentle, politically correct, virtual, hug.

Promiscuity by people who are also trying to live as Christians usually polarizes them in one of two directions. Both are pretty horrible. People either trivialize their behavior and claim that hedonism (living for pleasure) is good. But, after the tingling of the nerve endings has finished, they can, when cold reality dawns, not feel very good at all.

The other extreme is to feel massive debilitating guilt, guilt that stops them seeking intimacy with God in prayer. This, of course, begins a spiral dive away from God's presence, which can lead to loss of faith…and loss of destiny.

But what happens if you mess up?

Talk to Jesus about your feelings and ask for his love, assurance and wisdom. Please promise me: Don't ignore him. This is the time when you need to know his love the most. Jesus had huge compassion on women who had messed up (Luke 7:36-50; John 4:3-26; 8:1-11). And there's no reason to believe the same isn't also true for men.

Here's a hint to prevent 'stinking thinking' that will sabotage your inner wellbeing: *Don't compartmentalize!* In other words, don't have your Christian life in one pigeonhole, and your sexual life in another. You'll end up schizophrenic. The reality is, you can't serve two masters. (Jesus said this when he talked about being careful not to love money more than God, see: Matthew 6:24.)

Poor self-esteem and guilt can lead to people self-medicating on booze, drugs or chocolate. Sadly, it only adds to the problem because the root cause has not been addressed. To truly address it, you will need to chat to the one who loves you the most – God.

Some feel so inadequate that they need alcohol to embolden themselves before they go to a party. Whoops! You will be presenting an artificial 'you' to others, and your moral defenses will be down, making you vulnerable to being used (sexually victimized). You are also likely to do something you'll regret.

I'm not moralizing, honest. This is reality. I want the best for you.

If there is a hook-up culture that your community expects you to participate in, you have a decision to make. You can either go along with it because you don't have the self-confidence to stand against it, or you can take seriously the boasts you made earlier in life when you said that no one would ever force you to conform, and that you would go your own way. Sure, it's a mantra that can have selfish, egoistic overtones, but in this instance, it can prove helpful. Will you be conformed, or won't you? Will you be the person you want to be, or will you let others persuade you to be like them. Who will win?

If you are going to win, you will need to get your roots deep down into Jesus and hang out with a Christian community that will help you be the person you want to be.

It's worth remembering one other thing. It is this: God gets angry when he sees abuse, victimization and bullying. His one solution to sin (for that is what it is) is extreme: he kills it off (or will kill it off). He won't allow any of it into his eternal kingdom. You, however, have been reserved for his kingdom before time began, so do all you can to realize your intended destiny.

Have I told you that God keeps on forgiving? It's true. As long as the prayer of repentance is sincere, God will always forgive (Matthew 18:21-22; 1 John 1:9). So, always seek his face. Promise me that.

There is very little that is harder to manage than your sexuality, so manage it well.

I've said enough.

If you want to know more, read on…but a warning: things necessarily get a bit explicit and gritty.

A Bible study on sex

The sex drive is God's gift to us, and it is a beautiful one. It's worth beginning our study with this fact, as you can get the impression that sex was invented by the rock industry. As sex was God's idea, it would be very wise to discover how he intended it to be used. I say this because the gift of sex is, as I've said, the hardest gift you will ever be given to control.

The sex drive has many components. It is a primal urge to continue our genetic identity – a grope for eternity. The sex drive is also driven by our hormones, which beckon us to fulfill the function for which our sex organs have been designed. Psychologically, the sex act also expresses the reality (or illusion) that your sex partner considers you to be significant – worthy enough to be let into their most private and precious place. In other words, it meets that most basic need we all have of feeling honored, appreciated and significant.

However, sex only reaches its most sublime expression in the context of love that is committed, consistent and authentic. Sex in this context will cement and grow both intimacy and joy in a relationship.

God's idea of sex is therefore a lot more than using someone else's body to masturbate in. He intends it to be a great deal more than a mechanical act. Unless there is a loving, committed, mutually honoring quality to it, it will be a pale reflection of what God intends the gift of sex to be.

People have sex for a variety of reasons. At its worst it can be the expression of a neurotic need for control. Only marginally better – it can be motivated by a need for self-gratification – a need that has little regard for what is best for the sexual partner. This violation of the intrinsic worth of someone usually results in the partner developing a poor self-esteem and an unconscious self-contempt. This can end up expressing itself in them living a self-destructive lifestyle.

It is also a truism that you cannot abuse another without abusing yourself.

What makes great sex?

Three things contribute to great sex.

The first is visual stimulation. Males particularly are visually driven. There should be a visual sexual delight in seeing each other's bodies.

The second is physical stimulation (stroking, caressing and intercourse). Talk to each other about what works best for you.

The third is emotional stimulation. This comes from knowing your partner loves you, knowing your partner thinks you are worthy, and knowing that you are giving your partner pleasure.

No sex is ever perfect, but if you get these three things mostly right, you will have a healthy and fulfilling sex life.

When sex doesn't work well, don't despair. Talk together about the reasons and decide what you will do to improve things. Laugh at your mistakes, keep the joy, and keep communicating.

Let me also add that a good sex life does not spring from a vacuum. Good sex results from good romance. Women particularly need time for intimacy and romance before sex. Therefore, take time to be tender and time to talk.

. . .

Frequency of sex

There are two extremes to avoid. The first is being over-demanding with sex. The second is not being generous in giving sex. Let love guide you into what is best. Lacking generosity in sex and repeatedly denying sex is dangerous. If this is prolonged over a long period of time (without good reason), you risk ceasing to be an object of sexual desire to your spouse – and that can lead to mental, if not physical, infidelity. So, don't be someone who routinely criticizes or complains when it comes to sex. Both criticism and complaint are deadly to a good sex life...and will kill off intimacy.

All sex comes in the context of everything else that has happened during a day. Here's the crucial point: Never use sex as a prize for your partner's good behavior; or withhold it for bad behavior. Obviously, there are limits to this, but do what you can to keep sex out of the fight. Why? Because good sex helps reset and reestablish emotional intimacy.

Your body

Your body is "good," so don't be ashamed of it (Genesis 1:27,31). Note: modesty should not be confused with shame. Think of your body as a temple in which God lives by his Spirit (1 Corinthians 3:16; 2 Corinthians 6:16; Ephesians 2:22). The Bible encourages us to give our body as a living sacrifice to God (Romans 12:1-2).

It's worth pondering for a moment on what that means.

One of the things it means is that you should, as I've already said, give some thought to what you wear. In other words: dress to be beautiful, but avoid being too sexually provocative.[1]

When people go shopping, they are, in a very real sense, buying their identity. They want their clothes to make them feel a particular way and to advertise a 'look'. It is therefore perverse to buy a look and then object when people recognize it. The reality is, visual clues begin a conversation in the mind. This, let me hasten to say, is *never* an excuse for anyone to take sexual liberties. Clothes do not give permission... but they can give people ideas.

It should be said very clearly, however, that it is neither possible nor desirable for women to hide their sexuality completely by how they dress.

Paul's first letter to Timothy gives some good clues on how to dress. He suggests: modestly, rather than immodesty; decently, rather than indecently; and appropriately, rather than inappropriately (1 Timothy 2:9-10).

When Adam and Eve sinned and became sexually intoxicated with each other, God knew that trying to cover themselves with a few fig leaves was never going to do the job. That's why he improved their wardrobe by giving them clothes of animal skins (Genesis 3:6-7,21). So, learn the lesson. Don't buy fig leaves!

Note what the Bible calls true beauty:

> *Your beauty should not come from outward adornment, such as braided hair and the wearing of gold jewelry and fine clothes. Instead, it should be that of your inner self, the unfading beauty of a gentle quiet spirit* (1 Peter 3:3-4).

Be wise

The Bible says that we are to "flee" from the idea of immorality. In other words don't put yourself in situations where there is great pressure to sin (1 Corinthians 6:18). Be wise (Proverbs 2:12-18). Like a quarrel, once you start, it is difficult to stop (Proverbs 17:14; 26:11; 27:12).

This prompts the question: What level of 'petting' do you think is appropriate before marriage?

It's not an easy question.

Whatever else: avoid being a sucker for seduction (2 Peter 2:18-19; James 1:14-15). Be careful. The hormonal make-up of men means that certain stimuli will invariably produce sexual arousal. Some researchers also claim that the hormone-amended brain of males makes them less inclined to monogamy than females. This does not excuse bad male sexual behavior but it does suggest that men have to be particularly careful.[2]

Sexuality is a potent thing. It can be wonderful, or it can be demeaning, abusive and something that is not at all special. The challenge of 1 Thessalonians 4:3-7 is for us to develop the maturity to control our sexuality, so that it does not become a tyrant that sabotages healthy relationships.

Note: 'control' does not mean suppression or denial of one's identity. It means being who you were *meant* to be.

Finally, be stable. Know who you are and understand your sacredness to God. It is often the unstable who are most easily seduced (2 Peter 2:14).

In everything, know God's love and forgiveness

The sex drive is a powerful force, and we all make mistakes. Fortunately, God's love is such that he promises to forgive us when we come to him in repentance. God always offers us a fresh start. In everything, know God's love and forgiveness.

Sexual immorality

The Bible often links immorality with a deliberate choice to disobey God (Romans 1:18-32). But is this always the case? What about unmarried couples who have sex, and claim to be passionately in love? Isn't that beautiful?

The Bible teaches that not all loves are the best loves God wants for us. The intense heady and passionate love that can occur, particularly between adolescents, is still not of the quality to allow sexual intercourse in God's best plan for us. God ideally wants to reserve sexual intercourse for a love that is as passionate, but which also has been tested, and which commits for life.

There are a number of myths about life that have been promoted by the media. Here are some of them:

You'll be happy if you get whatever you want.
It's not true.
Any sexual activity between consenting adults is okay.

It is not. Sex that is demeaning or exploitative, which is not expressive of love and commitment, is destructive.

You can have it all.

You can't, and it wouldn't be good for you if you could.

You shouldn't have to wait for anything.

The culture of our time insists on instant gratification. In reality, this is gross immaturity. It is something two-year-olds insist on, not adults.

There is never any reason to feel guilty.

Sometimes guilt is healthy and points to something in our life that needs healing.

The Bible advises us not to be misled.

> *Don't always believe everything you hear ...for there are many false teachers around* (1 John 4:1).

> *See to it that no one takes you captive through hollow and deceptive philosophy, which depends on human tradition and the basic principles of this world rather than on Christ* (Colossians 2.8)

God calls us to be holy, i.e. a people without any hint of immorality. "But among you there must not be even a hint of sexual immorality, or of any kind of impurity, or of greed, because these are improper for God's holy people" (Ephesians 5:3). God doesn't say this to spoil our fun; God says it because immorality will spoil us.

Having unprotected sex with someone who is not your faithful, life-long spouse makes about as much sense as playing Russian roulette. Keep sex for marriage. Condoms are good but they are not always safe.

Incidentally, the human male's seminal fluid contains a special molecule (TGF-beta) that teaches the female immune system over time not to reject the male DNA, and so allow conception. This means that sexual faithfulness to one partner assists conception.

Immorality can be appealing, but it always has consequences

(Proverbs 5:3-6; 6:23-35). If love doesn't have moral boundaries (so that it reserves sexual intimacy for your spouse) then your love for your spouse is not special, and you are just a self-obsessed hedonist.

Here are some more truisms:

Love without commitment is not love; it is selfishness.

Romance without commitment is not romance; it is seduction. If you are not committed, you don't love – you are just faking love. When love does not honor its commitments, it is simply temporary emotionalism. Real love prefers, sacrifices, protects, and is loyal. If it is something partial, provisional, and non-committed, then it is not true love.

Atheism's not-so-good track record

Let me tell you the story of atheism's leading philosophers.

Jean-Paul Sartre once had four mistresses. He negotiated with his printer to have different names appearing in a quarter of one of his book's print runs, so that each mistress would think that they were the only one to whom the book was dedicated.

Bertrand Russell was infamously serially unfaithful to his four wives.

Friedrich Nietzsche died early, probably of syphilis as the result of going to brothels.

Perhaps these sad tales should not surprise us. The atheistic Enlightenment philosopher, David Hume, (1711-1776), said that: "reason is, and ought only to be, the slave of the passions."[3]

Oh dear!

Whatever else this teaches, factor in a person's world-view when choosing a life partner. Do they value fidelity, and do they have a foundation strong enough to live it out (2 Corinthians 6:14)?

It is a reality that the best predictor of promiscuity *in* marriage is promiscuity *before* marriage.

So please choose your life partner well. If you agree to have a partner who is not a Christian, he or she will not understand you at the deepest level of your soul, and will expect you to go along with society's promiscuous norm. Yes, I know she's/he's gorgeous, but guard your heart. You *are* able to choose. And God has given you the brains to look beyond things that are skin deep. Don't team up with someone who cannot share your values, your soul, your spiritual journey, and your intended destiny. Do yourself a favor!

'Try before you buy' (sex before marriage)

Some people are living together first to see if they are compatible before they get married. The problem with this is that the very thing that makes marriage work, i.e. commitment, is not there. There is therefore not the same incentive to make things work. This is poor training for marriage and probably explains why *Cleo* magazine (not usually the greatest source to go to for learning!) reports that living together before marriage increases the likelihood of divorce in the first two years by eighty percent. [4]

The best sex does not come from the greatest number of sexual liaisons or the most inventive sexual gymnastics. It doesn't just come from stimulated nerve endings. God designed sexual intercourse to affect much more of you than that. Sex was designed to be a life-unifying act. God's idea of sex is that it signifies a "one flesh" bond. The Bible says: "For this reason a man will leave his father and mother and be united to his wife, and they will become one flesh" (Genesis 2:24, quoted also in Matthew 19:6 and Ephesians 5:28).

Sex needs to take place in the context of two things. First: it requires you to "leave" your parents, i.e. to be emotionally and financially independent of them. In other words, you need to grow up and be an adult in your head as well as in your body.

Second: it requires you to be "united to" your spouse. This means being committed to and loving the person you are going to marry.

These two things provide the context for what follows – sex, (which is what "one flesh" means).

Godly sex should be a celebration of your commitment to each other. It is something you do together and share with no one else. It grows the bond of intimacy between you that makes you both feel cherished and special. So, please don't cheapen sex by letting it be a physical act that lacks an emotional and social foundation. Otherwise, it will be 'I use you', rather than 'I choose you'. It will be waking up beside a stranger rather than a soul-mate. So, don't engage in a life-unifying act without a life-unifying intent – or you will risk wounding your inner spirit.

If someone has been promiscuous before marriage, it will be harder for their marriage partner to trust him or her in marriage, for they have never proved themselves capable of sexual discipline. If you have sex before marriage, it also means that nothing unique is brought to the marriage. Your virginity has already been given away. And this is a pity. It is a valuable possession that should not be given to just anyone.

Sexuality is a potent thing.[5] Protect it with self-control, and let your expression of it be all that God wants for you. The apostle Paul writes: "It is God's will ...that each of you should learn to control his own body in a way that is holy and honorable, not in passionate lust like the heathen who do not know God" (1 Thessalonians 4:4).

Is the Christian ideal of 'celibacy in singleness and faithfulness in marriage' just a Western, cultural imposition?

Some may be tempted to suggest that celibacy in singleness and faithfulness in marriage does not reflect biblical truth, but is merely a product of outdated Western culture. They point to the different sexual ethics of some Biblical leaders in the Old Testament, such as King David and King Solomon, who amassed a considerable number of wives between them (2 Samuel 5:13; 1 Kings 11:1-3).

David and Solomon certainly did have many wives. What is equally true is that this led to strife rather than blessing. Polygamy caused Solomon to lose his faith (1 Kings 11:3), and Michal, one of David's many wives, ended up despising her husband (2 Samuel 6:16).

Similarly, sex outside marriage, such as King David's adultery with Bathsheba, resulted in death and murder (2 Samuel 11:1-12:19); and Abraham's sexual liaison with his maid caused jealousy and strife (Genesis 16:1-5).

It has to be said that sex outside the model God set for humankind has never worked well. Today, sex outside of God's pattern still has a reputation for causing wounds and conflict.

Whilst it was (and is) the cultural norm in some nations to regard the number of wives as a symbol of status, celibacy in singleness and faithfulness in marriage has always been God's intention or his people. For instance, the Godly wisdom of Proverbs, although located in Old Testament times, has no hint of polygamy. Rather, it tells a husband to rejoice in his wife, to be satisfied with her, and be captivated by her love (Proverbs 5:18-19).

Jesus taught us that his command to "love your enemies" (Matthew 5:38-45) superseded Moses' law of an "an eye for an eye" (Exodus 21:23-25). In the same way, Jesus' teaching on marriage firmly put paid to any former cultural distortions in the status of marriage. Jesus valued marriage highly, and made it clear that neither adultery nor divorce (outside of abandonment, abuse and adultery) is acceptable to God (Mark 10:2-12, John 8:3-11).[6]

The Apostle Paul also echoed Jesus' teaching (1 Corinthians 6:9-10; 1 Timothy 1:9-10).

In conclusion, it can be said that faithfulness in marriage has been a consistent, Godly imperative in both the Old and New Testament (Deuteronomy 5:18; Mark10:19).

Adultery

Don't do it (Exodus 20:14; Proverbs 6:26-29; Malachi 2:13-15). Don't wish you had someone else's marriage partner (Exodus 20:17; Mathew 5:27-28). Simple.

Adultery violates the marriage covenant that has been made between two people (Proverbs 2:17; Malachi 2:14). God is intensely interested in relationships that are committed, because it models the relationship he seeks to have with us (Ephesians 5:28-32). So, don't break one up!

Thinking it

The development of sexual feelings in young people is quite natural and is part of growing up into an adult. Rejoice in it and don't feel guilty about it. We also have to face reality. The sex drive can be powerful, and it is not easy these days to keep sex for marriage – particularly as people are becoming sexually mature earlier, but are marrying later.

The Bible makes it clear that savoring thoughts about sex in the context of love is okay. However, savoring thoughts about immorality is not. So don't let yourself be inflamed with the idea of sexual immorality (Proverbs 6:25-26; Romans 1:27), or wanting to be enticed by it (James 1:14-15).

But here's a question: Does this mean that unmarried people can't fantasize about sex?

Not at all; to do so would be to deny our humanity. However, it will be wise to keep fantasies about sex under control. Certainly, don't cultivate thoughts of sexual immorality.

Every act of immorality begins with a thought...so control your thinking. Integrity comes from the proper management of attractions. Therefore, manage your desires well. Don't let them manage you! (1 Corinthians 6:12)

Masturbation

There are no specific references to this in the Bible, so we must be guided by biblical principles that have guided our thinking about sexuality generally.

Not everyone masturbates. However, most people do. So the question is: How should people manage it?

There are usually four reasons for masturbation. The first is for sexual experimentation. Masturbation plays an important part in an adolescent's discovery of their sexuality. Because of this, it is important that masturbation not be stigmatized.

The second reason is to fantasize about being loved, or being 'significant' in a world that may not have loved you much or accorded you much significance.

The third reason is to release sexual tension. Evidently, it takes about two days for the male testicles to fully replace ejaculated sperm. After two days, there may be a slight increase in sexual tension due to the hormonal activity associated with this. For some, masturbation is the only way to deal with sexual tensions, particularly for those who don't have a sexually active marriage partner.

The fourth reason is in order to escape boredom or to release the stresses of life. (If this is the case, it might be better to examine your lifestyle, seeking out the causes of the boredom or tension, then dealing with them.)

Whilst the quote (below) was written about boys, it is applicable to both sexes:

> *Because masturbation is such a natural part of an adolescent boy's experience, he is a veteran of sexual pleasure before he ever becomes involved in partnered sex. When he is drawn by his desire for love coupled with mature sex, a boy has to make a precarious crossing over a bridge from that intensely personal, rewarding and predictable fantasy exercise, to a real life girl with her own unfamiliar sexual and emotional terrain.*[7]

Masturbation is not something to be guilty about, but keep it under control, and don't let it become compulsive.

Pornography

Those who sell pornography exploit one of the most powerful drives that exists in humankind: the sex drive. It is a cheap shot. Curiosity, sexual excitement, loneliness, and a frustrated sex drive lead many into the pornography trap.

Pornography is not bad because Christians don't consider the human body to be beautiful (as claimed by some in the pornography industry). It is bad for five reasons.

First: It is predatory on one of the most powerful drives known to humankind. One of the things that makes it particularly predatory is that pornography has to get progressively more explicit and degrading in order to maintain the same level of sexual excitement. In this way, it is addictive, can be ruinously expensive, and take control of your life. Pornography is a predator that loves to attack the weak.

Second: It is a lie. Pornography pretends an intimacy and sexual fulfillment that does not exist in reality. Those caught up in pornography have a distorted view of real life that often results in them being unable to have healthy relationships with real women.

Third: It spoils lovemaking with your spouse. People caught by pornography are unable to divorce pornographic fantasy from the reality of lovemaking with their spouse. Those immersed in pornography can also dissipate their sex urge, so that they have little to offer their spouse in the way of sexual fulfillment. Sometimes, they even need to employ pornography in their lovemaking, so that their spouse is left unsure about who their partner is really making love to.

Fourth: The life of someone caught in pornography can be secretive, solitary, and unhealthy, as they can spend many hours looking at pornographic websites. This can lead to guilt and shame.

Fifth. It degrades women by presenting them as sex objects.

Oral sex

Evidently, about 70% of couples in the West have explored this expression of sexuality at some time.

The Bible is silent on this issue, so what can be said?

Oral sex is only okay if it is: 1) mutually enjoyed and mutually honoring; 2) something you have talked about together and agree on; 3) an intimacy-enhancing, bonding act that is helpful to your marriage.[8]

Oral sex should not define the value of a relationship. Neither should it be something that one partner does reluctantly. The reality is that some women who engage in it are not very enthusiastic about it, thinking it to be a bit degrading. Remember, some people's sexual acts can be motivated by a compulsive need to dominate (or be dominated) rather than from authentic love.

Although it should be the goal of every married person to

delight their spouse sexually and be generous, good husbands should not pressure their wives to do anything they do not enjoy.

Certainly, if someone engages in oral sex simply to keep their spouse faithful, it points to a deeper issue that needs to be fixed.

Managing sexuality[9]

There are three components to human sexuality: biological, psychological, and spiritual.

We are biological beings. Our sexuality is controlled by our DNA, which in turn controls the production of hormones that gives us our sex drive. Our sexuality is good and godly[10] but it does need to be managed.

Godly sex is designed for reproduction; pleasure and for building 'oneness'. Our brains are wired for sex. It feels great, so we want to get more. And quite naturally, we gravitate toward those things that give us pleasure.

The psychological influence on our sexuality comes from our family upbringing, our peer group, the culture of the society we live in, and from early childhood (and early adult) experiences. All of these things can give us a perception of what is acceptable to do sexually. It can also result in you having a perception about your sexuality that may or may not be true. So it is worth testing the validity of your feelings against the rational truth you know about yourself...and the truth you know about God's love.

All of us are the product of the relationships we have invested in; so let me encourage you to invest in a relationship with God. He is the one who guarantees your worth, and whispers wisdom into your heart.

We are also spiritual beings. The relevance of this is that if your sexuality has been corrupted because of things that have happened to you in the past (or in your family's past), it needs to be addressed. This can be done through prayer. Confess any sins (including those of your ancestors if necessary) and say to God that you choose to cut the ties to all things evil that are affecting you from the past.[11]

Let God know that you want to live for him now, and live in the freedom and forgiveness he gives.

Boundaries

You will need to manage your sexuality. This means adhering to boundaries that will keep you from doing things that will hurt yourself or others. If this is to happen, it will be important to identify the principles you want to live by. Here's some you might consider:

Determine to love and honor God in all things. Your body is a temple of the Holy Spirit (1 Corinthians 6:19). Therefore, do nothing that will defile it.

Keep your imagination under control. Guard your 'eye gate' (Job 31:1; Romans 12:2; Philippians 4:8; James 1:14-15).

Control who, and what, will influence you. Don't allow yourself to be deceived into doing bad things by people who may just be pretending to be godly (Jude 4). Always be guided by the consistent principles of God's word (2 Timothy 3:16).

Put an absolute priority on submitting to your partner, i.e. put a priority on doing what's good for them. Nurture the love you have for your spouse, and encourage your partner to grown in faith and character (Ephesians 5:21-27).

The Greek word for 'sin' used by the writers of the New Testament was *hamartia*. *Hamartia* literally means 'to miss the mark'. So, sin is not simply failing morally, it is missing the mark God intends for you...so avoid it!

Some questions for honest reflection

Here are some questions for you to reflect on when the time is right. I ask them only because they may help you navigate the way to the future you want.

1. Who are you? Is the essential 'you' simply the sum of your desires, or is there something deeper that defines you?

2. Does your freedom come from being controlled by your desires – and is that really 'freedom'?
3. Does your significance come from the number and status of your sexual partners, or could your significance come from something more profound – being loved by God?
4. Could you live as God wants you to, intentionally feeding godly relationships in defiance of your sexual desires? (Note: I'm not talking about 'suppression', I'm talking about 'choice'.)

Overcoming sexual wounding

When someone who is sexually wounded becomes a Christian, his or her sexuality doesn't change overnight. We still have memories, habits and emotional vulnerability as a result of our past. It is important to remember that becoming a Christian means that transformation has begun, but has not been completed. So, be gentle with yourself. Everyone is born immature, including new Christians. Immaturity is not bad. It is only bad if you elect to remain immature.

If you have become addicted to ungodly expressions of your sexuality, be honest to God about it. Remember that God is *for* you, not against you. Jesus wants to be your advocate, not someone who scolds. And you are not alone. Jesus has promised to empower you with the Holy Spirit. He is someone who stands alongside us and helps us in our weakness (John 14:15). [12]

The reality is: you are of inestimable value to God.[13] So, when dealing with sexual wounding, let any frustration at your weakness propel you toward God, not away from him (Romans 7:14-25; 1 Corinthians 9:24-27; 2 Corinthians 1:8-9).

Whenever you feel hurt or tempted lean back into Jesus. Jesus understands what you are going through. He was tempted in the same way we are (Hebrews 2:18; 4:15). This should remind you that it is no sin to be tempted. Savoring the idea of the sin is the problem. When you catch yourself doing that, back away. Why? Because it's the precursor to committing a sin (James 1:14-15).

How to get back on track

If you want to get back on track, the first thing to do is to admit to God that you've been addicted to the wrong things...and that you now want God to be in control of your life. Then ask God to help you with the issues you particularly have to face.

It is important to persist and be patient when bringing about change. Reversing addiction takes time. Initially, you may be convinced you are getting nowhere. But things will eventually change. Just as it took time to become an addict, it will take time for new ways of thinking to become ingrained. As part of this process, it will be important for you to make yourself accountable to wise and godly people with whom you can talk honestly – people who model what you want to be, and who will respect confidentiality.

Move from immaturity to maturity

If you are to become mature, there are two goals to aim for.

First: Take responsibility for yourself. Immature people are driven by impulses, urges, and appetites. They give no thought to consequences. When found out, they typically abdicate responsibility and seek to blame others, often seeking to portray themselves as the victim. Immature people are self-focused and have trouble empathizing with others.

The mature person, in contrast, is self-controlled. They understand consequences, take responsibility for themselves, and are free enough from their ego to serve others.

The second goal is to move from insecurity to security. Insecure people doubt their value. They are neurotic and anxious, always trying to win the acclaim of others in order to feel valued. Insecure people are constantly comparing, envying, and coveting, and tend to be controlling and manipulative.

Secure people, in contrast, are at peace with themselves. They are confident of their value to God, and so are free enough to bless, serve, and affirm others.

Fundamentally, only God can give you true security. Therefore, don't seek it anywhere else (Jeremiah 17:5-8).

Some straight talk to men

Men are sexual beings with a relentless sexuality, and there are great pressures today for that sexuality to be distorted. Learning to handle the pressure of male sexuality is one of the skills a man must acquire if he is to be successful in his personal life, home life, and in his spiritual walk with God.

We have to understand that because of the culture we live in, a perversion of God's idea of sexuality has washed up onto our doorstep. Family life is now under real threat. Moral sexual standards have fallen, and now almost all sexual encounters seen on film and TV are outside the context of marriage.

'Do your own thing'; 'stay committed only as long as you feel in love'; and 'deny yourself nothing'; are the mantras of our age. It is now the cultural norm for a man to go after sex as often as possible and as hard as possible. People are increasingly seeing themselves as social animals that have to give way to their animal instincts. Any thought of humankind being made in the image of God, with an innate moral creed, is fading fast from society's moral landscape. Sex is now a pleasurable recreational act devoid of commitment and responsibility.

Today's culture trains men to seek self-gratification rather than mutuality. This has helped make men vulnerable to seeking gratification through pornography...which can bring mental, if not physical, promiscuity into marriage.

It is therefore very difficult today for a Christian man to maintain his sexual integrity. It is certainly a battle for a Christian man to have a sense of dignity about his sexuality. Any person's sex life has a massive impact on their feeling of self-worth. We are, after all, moral beings, so when we do and think things we are ashamed of, we think less of ourselves, and can be tempted to withdraw from God.

The management of a man's sexuality is one of the biggest challenges he will face in life, and it is so for good reasons.

Men's brains are hard wired, at a very basic level, to respond to sexual stimuli. Their brains are physically different from those of women, and this means men think differently about sex from women. Male hormones, particularly testosterone, cause the differences that occur in the male brain. The brains of nine-week-old male fetuses are deluged with testosterone. Male brains are deluged again at adolescence. These hormones cause irreversible changes that result in men thinking and behaving differently from women.

Male hormones predispose men toward seeking power and dominance.[14] Men are generally more focused, more aggressive, and have better spatial skills. Women, in contrast, seek communication, complementarity, and association. They are generally more articulate, more capable of multi-tasking, and have more sensitive sensory abilities. No amount of rhetoric from the proponents of 'gender fluidity' can erase the biological fact that male and female brains are wired in different ways because of our hormones. This different wiring has a marked affect upon behavior – particularly sexual behavior. Put bluntly, the differences result in a tendency for men to seek sex, whilst women seek relationships.[15]

A Christian man will not feel fulfilled until he has been set free from toxic distortions of sexuality served up by society. I invite you to be free.

When a Christian woman marries, she is seeking to marry a man who will make her his top priority. A distorted sexuality will rob her of everything she hopes for in a husband. Paul's writing in Ephesians 5:22-27 makes it clear that it is the responsibility of the husband to set the spiritual culture of a home. Therefore, if you want the best, you have to be willing to fight for it, and establish it in the home.

How, then, should you manage your sexuality?

Seven factors are important:

God and Me

1. Know that it is possible to change. You can change and manage your sexuality well.
2. Know that God's plans for sex are good. Sex is a gift given to us by God.
3. Know yourself. Identify your issues and face them honestly. Resist the temptation to become schizophrenic and have a sinful and a godly compartment of your life. Bring both to the light of God's love, ministry and understanding all the time.
4. Know that managing sexuality is challenging. This is normal. It is perhaps significant that God caused his covenant mark (circumcision) to be placed on that most unruly member of a man's body!
5. Talk about it. Have the courage to talk to wise Christian men who manage their sexuality well.
6. Guard your eye gate. This is of key importance. Follow the example of Job who said, "I made a covenant with my eyes not to look lustfully at a girl" (Job 31:1). Guard what influences you. This means guarding whom you choose to socialize with, what you choose to watch, and what you choose to read.
7. Define your boundaries. Take charge and set yourself boundaries that you will not cross.

I think I've said enough.

I'm wondering how you are feeling at this point?

My fervent hope is that you are feeling emancipated and enabled rather than condemned.

My aim is to bless, so let me leave you with a blessing:

> *The Lord bless you*
> *and keep you;*
> *the Lord make his face shine upon you*
> *and be gracious to you;*
> *the Lord turn his face toward you*
> *and give you peace* (Numbers 6:24-26)

11

Life After Death, and Me

There is something awfully final about death. After the miracle of birth, death seems a bit of an anticlimax. There is no fanfare, just the lingering process of decrepitude for both body and mind. It is not at all glorious.

Any spiritual claim concerning humanity needs to make sense of both our beginning (why we exist) and our ending (why death exists). These two events peg out the limit of our existence and remind us that life is linear. It has a beginning and an end, and we journey from one to the other in the brief window of time allotted to us.

Death is certainly a mystery that has baffled humanity throughout history. Some of us dread it, a few of us welcome it...and all of us have to face it.

Most of us don't like the idea much. Many people, such as the poet, William Cary, had a fear of it. When he saw a canary singing happily in a cage, he thought gloomily that it could only do so because it didn't know it was going to die.

As I've said in an earlier book, *Who Ordered the Universe?*, death is a handy thing biologically, as it allows the evolutionary process to happen. Death clears the stage of old organisms, and makes space for new organisms to develop. The death of species less suited to an ecological niche allows better-adapted species to thrive. This process of selection drives the engine of biological adaptation and diversity that has resulted in you. It has also instilled in you an innate instinct to survive for as long as possible.

It is significant that this instinct does not switch off once we have done our biological duty, and our children have become adults. We don't then meekly surrender to death, calm in the knowledge that we have done our job. Instead, we become social burdens. In our aged state, we clog up supermarket queues, and consume more than our fair share of the community's health resources. Surely evolution should have taught us to get out of the way with the minimum of fuss as soon as our biological job was done! Curiously, it hasn't. We hang on to life as tenaciously as possible. We hate death, partly because of its uncertainty, and also because it ruptures the bonds of love we have formed.

The big question is: Have we invented God simply to give ourselves the illusion that there is meaning and hope after death – making the prospect of death more palatable?

All this was a mystery until one man, Jesus Christ, defeated death and was resurrected. This did not happen in a myth: it happened in history. It did not happen in fiction: the resurrection accounts of Jesus stand up to forensic investigation.

Whatever else Jesus does, he throws our feelings about death up in the air...and reorders them rather beautifully.

The strangeness of death

It's strange seeing a dead body. I had to get fairly used to seeing one early in my adult life when I worked at a temporary job in the geriatric ward of a hospital. Later on in life, I became more familiar with death in my work as a pastor. I found it distinctly odd watching the phenomenon called 'life' trickle away...turning a friend into a corpse. The weird thing is that the body, at the point of death, contains all the elements necessary for life to exist – and yet there is only death.

So, what is the mysterious life force that breathes fire into the unlikely pile of atoms that make up your body? And, more intriguingly, why does this life force exist? These musings bring to mind a comment by St. Augustine: "And men go abroad to admire the heights of mountains, the mighty waves of the sea, the broad tides of rivers, the compass of the ocean, and the circuits of the stars, yet pass over the mystery of themselves without a thought."[1]

Why does death exist?

If we have looked at the cosmos and concluded that God exists, then we are forced to consider the question of death in relation to that God. What role does death play in God's big plan?

Two things need to be understood about God. The first is that God is love. In fact, God is the most perfect definition of love that exists. The second thing is that God is holy. He is the most perfect definition of holiness that exists. It is important to realize that the love of God, and the holiness of God, are not in tension. They don't cancel each other out through trying to make room for each other in God's essential nature. Both exist fully and perfectly in God...and both express themselves in God's creation. It works like this:

God's holiness means that he has a zero tolerance for evil. Evil is not something God will overlook or accommodate, as it challenges God's very nature. God, therefore, has one answer to sin, as we've said earlier: He kills it off. Not even the tiniest sin is allowed to exist in God's kingdom. And God's way of ensuring sin is killed off, is to institute the reality of death.

This truth is taught at the very start of the Bible. There, we read that Adam and Eve rebelled against God by trying to grasp at God's knowledge (so they could be like God), and also grasp at a forbidden mango. (The Bible doesn't specifically mention an apple. It just mentions "fruit." And let's be honest: who would be tempted by just an apple!) But let's get back to our story.

Before the mango was picked, we read that Adam and Eve lived easily in God's company, and significantly, there was no mention of death. However, after they rebelled, God cursed them with a terrible consequence – suffering and death (Genesis 3). Death was God's way of ensuring that sinful humanity would not be locked into their sinful state for all eternity. Humanity, and all living things that shared our fate, would die. That's why creation itself, and not just humanity, waits eagerly for redemption (Romans 8:19-23).

Death is God's act of 'un-creating'.

The Bible goes on to teach that those with any trace of sin are condemned by God's judgment...and face death (Romans 6:23). This unpalatable reality is made even more ghastly by the knowledge that every one of us has sinned. None of us is perfectly holy (Romans 3:23).

However, the good news is that because God loves us so much, he chose to rescue us back to himself by sending Jesus to die and pay the penalty for our sins, making us eligible for eternal life with God. All we have to do is accept God's love, accept Jesus' death on our behalf, and accept God's lordship of our lives. So, 'the gospel' (which literally means 'good news') is all about cheating death. Jesus said: "Whoever hears my word and believes him who sent me has eternal life and will not be judged but has crossed over from death to life" (John 5:24).

But: How does all this play out? What happens when we die?

What will happen to those who die?

The Bible makes it clear that Jesus was the first one resurrected. He is called, rather delightfully, the "firstfruit" (1 Corinthians 15:20). In this sense, Jesus is the pathfinder, the one who shows that resurrection life is possible.

The challenge for us is to die to self and live for Christ. The apostle Paul's term for this is to be "in Christ," a term that he used often. The relevance of this is that if we are "in Christ," we share in his death (meaning that our sins get killed off) and, crucially, we also share in his resurrection (Romans 6:3-6).

The big question is, of course: When do we get to be resurrected like Jesus? Does this happen when we die?

No it doesn't.

Resurrection (for the godly) will not occur until after Jesus comes again to judge the living and the dead...and inaugurate something entirely new: God's kingdom (1 Thessalonians 4:16-18). This, as I've said earlier, is God's end game. (Jesus inaugurated God's kingdom when he first came, and this kingdom will be consummated when he returns.)

So: What happens to those who die before Jesus returns? The answer to this should be of some interest because it will probably include you!

Let's remind ourselves of another story – the story of the two criminals who were crucified either side of Jesus (Luke 23:32-43). The first criminal scorned Jesus. The second criminal rebuked the first criminal, and asked Jesus to remember him when he returned to his kingdom.

Jesus replied to him saying: "I tell you the truth, today you will be with me in paradise."

What was Jesus referring to when he said 'paradise'? He couldn't be referring to the coming Kingdom of God, because that won't be consummated until Christ returns. It would therefore seem that 'paradise' is a waiting place. In other words, when those who are faithful to God die, their final judgment is anticipated by the fact that they go to heaven (or paradise). This is a glorious place where they wait (sometimes with a bit of impatience, see: Revelation 6:9-11) for Jesus to join a new heaven with a totally transformed Earth – and combine them together to form his eternal kingdom (Matthew 19:28; Revelation 21:1-3).

When Jesus comes again to do this, *both* the living and the dead will be resurrected (John 5:28-29; Acts 10:42). Those who are righteous will be judged and rewarded for what they have done (Matthew 6:19-25; 10:42, 25:31-46). Then they will be invited to take their place in God's kingdom.

What happens to those who spurn God?

Those who have chosen to reject God's lordship follow a similar pathway, albeit one with a very different outcome. Their eternal status after death is anticipated by the fact that they are sent to a place of punishment (Luke 12:47-48; 2 Peter 2:9), sometimes called "Hades" (Revelation 20:13). [2] Whatever this place is, it will be a place of regret (Luke 16:19-31). When Jesus comes again, they too will be resurrected, judged, and required to face the final consequence. The final consequence is referred to in the Bible as the "second death" (Revelation 20:6).

Christians are divided as to what the "second death" actually is. Some think the ungodly will be finally annihilated (which makes good sense of the word "death"), while others think there is some form of eternal punishment. Whatever we believe will happen, must be consistent with the just and compassionate nature of God.

The idea that the ungodly are annihilated is consistent with those Scriptures that teach that evil will be completely destroyed (Matthew 10:28; 2 Peter 3:7). However, believing that the ungodly will be annihilated requires you to treat the language of eternal torment in Scripture (Matthew 25:46; Luke 16:22-23; Revelation 14:11; 20:10-15) as metaphorical. In other words, it means understanding that eternal absence from God (because of annihilation) actually *is* eternal torment. Certainly, it is eternally significant!

When talking about God's judgment, it is important to remember that God's agenda is for us to be saved, not sent to hell (1 Timothy 2:3-4; 2 Peter 3:9). God did not intend anyone to go to hell (1 Thessalonians 5:9). The very reason Jesus came was to stop that happening. Hell was designed primarily for the Devil and his evil spirits, i.e. those who were the antithesis of God (Matthew 25:41). Only those who deliberately reject God's love and lordship go to hell.

The frightening thing is: God does not force his will on anyone, and will respect anyone's decision to have nothing to do with him – both now and in eternity. C. S. Lewis put this well when he said that *"the gates of hell are locked from the inside."* [3]

The anticipatory judgment of God (sending people either to heaven/paradise or hell/Hades) would be unfair, if the one making that judgment was anyone other than God. What makes God's judgment fair is the fact that he stands outside of time. In other words, the past, present, and future are equally clear to Him. As such,

God's anticipatory judgment is a sure indicator of the verdict he will deliver at the final judgment (Matthew 25:31-46; Revelation 20:10-15).

Let's return to the question of whether or not hell is an eternal reality.

Revelation 20:10-15 speaks of those who contend against God being thrown into the burning lake. Some argue that this may simply refer to the method of their execution...and that Satan and his evil spirits are the only ones who are tormented eternally (Revelation 20:10). However, Revelation 14:11 seems to make it clear that those who align themselves with Satan will also be punished for eternity. As such, the "simply execution" argument lacks credence.

Matthew 25:46; Revelation 14:11 and 20:10-15 can only be made consistent with annihilationism if it is understood that the language is, as we've said before, figurative rather than literal.

Whatever is understood, two things must always be taken into account. The first is that God is perfectly loving and just. We, who God created, are not going to have a better idea of justice and love than the God who created us. The second is that real gratuitous evil should receive no mercy from any God who is good.

Eternal rewards

I noted earlier that C.S. Lewis has suggested that the gates of hell are firmly locked on the inside. I wonder whether you agree. The idea certainly highlights the truth that humankind's rejection of God is something that is freely chosen. However, it is not correct in suggesting that there is no regret in hell, i.e. that people are content to keep the doors shut. Jesus' teaching makes it clear that those in hell would dearly like to open the gates and escape if they could (Luke 16:19-24).

The Bible is consistent in saying that we will all face God's judgment when we die. Specifically, it says: "people are destined to die once, and after that to face judgment" (Hebrews 9:27).[4] For the Christian, judgment holds no terror, as they have been given Christ's righteousness when they put their faith in Jesus (John 5:24). Death is not something that needs to be feared (1 John 4:17). Christians will, however, be judged in order to determine any special rewards (Mark 9:41; Ephesians 6:8).

Things are not so rosy when we consider hell. Jesus' teaching makes it clear that hell is a reality worth avoiding! He sometimes used the vivid imagery of the "fires of hell" to make this plain (Matthew 5:22; 18:9). Personally, the idea of missing out on eternity with a God of love, purpose, humor, and creativity, is too terrible to contemplate. Many agree with me. That's why Christians put a priority on telling others about Jesus – so they also can put their faith in him.

God's justice

It is deeply disturbing to think of people who knowingly reject God being disbarred from God's presence in eternity. The question it raises is one of justice.

If we consider the issue of God's justice, it will mean exploring the question of culpability. In other words, it means exploring the degree to which people are responsible for their eternal destiny.

We need to be careful when exploring this subject, because we do not want to arrogantly make judgments on God's judgment. After all, who are we to sit in judgment of God? (Job 40:1-80). To do so would be absurd, as God is the final definition of what is just. No: What we are seeking to do is to understand the principles behind God's judgment.

It is fair to say that we will never be able to understand everything as God does, and so there will inevitably be things that we don't fully understand.

What we can say is that the universe is shot through with signs of 'mind' (Psalm 19:1-4; Acts 14:17; 17:26-27). As such, the Apostle Paul believed it was reasonable to expect people to ponder the existence of creation, and let this introduce them to the possibility of God. In fact, he believed people were culpable if they did not (Romans 1:20-22).

Paul's comment in Romans 1:20-22 that people are "without

excuse" if they don't acknowledge God in the evidence of creation, has been dismissed as poor reasoning, something that was typical of the primitive thinking that existed in Paul's time.

Some care should be taken before we dismiss Paul's thinking and consign it to the waste bin of historical anachronisms. It is indeed true that Paul speaks from the perspective of the worldview of his time – but as is typical of Scripture, things of eternal significance are being said here that are true for all cultures and all times. The eternal principle it teaches is this: It is our responsibility to notice the world around us...and allow what we see to prompt questions about why it exists, and what our part in the grand scheme of things might be.

If people do not want to believe, that is their prerogative, but they can't justifiably claim a rational mandate for doing so. Willful atheism should never masquerade as carefully researched intellectual objections to the idea of God.

The other piece of evidence that commends the truth of the Christian gospel is Jesus. When God came to earth as Jesus, it did not just add another religion to the plethora that already existed. Rather, his coming was a sovereign initiative of personal revelation that supplanted all human attempts to reach God through man-made religions.

Until Jesus came, the 'mind' behind the universe remained hidden, and it stayed hidden until God chose to reveal himself to us as Jesus. When the time was right, Jesus came in history – and his historicity can be checked against the records of non-Christian historians who wrote about him at the time (see Chapter 3).

The significance of this is: if people choose to ignore Jesus despite evidence of Jesus' life, death, and resurrection, then there is a degree of culpability to their ignorance (John 3:18).

Quite how this translates into their eternal destiny, we'll leave to God. He is infinitely more just and compassionate than you and I will ever be. The biblical principles we've uncovered should, however, serve warning that willful atheism is no excuse for remaining ignorant of Jesus (John 10:13-14).

. . .

Did God create evil?

If God created everything, then surely that means God created evil. And if God created evil, he can't eternally condemn evil people — for to do so would be to eternally condemn a quality that arose from within himself.

Is this assertion right?

It is probably helpful to think of the issue in this way. Sin and death are not things that God caused to exist or is responsible for. Sin and death are caused by the absence of God in the same way that cold is caused by the absence of heat. Where God is, sin and death cannot exist.

Is God fair condemning people to hell?

We've been talking about whether God is fair and just in condemning people to hell, and we've cited many Bible passages. Let's also uncover the key truths within which the answer to this question can be found in one of our octagons.

The question is: Is God fair in condemning people to hell?

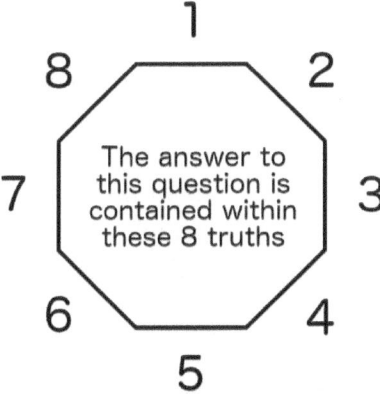

1. God is the perfect definition of justice.
2. God is the perfect definition of love.
3. God's holiness requires that cruelty, injustice, lack of love

and lack of truth be killed off. It is important that they not continue to exist eternally.
4. God stands outside of time so he already knows who will accept his love and lordship. In this regard, it can be said that you are predestined. However, it is still your free choice to accept him or not.
5. God's desire is for us to live with him in his eternal community. Only we can disqualify ourselves from it.
6. God has made provision for us to live with him in his eternal community by sending Jesus to die for our sins. All we have to do is accept him as our Lord and Savior.
7. Jesus reveals the character of God, and the truth and reality of the resurrected life.
8. God has given reasonable evidence of his existence in the wonders and order of the universe. It is willfully perverse to ignore it.

I hope that summary helps.

Our call to mission

The reason you and I are still alive on this planet is so that we can tell others about Jesus. It's that simple. All Christians are called to mission (John 20:21; Matthew 28:18-20 and Acts 1:8). The Swiss theologian, Emil Brunner, put it well when he wrote: "The Church exists by mission, just as a fire exists by burning."[5]

A rather obvious disincentive to telling other people about Jesus (by words and actions) is the conviction that hell does not exist.

To help answer the question this poses, let's construct another octagon.

The question we want to surround with truths we can be sure of is: Why evangelize?

God and Me

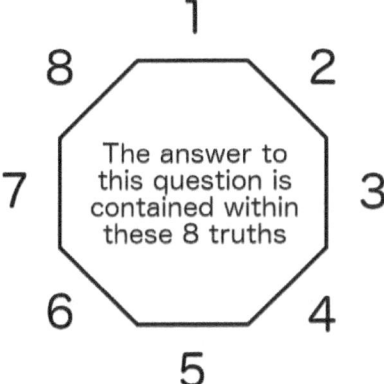

1. God chooses to work through his people, the church, to make himself known to those who don't yet know him (2 Corinthians 5:20).
2. Christians tell others about the truth of God in obedience to God's command to do so (Matthew 28:18-20).
3. Some people don't evangelize because they are not sure Jesus is the only way to God. The answer, of course, is to connect with God and be sure (1 Peter 3:15).
4. Mission is the heart of God. He doesn't want anyone to perish (2 Peter 3:9). We partner with Jesus in mission when we evangelize (Matthew 9:35-10:1,7-8,16).
5. Hell (eternal disqualification from God's presence) will be a self-chosen reality for many people (Matthew 7:13-14). Revelation calls this the "second death" (Revelation 2:11; 20:6,14). Know its reality and make it hard for people to choose it.
6. We are empowered by God's Holy Spirit to evangelize (Acts 1:8)
7. Sharing your faith grows your own faith (Philemon 6).
8. Hell (where evil is killed off) has to exist if God is to remain holy by not ignoring evil or accommodating it. God's judgment has to be a reality (Hebrews 9:27).

The thing to notice is that God is a missional God. He came to us as Jesus, on mission. It should therefore be of no surprise that those who follow Jesus are called to share in the mission of God.

Barriers to mission

As mission is of central importance, it's worth pausing for a moment to consider personal and theological objections people can have that prevent them from sharing their faith with others.

Let's begin with personal objections. Here they are:

1. The worthiness barrier. (I am not good enough to share my faith with any integrity.)
2. The motivational barrier. (I don't care that much about doing God's mission.)
3. The persecution barrier. (I am fearful of persecution and the derision of others)
4. The ability (or knowledge) barrier. (I don't know how to share my faith.)
5. The social (or connection) barrier. (I'm not in contact with any unbelievers.)

A right understanding of Jesus should fix most of these issues. This brings us to the theological barriers:

1. God doesn't exist.
2. Hell and heaven don't exist.
3. A loving God would not condemn anyone to an eternity in hell.
4. We have no right to share our faith with others. Faith is a personal and private thing. Intruding on other people's beliefs is rude. There is no God-given imperative for us to share the gospel with others.
5. All religions, sincerely held, will get you to God.
6. Morality rather than theology is what matters to God.

Again, a right understanding of Scripture should fix these issues.

Some churches don't preach about Jesus' second coming, preferring only to speak about meeting Jesus after we have died. Therefore, we need to ask: What are the specific references that teach that Jesus will come again?

First of all: Jesus said so (John 14:1-3,28; Revelation 22:20). Secondly: God's angel (mentioned in Acts 1:9-11) said so. This passage tells us that Jesus will return in the same way as he left, i.e. in the clouds. (This is also taught in Revelation 1:7.) Thirdly: The Apostle Paul said so (1 Thessalonians 1:10; 2:19; 3:13). Finally: The writer of the book of Hebrews said so (Hebrews 9:28).

I hope that covers it.

People have been trying to predict when Jesus will return for centuries. Jesus, however, made it clear that trying to do this is a useless exercise, because only the Heavenly Father knows when it will be (Matthew 24:36; Acts 1:6-7). Jesus does, however, urge us to read the signs of the times, so that we know that the time of his second coming is getting nearer.

> *He told them this parable: "Look at the fig tree and all the trees. When they sprout leaves, you can see for yourselves and know that summer is near. Even so, when you see these things happening, you know that the kingdom of God is near"* (Luke 21:29-31).

The obvious question that follows from this is: What are the signs of the times we need to watch out for?

Jesus gives a fairly comprehensive list in Matthew, chapter 24. Here it is:

v.5) Many will come claiming to be the Christ.

v.6) There will be wars.

v.7) There will be famines and earthquakes.

v.9) Christians will be persecuted.

v.10) Many will be deceived and will turn away from Christ (see also: 1 Timothy 4:1-2; 2 Timothy 3:13; 4:3-4).

v.11) False prophets will deceive people.

v.12) Wickedness will increase. People will be: lovers of themselves; lovers of money; boastful; proud; abusive; disobedient to their parents; ungrateful; unholy; without love; unforgiving; slanderous; without self-control; brutal; not lovers of the good; treacherous; rash; conceited; lovers of pleasure rather than lovers of God; having a form of godliness but denying its power (see also: 2 Timothy 3:1-7); scoffers (see also: 2 Peter 3:3-4).

v.12) The love of most will grow cold. Many will think their world is one of "peace and safety" and will become complacent (see also: 1 Thessalonians 5:3).

v.14) The Gospel will be preached to all nations.

v.29) The sun will be darkened, and the moon will not give its light, the stars will fall from the sky, and the heavenly bodies will be shaken. Note: It's always difficult to know how literally we should take this. Is it poetic metaphor? Is it God rattling the cosmos? Is it a volcano or a meteorite crash throwing up dust? What do you think?

v.30) The sign of the Son of Man (Jesus) will appear in the sky. Jesus will return in glory (see also: 2 Thessalonians 1:7, Revelation 1:7). The nations will mourn because they weren't ready for Jesus (see also: Revelation 1:7).

v.31) Angels will gather all Christians, dead or alive, at the sound of a trumpet. This is sometimes referred to as "the rapture" (See also: 1 Corinthians 15:51-52; Colossians 3:4; 1 Thessalonians 4:16-18).

Christians are therefore alert to these things as they wait. But as they wait, they get on with mission.

Wrapping up

I was once asked to visit an old man who was dying in hospital. I was warned that I might expect a chilly, if not outright antagonistic welcome, as the man had been vehemently anti-God for his entire life. He grew up in Holland and had witnessed the savagery and senseless death of many innocent people in World War II. He'd nearly died himself when he dared to creep out one evening to collect some firewood. A German fighter plane saw him and attempted to strafe him.

I sat beside his bed, held his hand, and said: "This is the real deal. I've got very little patience for theological games...and you have no time for them. You've been told you will die in the next day or two. Do you really want to die without hope and without peace? Do you want to go to the doors of death still clutching the bitterness in your heart that has been so corrosive of joy?"

I then shared the story of Jesus with him.

To my great delight, he listened.

Then the miracle happened. His face softened in a way that I'd never seen before. He smiled and closed his eyes.

Twenty-four hours later, he was dead.

I have to say; he cut it pretty fine. But, what a waste it would have been to have lived a whole life with bitterness, rather than joyful hope.

Please don't make the same mistake. Don't miss out on the promise of God. God has assured us in Scripture that his kingdom will be beyond imagining. The apostle Paul writes, "However, as it is written: 'What no eye has seen, what no ear has heard, and what no human mind has conceived' – the things God has prepared for those who love him" (1 Corinthians 2:9).

So, please don't miss out on it.

12

A Personal Note

May I finish this book on a personal note – so you might know a little more about the one who dares write to you?

I am dying of cancer, which is perhaps relevant to the substance of this book. Whatever else death does, it certainly tests the worth of the worldview you have lived by. Is what you have believed well founded and adequate? Is the hope of a destiny beyond this grief-stricken world grounded in truth?

So, what can I say?

Let me begin by assuring you that I am neither good nor brave. Like you, I rely on the undeserved love of God who has done so much to woo my love. As death comes closer, I can do nothing other than wrap myself a little tighter in God's word (Scripture) and let myself lean back further into his love. To have God whispering to my heart at this time is very special. This is particularly so at the moment. I am writing this as the COVID-19 pandemic plays out and may mean that very few people will see me to the door of death. I could so easily be lonely. But if you know God, you are never alone – and his promises mean that the prospect of death holds no fear.

God and Me

If I had ignored God's self-revelation in the cosmos, and ignored Jesus Christ, then fear and uncertainty would perhaps be reasonable. But God *has* revealed himself to me, and this has changed everything. It has resulted in me knowing that life is purposed, and that I have been in an adventure that is part of something very big.

A voice from the future

Have you ever wondered, in a whimsical moment, what an old 'you' might say to the young 'you' that once stood on the threshold of adult life?

Rather extraordinarily, I was able to do just that. When I was seventeen, I used to write the occasional poem. One of them was called, 'Shakespeare's Player', and I never finished it. The poem expressed the typical angst and uncertainties of a young man.

Fifty years later, I rediscovered the poem, and was able to finish it. So...a sixty-seven year old 'me' was able to reassure the seventeen year old me (in a poem, at least). It was a heart-warming, if slightly bizarre, experience.

This is the poem:

Shakespeare's Player

As Shakespeare's player struts and frets his hour upon the stage,
I search the stage of life for friends to lend my patronage.
And having chosen sect or clan, I'll then assume their idioms
to stay with them and strive to keep rebellion to a minimum.
I arm myself with all their necessary personalities,
and with the wardrobe act each part—accepted frivolities.

Am I doomed to forge myself on fellow man or deity?
And if on God, must all pride change to humble, base servility?
Will nothing stay to fuel the fires of glory or successfulness?
Because with God, I might lose out and suffer in my
    humbleness;

then try and calm neurosis by my biblical researches,
and be a priest with lost ideals, and preach in empty churches.

Have churches too all lost their cause as everything decays—
and rots to make a playground for the pigeon's deft displays?
Am I just a fluke of fate, an accidental outcome?
of swirling galaxies in space that spilt some cosmic
  breadcrumbs.
and who will say what right is good and whether there is
  meaning,
or whether I'm an accident—a thought that is demeaning?

This was the young man's angst I had when life was still
  ahead,
but now I'm old, I can report, God understood my dread.
"Give yourself to me," he said, "I've won for you a place…
beside me in eternity where you can see my face.
Your life on earth will test you and refine you for the story…
that is yours when you come home and see me in my glory."

Sampson's last prayer

Quite how a mildly dyslexic, academically lukewarm, absent-minded Australian should end up championing the validity of faith in God is a mystery. I hope it is one that gives you confidence, because if God can use me, he most certainly can use you.

Some of you will know the story of Sampson in the Old Testament. Like me, Sampson was a very imperfect fellow. Despite this, God empowered him to protect the Hebrew people from those who wanted to exterminate them.

At the end of his life, Sampson was not in great shape. He had been blinded by his enemies and was shackled as a prisoner. One day, his tormentors brought him out so they could gloat over his downfall. Like Christians today, he had become an object of scorn and ridicule.

Then Sampson prayed one last prayer. He prayed for the strength to push over the two central pillars holding up the giant edifice built by those who scorned his God.

Why do I tell you this?

Because I too have prayed...and am reaching for the two pillars of 'anti-theism' and 'untruth'...and I'm starting to push.

Notes

Introduction

1. Blaise Pascal, (*Pensées*, 1670).

1. The Cosmos, Meaning, and Me

1. The English cosmologist, Paul Davies, cites the work of the Australian physicist, Brandon Carter, who discovered that the universe needs to contain both radiative and convective stars if it is to be life-friendly. Carter worked out that in order to get both sorts of stars, the ratio of the strengths of the electromagnetic and gravitational forces needs to be 1040. (See: Paul Davies, The *Goldilocks Enigma* [London: Allen Lane, 2006], 164.)
2. John Polkinghorne, *Quarks, Chaos and Christianity* (London: Triangle, 1994), 30.
3. Some have claimed that the law of 'cause and effect' is not inviolable because things might both happen and not happen in the quantum world. I would argue that this is not the case as quantum reality and the laws that govern it must first exist, i.e be the cause, if anything is to happen in the quantum world.
4. Fred Hoyle, "The Universe: Past and Present Reflections," pp.1-3 in *Annual Review of Astronomy and Astrophysics*, 20 (1982).
5. Stephen Hawking, quoted in: J. Boslough, *Stephen Hawking's Universe* (New York: Simon and Schuster, 1983), 30.
6. Geraint Lewis, "A universe made for me? Physics, fine-tuning and life," *Cosmos* Newsletter, 18th December, 2016.
7. Martin Rees, *Just Six Numbers: The Deep Forces That Shape The Universe* (1st American ed. New York: Basic Books, 2001), 4.
8. Paul Davies, *The Goldilocks Enigma* (London: Allen Lane, 2006), 166-167.
9. *Ibid.* 167-170.
10. *Ibid.* 166-170.
11. "There is a God, leading atheist concludes," NBC News, 9th December, 2004.
12. Anthony Flew with Roy Abraham Varghese, *There Is A God: How the World's Most Notorious Atheist Changed His Mind* (New York: Harper Collins, 2007), 155.
13. Gerald Schroeder, "Has Science Discovered God?" http://science.lenicam.com.

    The thinking of Gerald Schroeder played a key role in changing the philosopher, Antony Flew, from being an atheist to someone who believed in God's existence.
14. Brian Cox, *The Universe with Brian Cox* (film), Series 1, Episode 4, "Heart of Darkness: Black Holes," 2021 (see: 41 - 50 minutes). https://view.abc.net.au/video/ZW3171A004500
15. *Ibid.*
16. *Ibid.*
17. Alexander Vilenkin cited in "Why physicists can't avoid a creation event," by Lisa Grossman, *New Scientist* (January 11, 2012).

Notes

18. Alexander Vilenkin, *Many Worlds in One* (New York: Hill and Wang, 2006), 176.
19. Terry Pratchett, *Lords and Ladies* (Discworld Novel, 1992).
20. Anthony Kenny, *The Five Ways: St. Thomas Aquinas' Proofs of God's Existence* (New York: Schocken Books, 1969), 66.
21. ABC Science Online, "The Big Questions: In the Beginning," Interview of Paul Davies by Phillip Adams, http://aca.mq.edu.au/pdavies.html.
22. John Polkinghorne, "Eschatology: Some Questions and Some Insights from Science," pp 29-41 in *The End of the World and the Ends of God*, J. Polkinghorne and M. Welker (eds.), (Harrisburg, PA: Trinity Press, 2000), 34.
23. Paul Davies, "Taking Science on Faith," *New York Times*, 24th November 2007.
24. Anthony Flew with Roy Abraham Varghese, *There Is A God: How the World's Most Notorious Atheist Changed His Mind* (New York: Harper Collins, 2007, p.80), 137.
25. David Hilbert "On the Infinite", a lecture delivered June 4, 1925, before a congress of the Westphalian Mathematical Society in Munster. Translated by Erna Putnam and Gerald J. Massey from *Mathematische Annalen* (Berlin) vol. 95 (1926), 161-90.
26. Richard Swinburne, "Design Defended," *Think* (Spring 2004), 17.
27. Colin Russell, quoted in Alister McGrath *Science and Religion* (3rd ed), (Hoboken, NJ: Wiley-Blanckwell, 2020), 22.
28. Paul Davies, *The Mind of God: Science and the Search for Ultimate Meaning* (New York: Simon & Schuster Ltd., 1992), 16.
29. Aristotle described God as the 'Unmoved Mover,' i.e. someone who was the prime cause of all motion in the universe, but is himself never moved. God moved the heavenly bodies furthest from Earth so they circled the Earth in a perfect circle. Their movement caused the sun, moon, and stars nearer to Earth to also move in circles around the Earth. At the center of the universe was the Earth, which did not move—much like rubbish caught in a whirlpool collects at the center and does not circle.

    Aristotle believed that physical matter was made up of a combination of four 'coruptable' elements: earth, wind, fire and water. He called the fifth element that filled outer space, 'aether' (or 'quintessence').
30. Paul Davies, "Taking Science on Faith," *New York Times*, 24th November 2007.
31. *Ibid.*
32. Max Planck, *Religion and Natural Science* (Lecture Given 1937) *Scientific Autobiography and Other Papers*, F. Gaynor (tr.), (New York, 1949), 184
33. John Polkinghorne, *Science and Theology: An Introduction* (London: SPCK, 1998), 72.
34. Albert Einstein, *Lettres a Maurice Solovine reproduits en facsimile et traduits en francais* (Paris: Gauthier-Viars, 1956), 102-103.
35. Thomas Nagel *The last Stand* (New York: Oxford University Press, 1997), 130.
36. Since this text was first drafted, it has come to light that Ravi Zacharias' engaged in significant sexual misconduct. This has come as a terrible shock to many and it has resulted in his legacy being discredited. This is a salutary lesson. Every Christian (particularly those in leadership) must live a congruent Christian life.

    As he was a good apologist before he became a bad Christian, so his words will still be quoted in this work.
37. Neil Ormerod, "The metaphysical muddle of Lawrence Krauss: Why science can't get rid of God." See: See: https://www.abc.net.au/religion/the-metaphysical-muddle-of-lawrence-krauss-why-science-cant-get-/10100010 Uploaded: Monday 18 February 2013 3:36pm.

Notes

38. Reported in: Howard P. Kainz, *The Existence of God and the faith-instinct*, (Cranbury, NJ: Rosemont Publishing, 2010), 21.
39. Deism is belief in a supreme being, but not one that can be known personally or which engages with humanity in any supernatural way.
40. Alice Calaprice, *The Ultimate Quotable Einstein*. Princeton NJ: Princeton University Press, 2010), p.340. Einstein said this in a letter to M. Berkowitz, 25th October, 1950.
41. Walter Isaacson, *Einstein: His Life and Universe*. (New York: Simon and Schuster, 2008), 390.
42. Albert Einstein, "Notes for an Autobiography," pp.9-12 in *Saturday Review of Literature*, (New York: November 26, 1949), 9.
43. Alice Calaprice *The Expanded Quotable Einstein*, (Princeton University Press, 2000), 214.
44. Albert Einstein, quoted in Timothy Ferris, *Coming of Age in the Milky Way* (New York: Morrow, 1988), 177.
45. Louis Pasteur, quoted in an article entitled "Is Darwinism On Its Death-bed?" *The Literary Digest* (New York: Funk and Wagnalls, 18 October 1902,) Vol. 25, No 16, 490.
46. James Clerk Maxwell "The Theory of Molecules," pp.276-290 in *The Popular Science Monthly*, January, 1874, Vol. IV, No 79, 289.
47. Charles Darwin in a letter first published in 1887 by his son Francis Darwin (F. Darwin [ed.], *The Life and Letters of Charles Darwin*, 2 vols [London, 1887, Vol 1], 304).
48. Charles Darwin, *On the Origin of Species By Means of Natural Selection*, J. Carroll (ed.), (New York: Broadview Texts, 2003), 443.
49. Arno Penzias quoted in "Clues to Universe Origin Expected" by Malcolm Browne (New York Times, March 12, 1978), 1.
50. Arno Penzias, pp.183 - 202 in *'The God I Believe In,'* Joshua Haberman (ed.), (New York, Maxwell Macmillan International, 1994) 184.
51. Arno Penzias, quoted in chapter 16 in Henry Margenau and Roy Abraham Varghese, (eds.), *Cosmos, Bios, Theos*, (La Salle, Illinois, Open Court, 1992), 83.
52. Christopher Isham, "Creation of the universe as a quantum process." In Russell, R. J., Stoeger, W. R., and Coyne, G. V. (eds.), *Physics, Philosophy, and Theology: A Common Quest for Understanding*. (Vatican Observatory, University of Notre Dame, third edition, 1997), 378.
53. Werner Heisenberg, *Across the Frontiers*, Peter Heath (tr.), (San Francisco: Harper & Row, 1974), p.213.
54. Freeman Dyson, *Disturbing the Universe* (New York: Harper & Row, 1979), 250.
55. David Wilkinson , *Christian Eschatology and the Physical Universe*, (London: T&T CLARK, 2010), 21.
56. Bertrand Russell, "The Free Man's Worship," *The Independent Review* 1 (Dec 1903), 415-424. Title of essay changed after 1910 to "A Free Man's Worship."
57. Paul Davies, "Eternity: Who Needs it?" pp. 41-52 in *The Far-Future Universe*, George Ellis (ed.), (London: Templeton Foundation Press, 2002), 48.
58. Fiona Ellis, "God, Naturalism, and the Limits of Science," pp. 8-20 in *Are There Limits to Science?* Ed. G. Straine (Cambridge: Cambridge Scholars Publishing, 2017,), 17. This quote has been attributed to Werner Heisenberg but the original quotation in German is: "*Der erste Trunk aus dem Becher der Naturwissenschaft macht atheistisch, aber auf dem Grund des Bechers wartet Gott.*" (The source cited in Ulrich Hildebrand: 'Das Universum – Hinweis auf Gott?' in 'Ethos. Die Zeitschrift für

die ganze Familie,' Berneck, Schweiz: Schwengeler Verlag AG, No. 10, Oktober 1988, p. 10).

2. Creation, Evolution, and Me

1. J. Polkinghorne, *Science and Theology: An Introduction* (London: SPCK, 1998), 72.
2. Ian Tattersall, *Becoming Human* (Orlando, FL: Brace & Company, 1998).
3. Bill Bryson, *A Short History of Nearly Everything* (London: Doubleday, 2003), 254.
4. Fred Hoyle, "Hoyle On Evolution," *Nature*, 294 (12th November 1981), 105.
5. Anthony Flew with Roy Abraham Varghese, *There Is A God: How the World's Most Notorious Atheist Changed His Mind* (New York: Harper Collins, 2007, 124.
6. *Ibid.*
7. Paul Davies, "The Origin of Life, II: How Did It Begin?" http://aca.mq.edu.au/PaulDavies/publications/papers'OriginsOfLife_II.pdf.
8. Anthony Flew with Roy Abraham Varghese, *There Is A God: How the World's Most Notorious Atheist Changed His Mind* (New York: Harper Collins, 2007), 131.
9. *Ibid. 131.*
10. *Ibid.* 132.
11. Nick Hawkes, *An Apology for the Scientific Credibility of Faith* D Min thesis, Australian College of Theology, submitted February, 2004.
12. Augustine, *De Genesi ad litteram*, II.9, 1.21, E. McMullin, (tr.), "How Should Cosmology Relate to Theology?" pp. 17-57 in A. R. Peacocke (ed.), *The Sciences and Theology in the Twentieth Century* (London: Oriel Press, 1981), p. 19.
    Origen of Alexandria and Basil of Caesarea similarly advocated an allegorical understanding of Genesis 1, see: Adam Rasmussen, *Genesis and Cosmos* (Boston: Brill, 2019).
13. John Calvin, *Commentaries: Genesis*, Vol I, Genesis, chapter 1, verse 6 (Grand Rapids, Michigan: Baker Book House), 79.
14. David Berlinski, *The Devil's Delusion: Atheism and Its Scientific Pretensions* (New York: Crown Publishing, 2008).
15. Charles Darwin, *On the Origin of Species*, (London: John Murray, 1866 edition), 308.
16. Stephen C. Meyer, *Darwin's Doubt: The Explosive Origin of Animal Life and the Case for Intelligent Design*, (New York: HarperOne, 2013).
17. David Berlinski, "The Deniable Darwin," *Commentary*, Vol. 101, June 1996 No. 6.
18. Richard Dawkins, *The God Delusion* (New York: Bantam Books, 2006), 275.
19. *Ibid.* 37.
20. Charles Darwin in a letter first published in 1887 by his son Francis Darwin (F. Darwin [ed.], *The Life and Letters of Charles Darwin*, 2 vols [London, 1887, Vol 1], 304).
21. Francis. Darwin, *The Life and Letters of Charles Darwin* (New York: Appleton, 1898, Vol.2), 82.
22. Frederick Temple, "The Present Relations of Science to Religion": A sermon preached on 1 July 1860 before the University of Oxford. See: J. Brooke and G. Cantor, *Reconstructing Nature: The Engagement of Science and Religion* (Edinburgh: T & T Clark, 1988), 36.
23. Some of this section was informed by a talk given by Dr. David Wilkinson at Tabor College, Adelaide, South Australia, on 11th January, 2010. Dr. David Wilkinson is Principal of St. John's College, Durham University. He is not only a theologian, but is one of Britain's top astrophysicists.

Notes

24. Morris had been convinced by creationist thinking of the Canadian writer, George McCready Price.
25. *Footprints in Stone*, 1973 (film, produced by Stanley Taylor for Films for Christ Association, Inc. Mesa, AZ.) This film has since been withdrawn. For more, see: http://paleo.cc/paluxy/sor-ipub.htm
26. Percy J. Wiseman, *Creation Revealed in Six Days* (London & Edinburgh: (Marshall, Morgan & Scott, 1948).
27. Bernard Ramm, *A Christian View of Science and Scripture* (Grand Rapids, Eerdmans, 1954), 151.
28. John C. Lennox, *Seven Days That Divide the World: The Beginning According to Genesis and Science* (Grand Rapids: Zondervan, 2011), 48-51.
29. *Ibid*, 53.
30. *Ibid*, 59.
31. Gregory of Nyssa, quoted in: *Ancient Christian Commentary on Scripture: Genesis 1-11*, A Louth (ed.), (New Haven, CT: Institute of Classical Christian Studies, 2001), Genesis 1:26.
32. Adam Rasmussen, *Genesis and Cosmos* (Boston: Brill, 2019).
33. Galileo Galilei, *Lettere*, Einaudi, Torino, 1978, pp. 128-135.

3. Jesus, Evidence, and Me

1. Clive S. Lewis, *"Broadcast Talks"* (London: Geoffrey Bles, The Centenary Press, 1942), 50-51.
2. Michael Green "Why the Resurrection Matters" *Christianity Today* Vol.33, No.5, 29
3. Clive S. Lewis, *Fern-seed and Elephants and Other Essays on Christianity*, (Collins, Font Paperbacks, 9th Imp, 1986), 109.
4. Richard Dawkins, *The God Delusion*, (London: Bantam, 2006), 93.
5. Christopher Hitchens, *God Is Not Great: How Religion Poisons Everything*, (New York: Allen & Unwin), 120.
6. Hitchens, *God Is Not Great*, 115.
7. *Ibid*. 122.
8. The American explorer, Edward Robinson incorrectly claimed in 1841 that the Old Testament city of Japhia was Yafia. It was an understandable mistake given that Yafia is the same as Japhia in Hebrew.
9. *Nazara* literally means 'branch.' This was probably because King David was the 'branch' (descendant of) of his father, Jesse (1 Sam 16:1-13). In other words, it signaled that the town was a Davidic town, and was therefore thoroughly Jewish.
10. The research was conducted in 1962 by the Department of Archaeology of Hebrew University, Jerusalem, with the assistance of Southern Baptist Theological Seminary, Louisville, Kentucky.
11. The early church fathers, Justin Martyr (100-165AD) and Origen (185 – 254AD) both spoke of Nazareth, and both would have had contact with the *Desposyni* (people of the blood line of Jesus). However, the Jewish historian, Josephus, doesn't mention the city. This should not surprising given that Josephus only mentions 20% of the important cities in Galilee.
12. Ossuary box designated "Number nine."

Notes

4. History, Morality, and Me

1. Jean Twenge and Keith Campbell, *The Narcissism Epidemic: Living in the Age of Entitlement*, (New York: Atria Books, 2009).
2. Plato, *Laws*, Chapter 10.
3. I am indebted to Dr. Leonard Long (medical practitioner, philosopher, theologian and historian (retired) currently resident in Adelaide, Australia) for this historical information.
4. Donovan X, 18, 03, 02 (Cornell University).
5. Viktor E. Frankl, *The Doctor and the Soul: From Psychotherapy to Logotherapy*, R. and C. Winston (tr.), (New York: Knof, 1955).
6. Friedrich Nietzsche, *Human, All Too Human* (1878), 71. Hope.
7. David Berlinski, *The Devil's Delusion: Atheism and Its Scientific Pretensions* (New York: Crown Publishing, 2008), Chap. 2, "An Insult to Human Dignity."
8. Aleksandr Solzhenitsyn, "A World Split Apart," a speech given at Harvard's 327th anniversary, 8th June, 1978.
9. *Ibid.*
10. "Socialism is booming in popularity among young people, survey finds," ABC, Hack, See: https://www.abc.net.au/triplej/programs/hack/socialism-booming-popularity-among-young-people-survey-finds/11655582 (Posted Wed 30th Oct 2019, 6:19pm).
11. Jonathon Van Maren, "Atheists sound the alarm: Decline of Christianity is seriously hurting society." posted Nov 4, 2019, (https://www.lifesitenews.com/blogs/atheists-sound-the-alarm-decline-of-christianity-is-seriously-hurting-society).
12. David Bentley Hart, *Atheist Delusions: The Christian Revolution and Its Fashionable Enemies* (Yale University Press, 2009), xi.
13. J. Monod, *Chance and Necessity*, A. Wainhouse (tr.), (London: Collins, 1972), 167.

5. Philosophy, Truth, and Me

1. Robert Griffiths, quoted in: Tim Stafford, "Cease-Fire in the Laboratory," *Christianity Today*, April 3, 1987, 18.
2. Baruch Shalev, *100 Years of Nobel Prizes* (New Delhi: Atlantic Publishers 2003).
3. Christian Anfinsen, "There Exists an Incomprehensible Power with Limitless Foresight and Knowledge" pp. 138-140 in Henry Margenau and Roy Varghese, *Cosmos, Bios, Theos*, (Peru, IL: Open Court, 1997), 139.
4. Gregory Benford, "Leaping the Abyss: Stephen Hawking on Black Holes, Unified Field Theory and Marilyn Monroe," *Reason* 4.02 (April 20002), 29.
5. Erwin Schrödinger, *My View of the World* (Cambridge: Cambridge University Press, 1964), p.93.
6. Albert Einstein, *The Quotable Einstein*, Alice Calaprice (ed.), (Princeton, NJ: Princeton University Press, 2005), 238.
7. Anthony Flew with Roy Abraham Varghese, *There Is A God: How the World's Most Notorious Atheist Changed His Mind* (New York: Harper Collins, 2007), 86-87.
8. Stephen Hawking, *A Brief History of Time* (London and New York: Bantam, 1988).
9. Katharine Tait, *My Father Bertrand Russell* (South Bend, IN: St. Augustine's Press, 75th edition, 1996), 188.

Notes

10. Katharine Tait, *My Father, Bertrand Russell* (London: George Allen and Unwin, 1967), 79.
11. Bertrand Russell, in: Ray Monk, *Bertrand Russell, The Spirit of Solitude*, 1872-1921, (Free Press, 2016), xix. Russell wrote this in the preface of his *Autobiography*.
12. David Bentley Hart, *The Experience of God: Being, Consciousness, Bliss* (Yale University Press, 2014), Chap 1, part 1, first sentence.
13. *Ibid*. Final paragraph.
14. Anthony Walsh, *A Nation Divided* (Wilmington, DE: Vernon Press, 2019), 67.
15. Francis Bacon *Essays, Civil and Moral*, (1625), The Harvard Classics 1909 – 14, Chapter 16 "Of Atheism."
16. Books written by Richard Dawkins include: *The Selfish Gene* (1976), *The Blind Watchmaker* (1986), *River out of Eden* (1995), *Climbing Mount Improbable* (1996), *The God Delusion* (2006).
17. Anthony Flew with Roy Abraham Varghese, *There Is A God: How the World's Most Notorious Atheist Changed His Mind* (New York: Harper Collins, 2007), 79.
18. *Ibid*. 80.
19. *Ibid*. 80.
20. *Ibid*. 78.
21. David Bentley Hart, *Atheist Delusions: The Christian Revolution and Its Fashionable Enemies* (Yale University Press, 2009), 4.
22. *Ibid*.
23. David Bentley Hart, *In the Aftermath: Provocations and Laments* (Cambridge, UK: Eerdmans, 2009), xii.
24. David Bentley Hart, *The Experience of God: Being, Consciousness, Bliss* (Yale University Press, 2014), Part three, VI.
25. David Bentley Hart, *Atheist Delusions: The Christian Revolution and Its Fashionable Enemies* (Yale University Press, 2009), 7.
26. Arnold J. Toynbee, *A Study of History* (Oxford University Press, 1957).
27. David Bentley Hart, *In the Aftermath: Provocations and Laments* (Cambridge, UK: Eerdmans, 2009), 6.
28. Bruce Gore, in an interview with Lucas Miles. See: Episode 107—Bruce Gore on "Church History and Revisionist Theology (https://art19.com 55 minutes running time; quote taken from 27-28 minutes).
29. Bradley, D. F., Exline, J. J., & Uzdavines, A. (2016, March 17). Relational reasons for nonbelief in the existence of gods: An important adjunct to intellectual nonbelief. *Psychology of Religion and Spirituality*. Advance online publication.
    Exline, J. J., Park, C. L., Smyth, J. M., & Carey, M. P. (2011). "Anger toward God: Social-cognitive predictors, prevalence, and links with adjustment to bereavement cancer," *Journal of Personality and Social Psychology*, 100, 129-148.
30. *Time* magazine, 7th April, 1980.
31. Friedrich Nietzsche's book, *Thus Spoke Zarathustra*, is one such attempt at this bravado.
32. Rosemary Sullivan, *Stalin's Daughter* (London: Fourth Estate, 2015), chapter 10.
33. See: "A crisis of meaninglessness is to blame for the rise in suicides" (*Dallas News*, 25th June, 2018).
34. Anthony Flew with Roy Abraham Varghese, *There Is A God: How the World's Most Notorious Atheist Changed His Mind* (New York: Harper Collins, 2007), 88.
35. *Ibid*. 155.
36. *Ibid*. 89.

37. Paul Davies, "What Happened Before the Big Bang?" in *God for the 21st Century*, Russell Stannard (ed.), (Philadelphia: Templeton Foundation Press, 2000), 12.
38. In case you missed it earlier in the end notes: Deism is belief in a supreme being, but not one that can be known personally or which engages with humanity in any supernatural way
39. H. L. Mencken, *Minority Report*, 1956 (reprinted by Johns Hopkins University Press, 2006).
40. Anthony Flew with Roy Abraham Varghese, *There Is A God: How the World's Most Notorious Atheist Changed His Mind* (New York: Harper Collins, 2007), 150.
41. *Ibid.* 141.
42. Richard Swinburne, *The Existence of God*, (Oxford University Press, 1979), 152.
43. Charles Darwin, *The Origin of Species*, J.W. Burrow (ed.), (New York: Penguin Random House, 1982), 458.

6. Quantum Physics, Atheism, and Me

1. Boyle, Robert, *Some Motives and Incentives to the Love of God*, 1648, (Cited in: David L. Woodall, "The Relationship between Science and Scripture in the Thought of Robert Boyle" pp.32-39 in *Perspectives on Science and Christian Faith* Perspectives on Science and Christian Faith, 49 (March, 1997), 32.
2. Robert Boyle, T*he Excellency of Theology Compared with Natural Theology* (tract, 1772) in R. Boyle, *The Works of the Honourable Robert Boyle*, T. Birch (ed.), second edition, 6 volumes (London: Rivingtons), Vol 4, pp. 1-66.
3. Thomas Browne, *Relgio Medici* (1642), J. Winney (ed.), (Cambridge, 1983), part I, section 16, pp. 18-19.
4. Francis Collins in an interview with CNN on 3 April 2007.
5. Nick Hawkes, "Clues From Quantum Physics that Tell Us What Mathematics Actually Is," in the ISCAST Online Journal, *Christian Perspectives on Science and Technology*, (June, 2019) see: http://iscast.org/node/702
6. Paul Dirac, (May 1963). "The Evolution of the Physicist's Picture of Nature, *Scientific American*. Retrieved 4 April 2013.
7. Eugene Wigner, 1959, "The unreasonable effectiveness of mathematics in the natural sciences," Richard Courant lecture in mathematical sciences delivered at New York University, 11th May 1959.
8. Galileo Galilei *Il Saggiatore*, quote translated by R.H. Popkin in (*The Philosophy of the Sixteenth and Seventeenth Centuries* (New York: Simon and Schuster, 1966), 65.
9. John Polkinghorne, *Reason and Reality: The Relationship Between Science and Theology* (London: SPCK, 1991), 36.
10. Robert Jastrow, *God and the Astronomers* (New York: W. W. Norton, 1978), 116.
11. Paul Davies, "Taking Science on Faith," (*New York Times,* 24th November 2007), A17.
12. Niels Bohr, Quoted in Werner K. Heisenberg *Physics and Beyond* (New York: Harper and Row, 1971), 206.
13. Richard Feynman, *The Character of Physical Law* (Cambridge: MA, MIT Press, 1965), 129.
14. Eugene Wigner "Remarks on the Mind-Body Question," pp. 171-174 in *Symmetries and Reflections*, Bloomington: IN, Indiana University Press, 1967), 171.
15. John von Neumann, in Keith Ward, *Is Religion Irrational?* (Oxford: Lion Hudson, 2011), 21.

Notes

16. John Bell, *Speakable and Unspeakable in Quantum Mechanics* (Cambridge University Press, 1987), 143.
17. Colin Brown, *Philosophy & the Christian faith* (Downers Grove, IL: IVP, 1969), 65.
18. Lawrence Krauss, *A Universe from Nothing* (New York: Simon and Schuster, 2012).
19. David Bentley Hart, "Science and Theology: Where the Consonance Really Lies," (*Renovatio*, Zaytuna College, 5th June, 2018).
20. Albert Einstein, "Physics and Reality" in the *Journal of the Franklin Institute*, vol. 221, Issue 3, 1936. See also: Albert Einstein, *Out of My Later Years* (New York: Philosophical Library, 1950), 58.
21. Robbert Dijkgraaf "Quantum Questions Inspire New Math," *Quanta Magazine*, See: https://www.quantamagazine.org/how-quantum-theory-is-inspiring-new-math-20170330/
22. Zhengfeng Ji, Anand Natarajan, Thomas Vidick, John Write and Henry Yuen, *MIP*=RE* (Cornell University, submitted 13th Jan 2020). See: https://arxiv.org/pdf/2001.04383.pdf
23. For a simple explanation, see: https://www.sciencenews.org/article/how-quantum-technique-highlights-math-mysterious-link-physics
24. Stephen Hawking, *A Brief History of Time* (London and New York: Bantam, 1988), 174.
25. Richard Dawkins *The Selfish Gene* (Oxford University Press, 1976).
26. Paul Davies, "Taking Science on Faith," *New York Times*, 24th November 2007.
27. Paul Davies, "The Origin of Live II: How Did It Begin?" http://aca.mq.edu.au/PaulDavies/publications/papers'OriginsOfLife_II.pdf.
28. Robert Olby *Francis Crick. Hunter of Life's Secrets* (Cold Spring. Harbor, NY: Cold Spring Harbor Laboratory Press, 2009).
29. Stephen Hawking, *A Brief History of Time* (London and New York: Bantam, 1988), 174.
30. Richard Dawkins *The Selfish Gene* (Oxford University Press, 1976).
31. Paul Davies, "Taking Science on Faith," *New York Times*, 24th November 2007.
32. Paul Davies, "The Origin of Live II: How Did It Begin?" http://aca.mq.edu.au/PaulDavies/publications/papers'OriginsOfLife_II.pdf.
33. Robert Olby *Francis Crick. Hunter of Life's Secrets* (Cold Spring. Harbor, NY: Cold Spring Harbor Laboratory Press, 2009).

7. Suffering, Grief, and Me

1. Nick Hawkes, *An Apology for the Scientific Credibility of Faith*, Doctor of Ministry thesis submitted to the Australian College of Theology in 2004, 124.
2. John C. Polkinghorne, *Quarks, chaos and Christianity* (London: Triangle, 1994), 42-49. See also: J. C. Polkinghorne, *Scientists as Theologians* (London: SPCK 1996), 46-50.
3. Bruce M. Rothschild, "Diseases of Dinosaurs," *Scientific American*, 21 October 1999.
4. Irving Greenberg, "Cloud of Smoke, Pillar of Fire" in Eva Fleischner (ed.), *Auschwitz: Beginning of a New Era?* (New York: Ktav, 1977), 9.
5. Elie Wiesel, *Night* (New York: Bantam, 1982), 32.
6. Albert Camus, *The Plague*, Stuart Gilbert (tr.), (New York: Vintage International, 1991), 211.

Notes

7. Clive S. Lewis, *A Grief Observed* (first published under the pseudonym N.W. Clerk, (London: Faber and Faber, 1961).
8. Gilbert Meilaender, *The Taste for the Other: The Social and Ethical Thoughts of C.S. Lewis* (Vancouver, BC: Regent College), 125.
9. Stephanie Dowrick *Forgiveness and Other Acts of Love* (New York: Viking, 1997), 39.
10. Rick Warren, *The Purpose Driven Church* (Grand Rapids, MI: Zondervan, 1995), 361.

8. Other Faiths, Christianity, and Me

1. John Hick, *God and the Universe of Faiths*, (London: Fount/Collins, 1977), 166-167.
2. Collected Wheel Publications, Vol VIII, Numbers 101-115 (Kandy Sri Lanka: Buddhist Publication Soc., 1966), 277.
3. John Gilchrist, *Muhammad and the Religion of Islam*, (Roodepoort, South Africa: Mission Press, 1986), 65.
4. Peter Corney, "GenX and the Gospel," pp.27-28 in *On Being* Vol.21, No.8, Nov, 1994.
5. Russell Chandler, *Racing Toward 2001:The Forces Shaping America's Religious Future* (Zondervan, 1992), 205-206.

9. Church, Its Moral Failure, and Me

1. Roy Abraham Varghese, in *There Is A God: How the World's Most Notorious Atheist Changed His Mind*, Anthony Flew with R.A. Varghese (New York: Harper Collins, 2007), xxiv.
2. D. Myers, *A Friendly Letter to Skeptics and Atheists: Musings on Why God is Good and Faith Isn't Evil* (Dan Francisco, CA: Jossey-Bass, 2008).
3. Ravi Zacharias, *Light in the Shadow of Jihad* (Orlando, FL: Multnomah, 2002), 102.
4. Piero Scaruffi "Wars and Casualties of the 20th and 21st Centuries"
   See: https://www.scaruffi.com/politics/massacre.html Accessed: 20th May, 2020.
5. Frank Dikötter, *Mao's Great Famine*, (New York: Bloomsbury, 2010).
6. These accretions include the worship of Mary; a belief that the bread and wine given at Mass literally turns into the body and blood of Jesus; a belief in purgatory, the belief in the compulsory celibacy of priests, and the adequacy of ritual over sincerity.
7. The term 'Protestantism' is used here in the broadest sense to mean those churches protesting against Roman Catholic authority.
8. John Wesley, 'Thoughts Upon Methodism,' in Arminian Magazine, 1787), Works, vii, 315-317. (See: *Selections from the Writings of the Rev. John Wesley*, M.A., Herbert Welch [ed.], [New York: Eaton and Mains], 127.)
9. Some liberal Protestant denominations would still claim to put a priority on their mission to the poor, but in reality, this can amount to little more than hiring some non-Christian people to help them administer and disseminate government grant money. Whilst this is laudable, I respectfully submit that such activity is an inadequate measure of the health of any church denomination.
10. The tenth of John Spongs' twelve theses (or articles), see: John Spong, '*A Call for a New Reformation.*'

Notes

11. John Spong, 'The God Beyond Theism,' *The Voice* October 1999.
    See also: John Hick, 'Jesus and the World Religions,' in *The Myth of God Incarnate*, John Hick (ed.), (London, SCM, 1977)
12. John Spong, '*A Call for a New Reformation*,' see Article 2
13. Richard Niebuhr, *The Kingdom of God in America*, (Chicago: Willett, Clark & Company, 1937), 193.
14. Dietrich Bonhoeffer, *The Cost of Discipleship*, (New York: Collier, 1963), 47.
15. D.P. Gushee and G.H. Stassen, *Kingdom Ethics: Following Jesus in Contemporary Context*, (Downers Grove: IVP Academic, 2003).
16. The Roman Catholic Church has continued to be a significant entity throughout history because it allowed reformations of its own, most notably the first: The Counter Reformation of the sixteenth century. I submit that it is time for another.
17. The term 'Protestantism' is again used here in the broadest sense to mean those churches protesting against Roman Catholic authority.
18. Richard Dawkins, *The God Delusion* (New York: Bantam Books, 2006), 31.
19. A year before in October, 2003, a girl was sacrificed to a god in Chandpur, (also in the Bignor district of the state of Orissa) by people who wanted a god to give them a son.

10. Sex, the Bible, and Me

1. The Greek word *porneia* from which we get our word pornography, does not just mean bare flesh. It means dressing in a way that is sexually provocative.
2. It is perhaps no accident that the mark signifying a person's covenant relationship with God was circumcision for the Jewish male. The covenant mark was upon that member of the body notoriously difficult to keep under control!
3. David Hume, *A Treatise of Human Nature* (London: John Noon, 1739–40), II.3.3, 415.
4. *Cleo*, July 1986, 81.
5. It is perhaps no accident that the mark signifying a person's covenant relationship with God was circumcision for the Jewish male. The covenant mark was upon that member of the body notoriously difficult to keep under control!
6. Matthew's gospel records Jesus teaching that although divorce was allowed in the Old Testament (as a concession to the "hard hearts" of the Jews), it should ideally not happen. However, Matthew goes on to say that divorce is permissible in cases of marital unfaithfulness (Matthew 5:31-32; 19:3-9).
7. Dan Kindlon, and Michael Thompson, *Raising Cain*, (London: Penguin Books, 2000), 206.
8. Some choose not to engage in aural sex because they associate it with a past life of promiscuity lived outside of God's purposes. For them, it is therefore not a helpful act that builds their marriage.
9. Some of this teaching was inspired by talks by Sy Rogers at the *Lifewell* conference in Adelaide, August, 2009.
10. Human sexuality is celebrated, for example, in the Song of Solomon (in the Old Testament). Its sexuality was recognised by the ancient Jews who used to only let men over the age of 30 to read it!
11. Repent, and by so doing, change the history of your family. Let your healing echo in your generation and the next generation.
    Both the Greek and the Hebrew word for repentance literally means, 'to turn

around,' i.e. to turn 180 degrees and go down the opposite track. The Greek word *metanoeo* means to perceive in a way that causes you to change your mind and purpose. The Hebrew word *shûwb* also means to go back home. Repentance is means choosing to come home.
12. The Greek word used to describe the Holy Spirit literally means, 'one who speaks in favor of another,' or 'one who stands alongside.'
13. The severity with which Jesus viewed people saying *"raca"* to anyone (Matthew 5:22) is explained by the fact that the Aramaic word *raca* did not only mean 'empty head', or 'fool' but it meant 'worthless.' The concept of anyone being worthless is abhorrent to Jesus.
14. Anne Moir & David Jessel, *Brain sex: the real difference between men and women* (London: Mandarin, 1989), 7.
15. *Ibid.* 101, 107.

11. Life After Death, and Me

1. Augustine, *Confessions*, X, 29.
2. It may be that the place of "punishment" (or Hades) is the same place called the 'Abyss' in Revelation 20:2-3. The Abyss was where Satan was imprisoned before being released briefly before being recaptured and finally condemned (Revelation 20:10).
3. Clive S. Lewis, *The Problem of Pain* (London: The Centenary Press, 1940), 127.
4. See also: Romans 14:10; 2 Corinthians 5:10.
5. Emil Brunner, *The Word and the World* (London: Student Christian Movement Press, 1931), 108.

Acknowledgments

I wish to acknowledge the friendship and wisdom of Dr. Leonard Long (medical practitioner, philosopher, historian and theologian) who has been a rich source of information for this book.
As iron sharpens iron, so one person sharpens another (Proverbs 17:17).

About the Author

Dr. Nick Hawkes is a theologian, award-winning writer, and communicator. He has been a guest lecturer at a number of theological colleges and has written and recorded over 800 "thoughts for the day" for Christian radio—both in Australia and the UK.

Nick has five degrees in the disciplines of science and theology – including two doctorates. He writes theological resources for the Christian church.

Nick also writes novels that feed the heart, mind and soul, (the 'Stone Collection,' see: author-nick.com).

Also by Nick Hawkes

There are ten novels in "The Stone Collection" that feed the heart, mind and soul:

The Atlantis Stone

The Peacock Stone

The Fire Stone

The Dragon Stone

The Celtic Stone

The Syrian Stone

The Viking Stone

The Pharaoh's Stone

The Martyr's Stone

The Scorpion Stone

www.ingramcontent.com/pod-product-compliance
Lightning Source LLC
Chambersburg PA
CBHW030252010526
44107CB00053B/1680